MW01701127

About t

Francis Ansah is a communication consultant and career coach with Associate Certified Experts Career Coach (ACECC) designation. He also specialises in biography and memoir writing, and provides life coaching services to students and professionals.

‘The foundation of life’s achievement is a sound mind in a healthy body, driven by a sense of purpose.’

-- Francis Ansah

What people are saying about *Sense of Purpose Through College and Career:*

Elizabeth Mensah

My son has performed poorly since primary school, and he hasn't improved in Junior High School. My husband and I have tried every intervention, but to no avail. I got worried that he would have a shaky future, but after reading a sentence in this book that says: 'The foundation of life's achievement is a sound mind in a healthy body, driven by a sense of purpose,' my fears are now allayed. This book also draws my mind to my son's ability as a polyglot, and he's so excellent at persuading people that he can sell ice to Eskimos. These are his God-given potentials, and after reading every chapter of this book, I do not doubt that he'll become a successful entrepreneur. The content is reassuring, and I enjoyed reading every bit of it.

Emmanuel Koney

I was a standout student and topped every class I sat in at school. However, reading Francis Ansah's *Sense of Purpose Through College and Career* has got me thinking. I admit that though I'm an academic achiever, I'm not a genius in any field, and I should aim to be one! While reading, I came across the profiles of Albert Einstein, John Gurdon, Winston Churchill, Hedy Lamarr, and Madam C.J. Walker. For the first time, I've learnt that Albert Einstein was average in school, John Gurdon and Winston Churchill were dunces, Hedy Lamarr never went to college, and Madam C.J. Walker was unschooled. Yet, their ingenuities were groundbreaking, and their successes were phenomenal. This made me realise that being a genius is more worthwhile than merely being smart in school. *Sense of Purpose Through College and Career* is a classic and has imbued me with a sense of ingenuity. I'm confident it'll inspire other readers the same way, and I recommend it as a must-read for all graduates and undergraduates.

Kevin Smith

I've never been phenomenal in school, and my best performance as a student always placed me below average. After I barely graduated from university, I found myself not being forceful enough and lagging behind. Besides, I was made to feel in my early school years that I didn't count, but reading this book has enlivened me. It has also made me realise that we're all different, and what it takes to succeed in a career is distinct for everyone. For instance, whereas some people's career accomplishments can be linked directly to their phenomenal performance in school, most extraordinary achievers draw on their aptitudes and passions, which are usually unrelated to how well they performed in school or even what they studied in college. Fortunately, I have an aptitude for a skill, and I've begun developing it in order to change my career. I'm optimistic that I'll be accomplished on this new career path and live a satisfying life thereafter. Francis Ansah's *Sense of Purpose Through College and Career* is a masterpiece and has restored my confidence.

Edwina N.K Quarcoo

I read Francis Ansah's *Sense of Purpose Through College and Career* through two lenses. First, as a copyeditor, I couldn't help but get enthralled by the diction and thesis of every chapter. Second, as a 16-year-old me who knew that she needed direction on her career path but didn't know where to begin, who to talk to, or what to do. Supposing you're like my past self, then you became a product of an education system that made you confused and uncertain about your future. In that case, I urge you to grab a copy of *Sense of Purpose Through College and Career*. Because not only will this book help you to resolve your confusion, but it'll put you on the career path where you'll most likely be accomplished and fulfilled.

Samuel Cole

Though I've had a passion for computing since my teens, I couldn't make it to the university to study computer science because I failed science and math. Taking several resits didn't improve my grades, so I gave up until I came across Francis Ansah's *Sense of Purpose Through College and Career*. While reading, I realised that I could learn coding on my own terms. I immediately contacted some developers, and one agreed to mentor me while I studied from textbooks and the internet. The learning curve has been worthwhile, as I'm already a member of a software development team. *Sense of Purpose Through College and Career* has transformed my life, and I recommend it to every student.

Ama Asamoah

I dream of becoming a chartered accountant, but I find myself studying something different. I nearly abandoned my passion for accounting until I came across Francis Ansah's *Sense of Purpose Through College and Career* book. After reading, I was inspired to take a professional ACCA course in addition to my studies. So, I enrolled in a private ACCA class, and I hope to complete it by the time I graduate from university. *Sense of Purpose Through College and Career* is a real eye-opener, and I recommend it to every student.

Maxwell Agyei

After reading *Sense of Purpose Through College and Career*, I reflected on my science career trajectory and the qualifications I've garnered over the years and found myself short of ingenuity. I've always thought that academic achievement was enough to advance civilisation until this book made me understand that ingenuity is what counts. Now that my eyes are open, I want to learn how to develop a vaccine for malaria, find a cure for diabetes, or invent something to further human longevity. It wouldn't be easy, but it's not impossible if we all begin to think about solving a problem. This book is a transformative piece of high merit, and I encourage every parent, teacher, and student to grab a copy.

Sumaila Aziz

Having read *Sense of Purpose Through College and Career* as a teacher, I've understood that failure in school can translate to phenomenal success after school, and it's very wrong to belittle a non-performing student's ambition. This book has made me realise that no matter how poorly students fare in school, they can still find their purpose after school. And if any of them fail in life, it won't be because they didn't perform well in school but because they lacked a sense of purpose. I highly recommend this book to all teachers.

Suzan Gyan

Initially, I thought *Sense of Purpose Through College and Career* was one of the numerous motivational books with impractical content, so I was hesitant to read it. But I took a glimpse at the blurb, and it was engaging. I then read the first sentence of the introduction, the second, third, and so on, and I was enjoying everything I was reading. The content is so practical and stimulating. How I wish I had this book when I was in college! But now, as a professional and a parent, it has been an inspiration to guide my own career path and that of my children. I recommend Francis Ansah's *Sense of Purpose Through College and Career* to every parent.

Victor Asante

Such a relevant book written by a career coach and startup consultant has clarified the way forward in my career and entrepreneurial endeavour. And I couldn't be more thankful to Francis Ansah for his insight, which has helped me avoid a career blunder and an entrepreneurial mishap. I encourage every student and professional to grab a copy of this book.

Sam Laryea

Whilst it seems to some people as though the essence of higher education is centred on credential collection, Francis Ansah steers our perspective toward ingenuity and problem-solving as the true essence of higher education, and I absolutely agree with him. More so for averring that ingenuity isn't just for top performers and students at prestigious universities but can be achieved by anyone with a sound mind and a healthy body. This aspect leads to one conclusion: anyone, regardless of their level of education, where they received their education, or their academic performance, can be successful if they have a sense of purpose.

SENSE OF PURPOSE

THROUGH

COLLEGE AND CAREER

Francis Ansah
Associate Certified Experts Career Coach
(wa.link/mycareercoach)

ISBN: 978 – 9988 – 2 – 4086 – 8

Dedication

To Doris Ampofo, with love and appreciation

Foreword

Thank you for taking the time to delve into *Sense of Purpose Through College and Career*. Through its pages, you'll be able to learn more about how college education, apprenticeship or mentorship, and self-learning can help you develop proficiency and progress in your career, especially if you can effectively combine two or all three of these approaches.

In this book, I've written about my own experiences as well as the experiences of achievers and extraordinary achievers who left their marks in this world. My goal is to give you a well-rounded view of the different ways to move up in your career and to inspire you to take the path that best fits your interests and goals.

I encourage you to take the time to reflect on the ideas and advice presented in this book and to consider how you can apply them to your own life. Whether you are a trainee, an undergraduate, a graduate, or a professional, I can assure you that there's an invaluable piece of advice for you in this book.

I hope that this book will serve as a valuable resource as you seek to find your own sense of purpose through college and career.

Francis Ansah

CONTENTS

Glossary of Terms and Acronyms

1. **ACCA:** Association of Chartered Certified Accountants.
2. **ACECC:** Associate Certified Experts Career Coach.
3. **Adversity Quotient:** It is a measure of a person's ability to deal with life's adversities.
4. **Allied:** Related to Britain and her allies during and after World Wars I And II.
5. **Antiquity:** The ancient past, especially the period of classical and other human civilisations before the Middle Ages.
6. **Apollo:** The Patron God of Troy
7. **Aptitude:** Herein used interchangeably with **talent**, it refers to a natural ability to do something.
8. **Behavioural Modernity:** A suite of behavioural and cognitive traits that distinguishes current Homo sapiens from other anatomically modern humans, hominins, and primates.
9. **Brainpower:** Mental ability
10. **Calling:** Herein used interchangeably with vocation; refers to a strong feeling of suitability for a particular career or occupation.
11. **Catamaran:** A type watercraft or yacht that has two parallel hulls.
12. **Circumnavigation:** Sailing around the world.
13. **Collective bargaining:** Negotiation between a group of workers and an employer over pay and working conditions.
14. **Collective punishment:** Punishment or sanction imposed on a group for acts allegedly perpetrated by a group member.
15. **College:** This term, along with 'university,' 'higher learning,' and 'higher education,' refers to institutions that provide tertiary education.
16. **Developer (IT):** A person who builds or creates software and applications.
17. **Experiential learning (ExL):** The method of gaining knowledge through experience. Experiential learning can include hands-on learning.
18. **Extremist:** A person who upholds extreme religious beliefs and is willing to be violent to express their faith.
19. **Finds:** A discovery of something valuable, typically something of archaeological interest.
20. **Fundamentalist:** Someone who believes in the strict adherence and literal interpretation of a scripture.
21. **Genius:** Someone with exceptional intellectual or creative prowess. Also used herein, it refers to creative ability.
22. **Go Public:** To have a company listed on the stock exchange.
23. **HOD:** Head of Department

24. **Ingenuity:** The quality of being clever, original, and inventive
25. **IPO:** Initial Public Offering is a public offering in which a company's shares are sold to institutional investors and usually also to retail (individual) investors.
26. **IPS:** I Promise School.
27. **Jason Bourne:** A movie character with impeccable self-defence skills.
28. **Juju:** A belief system in West Africa that involves the use of objects believed to contain supernatural powers.
29. **Kayaking:** The sport of paddling a kayak.
30. **Luminary:** A well-known person or someone who has achieved great success in a particular field.
31. **Mind projection fallacy:** It happens when someone believes that how they see the world is representative of how the world actually is, even going so far as to believe that imagined items actually exist.
32. **MIT:** Massachusetts Institute of Technology.
33. **Mojo:** A magic charm, talisman, or spell.
34. **Nazi:** Adolf Hitler's fascist German fascist party that ruled Germany from 1933 to 1945.
35. **Nobel Laureate:** A recipient of a Nobel Prize.
36. **Notary:** A person with the authority to perform certain legal formalities, especially to draw up or certify contracts, deeds, and other documents for use in other jurisdictions.
37. **Proclivity:** This term is used interchangeably with passion, inclination, and penchant; it refers to the tendency to choose or do something regularly; a predisposition towards something specific.
38. **Renaissance:** A period in European history spanning the 15th and 16th centuries, characterised by an attempt to revive and surpass the ideas and accomplishments of classical antiquity.
39. **Russian roulette:** [1]The practice of loading one bullet into the chamber of a revolver, spinning the cylinder, and then pulling the trigger while pointing the gun at one's own head. [2] an activity that is potentially very dangerous.
40. **Social functioning:** The ability of a person to communicate effectively and effortlessly with others.
41. **Talent:** A natural skill
42. **Torpedo:** A bomb designed to travel underwater.
43. **UCLA:** University of California, Los Angeles
44. **UPenn:** University of Pennsylvania.
45. **Zeus:** The supreme deity in ancient Greek religion.

PREFACE

The more the success stories of the world's ultra-successful hot shots are publicised, the more ordinary but ambitious people are inspired to develop their potential and turn their lives around. To achieve this turnaround, the latter are drawing on their brainpower to find solutions to problems, improve efficiency in systems, and supply human wants.

These endeavours have scaled up entrepreneurship, access to information, globalisation, open-access learning, and the successive rollout of user-friendly technologies by people with minimal or advanced education, and have thereby achieved success.

Their successes show that it is possible for anyone of a sound mind and in good health, with or without a college degree, to be creative and incredibly wealthy.

Furthermore, the growing popularity of the 'rags-to-riches' and 'dropout-to-tycoon' success stories in the West has enkindled a prevailing desire for ultra-success among the African youth as never before. This has led to some development in the startup ecosystem on the continent. According to a 2022 *Business Insider Africa* report, while South Africa, Kenya, Nigeria, Rwanda, and Egypt have gained recognition in the global startup ecosystem, Ghana and Cape Verde have also improved their rankings. This development was unprecedented!

Examining the education and career pathways of historical and modern luminaries, it can be inferred that the foundation of life's achievement is a sound mind in a healthy body, driven by a sense of purpose. Meanwhile, human ingenuity has been demonstrated with or without higher education since the beginning of time.

This makes me think of the best-selling authors who didn't have a degree in any language or literature, the business tycoons who didn't have an MBA, the many inventors who didn't have a degree, the tech stars who dropped out of college, and other successful geniuses who went to school for a short time or taught themselves.

Apparently, the farthest point people can reach in their lives lies in their sense of purpose, not necessarily in their educational attainment. Moreover, extraordinary accomplishments emanate from people's aptitudes and proclivities, not from their academic qualifications. Several examples have been discussed in this book.

In *Sense of Purpose Through College and Career*, Francis Ansah draws attention to the phenomenal potency of the human brain and inspires ingenuity in the reader. In his composition, he sets the tone for what it takes to accomplish a life purpose against the backdrop of the flawed paradigm of success that has been promulgated by the education system for many years. This way of thinking makes academic success seem like the only way to be successful, even though it's not always the best way for everyone.

Francis Ansah shows throughout the book that a person's talent and determination can take them far beyond their educational attainment. This is why some people who didn't finish high school can go on to achieve greater success in life than those who did. It's also why some people with few educational credentials, poor academic performance, or no formal education at all can surpass their more well-educated peers.

In this way, Francis Ansah argues that, just as with academic pursuits, any other career path can lead to success if the person who chooses it is enterprising and has a sense of purpose!

INTRODUCTION

Proficiency and Ingenuity Emanate from the Brain, not the Degrees.

We humans have an inherent desire to accomplish something worthwhile in our lifetime. At least, we desire acknowledgement for our contributions and thirst for recognition in our careers. Our career pathways are diverse, encompassing college education, science, technology, politics, entertainment, business, and even spirituality. College education, however, is the most acclaimed career pathway in human history. After all, it's the most mentally stimulating option, and everyone desires to be mentally stimulated.

The continuous encouragement of college education has snowballed intellectualism and rationalism over the centuries. Societies that delayed incorporating college education into their culture fell behind civilisation and were plagued by an ignorant populace. Those that embraced it early, in contrast, churned out civilisation, thereby fostering the notion that colleges are the fount of knowledge and human ingenuity.

In hindsight, it makes sense to think of college as a source of knowledge, but it's unclear whether a college education stimulates ingenuity. This is because humans were already ingenious before college education was founded.

Also, only a few geniuses with advanced degrees have emerged at present to have singularly achieved major scientific breakthroughs, as compared to the many geniuses in bygone years whose contributions were singularly achieved and without degrees. The reason is that the present-day education system encourages credentialism over ingenuity.

This, in turn, drives many learners to pursue certifications, in other words, credential collection, as the essence of their education. Conversely, geniuses draw on their brainpower and pursue applied knowledge and problem-solving skills. That's why they're ingenious!

Nevertheless, credentialism and ingenuity are both appreciable, though one is more worthwhile than the other. Credentialism, for instance, depicts the successful completion of higher education, the conferment of certificates, and the reliance on certifications as absolute proof of competence. To this end, Benjamin Bolger garnered a lot of degrees from some prestigious universities.

He began college at the age of 12 at Muskegon Community College and graduated with an Associate of Arts. He then transferred to University of Michigan and earned a Bachelor of Arts in Sociology in 1994. From there, he went on a study spree, earning a Master of Science in Sociology from University of Oxford in 1997, a Master of Philosophy in Sociology and Politics of Modern Society from University of Cambridge in 1998, a Master of Arts in Education from Stanford University in 2000, a Master of Arts in Politics of Education from Teachers College, Columbia University, in 2002, a Master of Science in Real Estate Development from Graduate School of Architecture, Planning and Preservation, Columbia University, also in 2002, a Master of Arts in Development Studies from Brown University in 2004, a Master of Arts in Liberal Arts from Dartmouth College, also in 2004, a Master of Arts in Coexistence and Conflict from Brandeis University in 2007, a Master of Arts in Humanities from Skidmore College in 2007, Doctor of Design in Urban Planning and Real Estate from Harvard University in 2008, and a Master of Fine Arts in Creative Writing from Ashland University in 2014.

Benjamin Bolger‘s academic achievements indicate that he's highly learned. To be ingenious, however, is a different ballgame.

Ingenuity is problem-solving and transcends academic credentials. It's the bedrock of civilisation, economy, and power, and has a direct influence on society. It's also a practical manifestation of human brainpower, and as often as societies have expected academic achievers to be ingenious, it's noteworthy that the most extraordinary achievers in the real world were usually not notable academic achievers or the top performers in school.

In fact, extraordinary achievers who attained higher education usually had ordinary grades, if not drab. They also include dropouts, the unschooled, and those with minimal education.

What these geniuses have in common is that they took to self-learning or apprenticeship/mentorship to hone their aptitudes and proclivities, either in addition to or without college education, and their accomplishments were phenomenal.

The Wright brothers were one of these geniuses: Wilbur completed high school but didn't receive his diploma, whereas Orville dropped out of high school after his junior year. Despite this, they learned aeronautics from textbooks and invented the first piloted airplane without ever attending college.

Cornelis Drebbel was an acclaimed inventor who distinguished himself by building the first navigable submarine in 1620. He also contributed to the development of measurement and control systems, optics, and chemistry. Cornelis Drebbel never attended college; his training was entirely by apprenticeship under Hendrick Goltzius.

Actress Hedy Lamarr's beauty and screen appearance made her the most sought-after actress in the United States, and she was often referred to as the Most Beautiful Woman in Films.

During World War II, Hedy Lamarr learnt that the Nazis could easily jam and divert the Allied torpedoes' trajectories. So, she came up with the idea of a frequency-hopping signal technology that could prevent the Nazis from detecting the Allied torpedoes. She then contacted her friend, George Antheil, to help her develop the technology, and together they invented and patented frequency-hopping technology in 1941. The technology would later become the precursor of secure Wi-Fi, GPS, and Bluetooth. George Antheil recounted:

> We began talking about the war, which in the late summer of 1940, was looking most extremely murky. Hedy said that she did not feel very comfortable sitting there in Hollywood and making lots of money when things were in such a state. She said she knew a good deal about munitions and various secret weapons… and that she was thinking seriously of quitting her studio occupation and going to Washington, D.C., to offer her services to the newly established National Inventions Council.

Interestingly, Hedy Lamarr had no formal training or college degree; she had an aptitude for invention and was primarily self-taught. She admitted: 'Inventions are easy for me to do. I don't have to work on ideas; they come naturally.' In 2014, Hedy Lamarr was inducted into the inventors' hall of fame.

With the ever-popular aphorism: 'Education is the key to development,' and its characteristic competitiveness in schools, students' academic performance has long been perceived as the pointer to their future success. In other words, if a student scores good grades, it's extrapolated that the student will have an opportune future, whereas dunces are expected to have a shaky future.

But this isn't the case in the real world, wherein inspiring GPAs can only take you so far but are never an indication of ingenuity nor necessarily a measure of proficiency and competence or whether you'll accomplish something extraordinary or even get ahead of someone.

In the real world, social intelligence trumps egghead smartness, and uneducated streetwise folks can, in many ways, outplay the most learned people who aren't streetwise. It's also noteworthy that lacklustre GPAs neither connote mediocrity nor incompetence, as many average students and dunces have turned out to be extraordinary achievers in their careers, just as their smart counterparts from school could be.

Prof. Albert Einstein and Sir Winston Churchill come to mind. Albert Einstein was average in school, and Winston Churchill was a dunce. However, years after their formal education had ended, they churned out groundbreaking accomplishments that cemented their status as geniuses.

So, the real world is a great equalizer because it has a lot of opportunities that can make anyone successful, no matter their background or level of education.

John D. Rockefeller, for instance, was born to a homemaker mother and a con artist father who led a vagabond existence and gained notoriety for shady schemes. After dropping out of high school, John D. Rockefeller studied bookkeeping at Folsom's Mercantile College for only ten weeks and had his first job as an assistant bookkeeper at the age of 16.

Beginning at the age of 20, he ventured into several business partnerships and founded the Standard Oil Company at age 31. He remained the largest shareholder of Standard Oil and became the richest man in the US, controlling 90% of the oil industry. He also gained enormous influence over the railroad industry, and his fortune earned him the status of the richest man in the world, with an estimated net worth of $900 million as of 1913.

This attests to the fact that the real world presents the opportunity for actual career training and practical experience. Here, finding a resourceful mentor and an enabling work environment—not a paycheque—is the best opportunity for career development.

In this regard, your eagerness to learn will triumph over any fancy degree or lacklustre GPA you have, provided you have a sense of purpose. A sense of purpose, in any case, is either self-conceived or inculcated, which can be achieved by self-motivation or coaching! It has nothing to do with how sharp or slow a person was in school.

There are also several instances where some future achievers were belittled because they weren't doing well in school. But parents shouldn't, under any circumstance, join the fray. Instead, they should be an unrelenting voice of encouragement to their children in order to offset those traumatic remarks some teachers might blurt at them—as Albert Einstein's teacher said to him: 'You will not amount to anything.'

This book, Sense of Purpose through College and Career, doesn't downplay college education, or for that matter, college degrees, but while it stresses the relevance of higher learning, it strikes a balance between college education, apprenticeship or mentorship, and self-learning.

You will also be encouraged to combine your academic knowledge with street smarts. This will enable you to quickly adapt to the real world of work. Furthermore, you'll be stimulated to pursue experiential learning by combining apprenticeship or self-learning with the knowledge you acquired in college. Your success in this endeavour will boost your competence and make you one of the finest in your field.

Throughout the book, the author talks about how amazing the human brain is and how effective self-learning and apprenticeships/mentorships are for skill development and career growth.

By the time you're done reading, you'll be convinced that drawing on your brainpower, or for that matter, your smarts, aptitudes, and proclivities, will make you an achiever and propel you further in your goals than the names of the universities you attended. Fortunately, everyone has a brain!

Before the word 'university' became part of the modern lexicon, science and technology were already dynamic, scholars were already in the system, and civilised societies were already in existence. For instance, before the founding of the first-ever university, the University of Karueein, in Fez, Morocco, in 859 AD, mavens such as Pythagoras (570–495 BC), Aristotle (384 –322 BC), and Archimedes (288–212 BC) were known geniuses in philosophy, science, and engineering.

Their ingenuity did come from a source where ideas are generated and thoughts are processed. This source could've only been their brains.

On September 13, 2002, a Futon salesman, Jason Padgett, was assaulted by two thugs outside a bar. He staggered to a nearby hospital, where he was diagnosed with a concussion and bleeding kidney, but upon recovery, he was found to have turned into a mathematics genius. Before his attack, he had an aversion to math and couldn't do algebra. But after his attack, he began seeing the world in a pixelated geometric shape. He also understood the concept of Pi (π) and could hand-draw complex fractals without having learnt to draw.

How did it happen? The human brain changes itself by creating new neural pathways when we learn something new. This ability of the brain is called neuroplasticity. By being pummelled in the head, a hardwired neural pathway for mathematical intelligence was created in Jason Padgett's brain in a rare and dramatic event, hence turning him into a mathematics maven overnight.

Similarly, on October 27, 2006, Derek Amato hit his head on the shallow bottom of a pool. As a result, he suffered a concussion, but upon recovery, he had transformed into a musical savant who could play the piano without ever having learnt to play! All of these things indicate that the brain is the source of human ingenuity and show how amazing our brainpower is.

While reading, you'll be inspired to take on an endeavour and commit to it with body, soul, and mind. This is how you'll live a life of purpose; hence, achieving a sense of purpose favours the most determined soul.

Lastly, the effectiveness of superstition and spiritual practices in advancing one's sense of purpose has been analysed and evaluated based on its alignment with reality. Upon reflection, it will be possible to discern whether this path is reliable or one that requires caution.

CHAPTER ONE

College Education and the Brain

The value of a college education is not the learning of many facts but the training of the mind to think. – Albert Einstein.

In 859 AD, in Fez, Morocco, the oldest existing university in continuous operation, University of Karueein, was founded. Two hundred and twenty-nine years later, University of Bologna was also founded. Centuries after the establishment of these pioneering universities, and the subsequent establishment of many others, universities have been regarded as the source of human ingenuity. However, evidence points out that ingenuity is inherent in humans, and college education doesn't necessarily engender ingenuity.

In our 300,000 years of existence as Homo sapiens, our early ancestors dwelled in the wild until some 50,000 years ago, when they exhibited behavioural modernity.

Because they were dexterous and had modified limbs to use tools, they continuously learnt to fashion tools for hunting and gathering. They didn't create their tools simply because the raw materials were readily available, nor did they do so because of their modified limbs, but rather because of their larger brains.

The human brain has a well-developed cerebral cortex, which allows for abstract reasoning, motor functioning, language processing, personality development, planning, and organisation. These qualities set humans apart from other animals.

As time passed, our ancestors became increasingly curious about their environment and set out to explain and manipulate events. This led to the development of religion, mythology, the arts, philosophy, science, and technology.

They also endeavoured to spread across the earth's surface and establish their dominance. This led to their migration from one part of the earth to another, and they settled wherever they could adapt and procreate. They then organised themselves into groups based on shared interests and eventually established highly structured and advanced societies.

At the dawn of civilisation, our ancestors grew in complexity with diverse tastes and interests. Due to the waves of migration and growing population, their demand from their natural environment outstripped supply. This necessitated further inventions to augment their basic needs of life. They, therefore, became inventive out of need and necessity, and their inventiveness culminated in the first civilisation.

The diversity of the human intellect grew in direct proportion to population and adversity. Whether natural or manmade, adversities expanded our ancestors' problem-solving skills and further stimulated their thought processes. This led to the continuous development of appropriate tools for relief, tranquillity, and defence.

Thus, endeavour and ingenuity were inherent in our forefathers. With their primitive knowledge and skills, they had, from time to time, changed their abode from caves, tents, and roundhouses to straight walls with windows. Thus, acquired applied knowledge and skill were critical for their survival and were initially taught by those who first conceived of the knowledge and skill.

After thousands of years, higher education was set up to help spread knowledge and skills even more. In any civilised demography, the spread of knowledge and skills doesn't only enlighten people, but also empowers them en masse. Besides, the more enlightened people there are, the more they'll be empowered, and the more civilised their demography will be. These attributes underpin the human problem-solving impetus and personal dignity.

The historical background of University of Bologna is telling. Also, the conclusion of the Brownsville Affair is a classic example of how intellectualism and rationalism were used to fight against human rights violations and restore dignity to those whose dignity had been imperilled.

The Brownsville Affair

On the night of August 13, 1906, on the street of Brownsville, Texas, bartender Frank Natus was shot dead. The same night, police Lieutenant M. Y. Dominguez was shot and wounded.

Irate White residents of the town immediately accused the Buffalo Soldiers, a segregated unit of African-American soldiers of the 25th Infantry Regiment stationed at nearby Fort Brown, of the shooting. Although all their

White commanders attested that every soldier was in the barracks on the night of the shooting, the city's mayor, Frederick Combe, and some White locals insisted that some Buffalo Soldiers had carried out the shooting.

The White residents even obtained spent bullet cartridges from army rifles and presented them as evidence against the Buffalo Soldiers. Despite the evidence that the spent bullet cartridges were contrived as part of a frame-up, investigators accepted the statements of the mayor and the White locals.

Consequently, the Buffalo soldiers were interrogated to name those responsible for the shooting, but they insisted that they were all in the barracks on the night of the shooting. Nevertheless, Captain Bill McDonald of the Texas Rangers narrowed his suspicion to 12 soldiers and attempted to tie the crime to them. But without proof, the court snubbed him. All the same, on the recommendation of the Army's Inspector-General, President Theodore Roosevelt ordered the dishonourable discharge of the 167 Black soldiers, withheld their pensions, and banned them from ever working in the military or civil service.

President Theodore Roosevelt's decision outraged both White and Black citizens. Leaders of major Black organisations, including Booker T. Washington, tried to dissuade the Administration from its verdict, but it fell on deaf ears and their plea was rejected.

How Intellectualism was Applied

Senator Joseph B. Foraker of Ohio then moved for an investigation into the matter, known as the *Brownsville Affair*, and filed a minority report favouring the soldiers' innocence. An additional report by four Republicans concluded that the evidence against the soldiers was too far-fetched to warrant their discharge.

On February 23, 1909, the Committee on Military Affairs passed a recommendation on a bill for the correction of records and reenlistment of the discharged soldiers of the 25th Infantry Regiment. Both houses passed the legislation, which was signed by President Roosevelt on March 2, 1909.

On March 6, when Senator Foraker was no longer in office, he was the guest of honour at a mass meeting at Washington's Metropolitan African Methodist Episcopal Church. In his address, he said:

> I have said that I do not believe that a man in that battalion had anything to do with the shooting up of 'Brownsville,' but whether any one of them had, it was our duty to ourselves as a great, strong, and powerful nation to give every man a hearing, to deal fairly and

> squarely with every man; to see to it that justice was done to him; that he should be heard.

In 1970, Historian John D. Weaver published The Brownsville Raid, which detailed the events and investigated the affair in depth. In the Brownsville Raid, Weaver argued convincingly that the Buffalo Soldiers were innocent of the crime and were interdicted without the benefit of due process of law as guaranteed by the US Constitution.

After reading the publication, Congressman Augustus F. Hawkins of Los Angeles introduced a bill that allowed the Defence Department to reinvestigate the matter and serve justice to the accused soldiers. In 1972, the US Army found the accused soldiers of the 25th Infantry Regiment innocent.

Explication

In every state of affairs, people's biases repress their intellect, and it's only a matter of time before the truth triumphs. When ill-intention backfires, not only does the truth save the innocent, but it also exposes the malice and incompetence of false accusers. This holds true in underhanded dealings wherein people scheme to gain personal advantage over a group's interest and thereby expose their incompetence and lack of principle.

Moreover, when spite, prejudice, and falsity take the lead, explanations fall short of logic and the dots don't connect, thereby putting the false accuser's competence into question. Such was the situation surrounding the Brownsville Affair, as well as the shame of the hands that sought to entangle the innocent Buffalo Soldiers.

In the end, the intellectual inquiry by Senator Foraker, Historian John D. Weaver, and Congressman Augustus F. Hawkins brought the Brownsville Affair to a reasonable conclusion, not because they vindicated the soldiers of the 25th Infantry Regiment, but because they allowed for due process as it should be in a civilised society.

Intellectualism, therefore, triumphed over a preposterous collective punishment against the Buffalo Soldiers. Conversely, if the regime at the time was totalitarian, those unfounded accusations would've sent the innocent soldiers to the gallows.

Education is the only key to Develop the Intellect

Knowledge makes a man unfit to be a slave. –Frederick Douglas

---

During the 11th century in Bologna (the capital of Emilia-Romagna) in northern Italy, a guild of foreign students, called Universitates Scholarium, were appalled by the city's laws that imposed collective punishment on foreigners for the crimes and debts of their countrymen. So they hatched a plan to repeal the absurd law!

They knew that their residency as foreigners in Bologna gave them little options to lobby city authorities for their cause. They were also aware of their limited rights, except that they could study and expand their intellect as far and wide as they wanted. So, they started a tutorial group.

Initially, they had no faculty or infrastructure of their own. They, therefore, hired scholars from the city's pre-existing lay and ecclesiastical schools to be their instructors. They also had their lectures in informal schools called *Scholae* and the subjects they studied included liberal arts, notarial law, theology, and scrivenery.

The *Universitates Scholarium* then expanded its membership to *Studium,* becoming a modern-day university. As a result, Bologna society began to respect and admire the city's learned class that had graduated from the *studium*. With time, the *studium* grew to influence collective bargaining with the city because the city derived a lot of revenue from visiting foreign students, who would leave if they weren't treated well. The foreign students were then granted significant rights and privileges, and with this new social norm in place, collective punishment eventually died out.

Understand: In any human institution, an error in judgment, malice, or sheer stupidity can entangle someone or trample on other people's rights. However, in a jurisdiction governed by the rule of law, a victim can argue his case out and extricate himself from the entanglement, but only if he's learned; otherwise, there must be someone else who is learned to act on his behalf. The essence of being learned is to be intellectual and more rational, which no other establishment has taught the masses but the college system. This makes the entire college experience worthwhile, adding to the strategic relationships that learners can forge among themselves. It therefore flaws any reason to downplay college education, even if it falls short of inculcating proficiency and competence in learners en masse.

Brainpower

> The human brain has 100 billion neurons; each neuron connects 10 thousand other neurons. Sitting on your shoulders is the most complicated object in the known universe. – Michio Kaku

It is inherent in our nature to seek a greater purpose in life, which implies that we possess a biological predisposition to pursue our goals and leverage our abilities. Years of research and introspection have provided sufficient evidence to demonstrate that our complete potential and capabilities are indeed hardwired in our brains, waiting to be realised.

The Human Brain

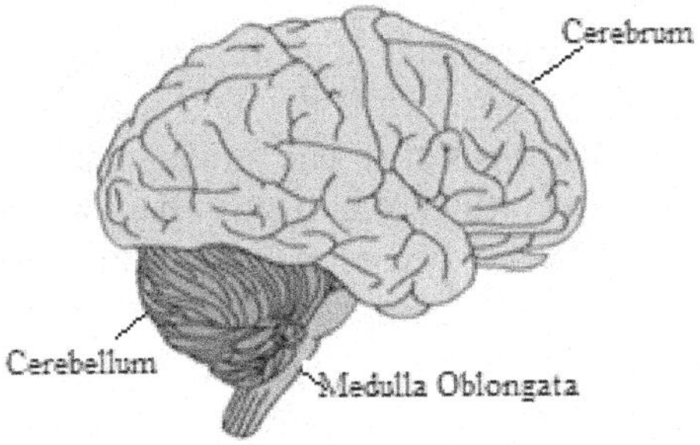

The human brain has three main parts: the cerebrum, cerebellum, and brainstem. The cerebrum is the largest part of the brain; it controls reading, thinking, learning, speech, emotion, and planned muscle movements such as walking. Its outer portion is called the cerebral cortex.

The cerebral cortex is divided into two cerebral hemispheres: left and right. The hemisphere has four sections called lobes: frontal, parietal, temporal, and occipital. Each lobe plays a distinct role. The frontal lobe controls reasoning, physical control, emotion, and language. It contains the motor cortex, which plays a role in planning and coordinating movement; the prefrontal cortex, which plays a role in higher-level cognitive function; and the Broca's area, which is crucial for language production. The temporal lobe controls memory, speech, and smell. The parietal lobe controls cognition, information processing, speech, visual perception, reading and writing, and mathematical computation. The occipital lobe processes and interprets everything we see.

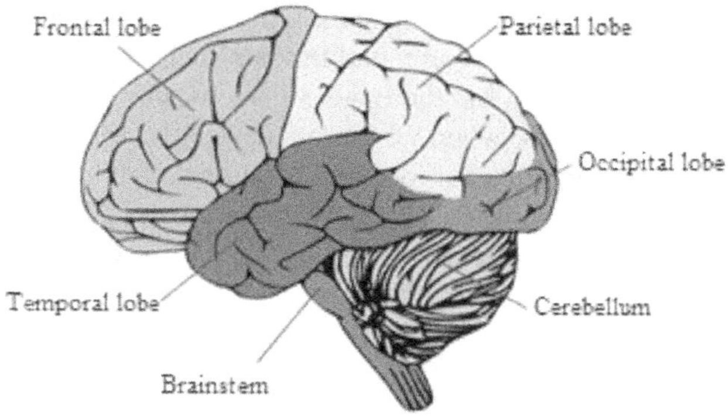

The brain has a network of neurons connected as neural pathways for the brain to function. Every neural pathway represents a certain knowledge, skill, or ability and can be hardwired. This attests to the brain's function as a wellspring of ingenuity.

Our early ancestors had symbiotic relationships in smaller leagues, such as nuclear families, and expansive leagues comprising several families. While they lived in caves for shelter, their next needs were food and clothing. So, they hunted and gathered and made clothes from plants and animals.

Ten thousand years into their existence, their hunting, gathering, and clothing-making skills progressed from novice to mastery. And every experience gained from each occupational adventure was worthwhile for self-improvement.

They could pluck a fruit with their hands and batter animals to death with clubs. But battering was strenuous; to make hunting convenient, they sharpened the ends of sticks with the edges of stones or rubbed the sticks against rocks till they had a piercing weapon.

Ingenuity began manifesting, and because one person conceived a trick at a time, the rest had to learn from that person by observing. This was how knowledge began to spread. Meanwhile, one invention led to another, thereby heralding the evolution of simple machines.

Explication

Throughout human history, we've always had the urge to be inventive and learn new skills. This desire stems from our need for a solution to a problem and to improve ourselves, thereby contributing to civilisation. And though modern life encourages schooling in order to sustain civilisation, it's worth noting that the structure of our brains already enables us to learn anything we desire to know—**including what we want to learn on our own**.

In the year 2000, a team of Brown University researchers taught some rats to grasp food pellets from a hole in a box. The researchers tested the rats after five days and found that not only had the rats' behaviour changed due to their learning of a new skill, but there were also changes in their brains.

This is similar to humans: when we learn a new skill, a large number of neurons amass in the brain's frontal lobe and become active to allow for the learning process. This also allows the frontal lobe to expand during the initial phase of assimilating knowledge and skills. Continuous practice makes the brain internalise the skill, and when this is achieved, the neural pathway for this skill moves to its appropriate functional area. For instance, though the learning of mathematical computation may begin in the frontal lobe, its final neural pathway is the parietal lobe.

When this happens, the neurons in the frontal lobe that amassed during the initial learning phase free up to make space for another skill to be learnt. After that, the frontal lobe reverts to its original size. A network of neurons then clusters together to remember that particular skill. This is typical of muscle memory. Example, bicycle riding, which is impossible to forget after years of learning to do it.

Every individual also has a distinct neural pathway. This accounts for the differences in our levels of intelligence and capabilities. It also explains why, among children with no training, we can still find those who draw so well, tell exciting stories, grasp mathematics with ease, or sing better than the rest.

Prodigy

A neural pathway becomes hardwired as a result of sustained learning, training, and practice. Some people, on the other hand, are born with pre-programmed neural pathways. This enables them to exhibit high performance at an early age without training. They're called prodigies.

Michael Kearney's outstanding cognitive ability would make one wonder if he was truly diagnosed with ADHD. The commonly known cognitive challenges associated with ADHD include absent-mindedness, difficulty focusing, forgetfulness, and a short attention span, often leading to learning difficulties. However, because Michael Kearney was prodigious, the hardwired neural pathway in his brain repressed the cognitive limitations he could've experienced due to ADHD.

Born on January 18, 1984, to an American father and Japanese-American mother, Michael Kearney began talking when he was four months old. When he was six months old, he said to his paediatrician: 'I have a left ear infection.' He began reading when he was eight months old and learnt the elementary school curriculum by the age of four. He entered college when he was six years old and graduated at the age of 10.

When Michael was four years old, he was tested with a multiple-choice diagnostic test for the John Hopkins Precocious Math Programme. Though it was his first attempt and he hadn't studied specifically for the programme, he aced the test.

In October 2006, Michael became a finalist in the trivia-and-puzzle game Gold Rush and won $100,000.00. In November of the same year, he won the grand prize of $1 million on Entertainment Tonight. Two years later, he contested on the show 'Who Wants to Be a Millionaire?' and won $25,000.00.

Talent

A study of modern and historical geniuses reveals that talent is a set of neural and physiological attributes that enhance proficiency and ease the acquisition of skills or knowledge. These attributes are the result of a distinct neural pathway in a person's brain. Although continuous learning and practice will eventually remap a person's neural pathway, a talented person already has his neural pathway mapped out, thereby enabling them to attain mastery with relative ease.

A typical route to becoming a professional actor is to attend drama school or take a formal acting class. Actor Aaron Paul, however, didn't take this route, nor did he take any other formal lesson in acting. Yet, his portrayal of Jesse Pinkman in the hit series, Breaking Bad, earned him several awards, including three **Emmys.**

Four-time Ironman triathlete world champion, Chrissie Wellington, didn't compete professionally until she was 30, but she won her first world championship less than a year later. Thus, talent allows a person to develop proficiency faster than someone without it.

To become a sniper in the army, a recruit must show good marksmanship in order to be noticed and selected for further training in a sniper school. How does the army expect an inexperienced recruit to show good marksmanship? The recruit must have already had a neural pathway mapped out for shooting. This neural pathway is the basis of our aptitudes, proclivities, and vocations.

When Craig Harrison of the British Army first used a sniper rifle on a firing range near a British military base in Split, Croatia, he felt the weapon in his hands as though it were merely an elongated AK-47.

This is to say that without prior experience, Harrison knew the first time that using the *Dragunov Sniper Rifle* (SVD) would be a piece of cake, and indeed, after firing his first shots at a tree, the tree split into two. There and then, he discovered himself as a marksman.

Without a neural pathway for marksmanship, he wouldn't have felt the Dragunov Sniper Rifle (SVD) in his hand as though it was an elongated AK-47, and his initial sniper shots would've been lacklustre. In 2009, he set a world record for the longest confirmed sniper kill in combat, at a range of 2,475 m (2,707 yds).

Annie Oakley's exceptional skill with guns may seem too amazing to be believed, but it is absolutely true. Even from a distance of 30 paces, she could accurately shoot and split a playing card held on its edge. She could also hit dimes that were tossed into the air and shoot a playing card thrown into the air before it even touched the ground.

During a stage performance on March 19, 1884, Annie Oakley confidently stepped onto the stage, lifted her riffle, and aimed at a burning candle. With a single shot, she extinguished the flame with a swift bullet, astonishing the audience. Not only that, she could also knock corks off bottles and slice through a cigar that her husband held between his teeth.

What's truly remarkable is that Annie Oakley achieved all of this without any formal training in marksmanship. Her exceptional shooting skills, thus, can only be attributed to her talent and, of course, practice.

Ingenium

There are only a few enlightened people with a lucid mind and style and with good taste within a century. What has been preserved of their work belongs among the most precious possessions of mankind. – Albert Einstein.

Some people possess rare brainpower that is unique to them and cannot be learned by other people. This type of brainpower is called *ingenium,* and it's what manifested in Einstein's cognition, Charles Hatfield's genius, and Thomas Fuller's calculative prowess.

Einstein, the Genius

Albert Einstein was a theoretical physicist with incredible cognition. His life's work elicited so much awe that when he died, other scientists wanted to know what was in his brain. A postmortem study of his brain revealed that his inferior parietal lobule (the part of the brain responsible for spatial cognition and mathematical thought) was wider than usual and seemed better integrated than the brains of ordinary people. He also had a fourth ridge on his mid-frontal lobe, the part of the brain responsible for planning and working memory. Other people have three ridges.

During his heyday, Einstein was widely venerated; when he spoke, people listened. In July 1939, physicist Leo Szilard persuaded him to write a letter to US President Franklin D. Roosevelt, urging him to develop an atomic bomb. With Einstein's guidance, Szilard drafted the letter, which was signed by Einstein and sent to President Roosevelt:

Albert Einstein
Old Grove Rd.
Nassau Point
Peconic, Long Island
August 2nd, 1939.

F.D. Roosevelt,
President of the United States,
White House
Washington, D.C.

Sir:

Some recent work by E. Fermi and L. Szilar, which has been communicated to me in manuscript, leads me to expect that the element uranium may be turned into a new and important source of energy in the immediate future. Certain aspects of the situation which has arisen seem to call for watchfulness, and if necessary, quick action on the part of the Administration. I believe that it is my duty to bring to your attention the following facts and recommendations:

In the course of the last four months, it has been made probable – through the work of Joliot in France as well as Fermi and Szilard in America – that it may become possible to set up a nuclear chain

reaction in a large mass of uranium, by which vast amounts of power and large quantities of new radium-like elements would be generated. Now it appears almost certain that this could be achieved in the immediate future.
This phenomenon would also lead to the construction of bombs, and it is conceivable – though much less certain – that extremely powerful bombs of a new type may be constructed. A single bomb of this type, carried by boat and exploded in a port, might very well destroy the whole port together with some of the surrounding territory. However, such bombs might very well prove to be too heavy for transportation by air.

The United States has only very poor ores of uranium in moderate quantities. There is some good ore in Canada and the former Czechoslovakia, while the most important source of uranium is Belgian Congo.
In view of this situation, you may think it is desirable to have some permanent contact maintained between the Administration and the group of physicists working on chain reactions in America. One possible way of achieving this might be for you to entrust with this task a person who has your confidence and who could perhaps serve in an official capacity. His task might comprise the following:

a) to approach Government Departments, keep them informed of the further development, and put forward recommendations for Government action. Giving particular attention to the problem of securing a supply of uranium ore for the United States.
b) to speed up the experimental work, which is at present being carried on within the limits of the budget of university laboratories, by providing funds, if such funds be required, through his contacts with private persons who are willing to make contributions for this cause, and perhaps also by obtaining the co-operation of industrial laboratories which have the necessary equipment.

I understand that Germany has actually stopped the sale of uranium from the Czechoslovakian mines which she has taken over. That she should have taken such early action might perhaps be understood on the ground that the son of the German Under-Secretary of State, von Weizsäcker, is attached to the Kaiser-Wilhelm-Institute in Berlin where some of the American work on uranium is now being repeated.

Yours very truly,
Albert Einstein

Eight days later, President Roosevelt replied to Einstein, informing him that he had constituted the Uranium Committee to study the proposal. They later developed the atomic bomb.

Earlier in 1918, when WWI had ended, a group of radical students stormed the University of Berlin and held the rector and faculty hostage. The situation was volatile, and a police confrontation was sure to end in tragedy. To avoid bloodshed, Einstein was called to negotiate with the students. When they saw him, they mellowed, and when he spoke to them, they listened. Peace was brokered, and the situation was resolved without tragedy.

Einstein knew of his ingenium and the reverence it elicited in anyone he beseeched. He also knew he would be deified and immortalised when he died; so, before his death, he asked for his mortal remains to be cremated and his ashes to be scattered in secret to prevent his grave from becoming a place of pilgrimage.

Charles Hatfield, the Rainmaker

In 1902, Charles Hatfield developed a secret formula comprising 23 unknown chemicals and stored them in a large evaporating tank. He announced that he could use his formula to precipitate rainfall, and after a succession of successful demonstrations, he earned the moniker, *the rainmaker*.

The year 1915 brought drought to San Diego, and the residents were perturbed. The members of the San Diego Wide Awake Improvement Club pressured the San Diego City Council to invite Charles Hatfield to intervene. Their primary demand was for Hatfield to precipitate enough rain to fill the Morena Dam reservoir.

When Hatfield arrived in San Diego, he met with the city council to negotiate his pay before building a tower beside Lake Morena. He finished building the tower in the New Year of 1916, and on January 5, he climbed to the top of the tower and dramatically released his secret 23 chemicals into the air.

Dark clouds emerged and began to gather, thereby mystifying onlookers. In a moment, the rain started, and it fell enough to fill the Morena Dam reservoir. But the rain didn't stop; it continued for at least a month, and caused flooding that destroyed bridges, farms, homes, and marooned trains, resulting in some 20 casualties.

Although the disastrous effect of the protracted rainfall led to a rift between the San Diego City Council and Charles Hatfield, his fame nonetheless soared, and people kept inviting him to precipitate rain for them. Charles Hatfield died on January 12, 1958, and took his rainmaking wonder with him to the grave.

Thomas Fuller, the Mental Calculator

In 1714, when Thomas Fuller was 14, he was enslaved somewhere in Liberia or Benin and shipped off to the US, where he became the property of Presley and Elizabeth Cox in Alexandria, Virginia.

The Coxes kept a total of 16 slaves, but they valued Thomas Fuller the most because of his ability to solve complex mathematical problems in his mind. Word spread about Thomas Fuller's genius, and when he was 70, William Hartshorne and Samuel Coates, both influential figures from Pennsylvania, visited Alexandria, Virginia, and sent for him.

When Thomas Fuller was brought to them, they challenged him with two questions they thought no human could work out in their mind. They first asked him how many seconds there were in a year and a half, and he answered in 30 seconds, '47, 304,000'. He was right. Next, they asked him how many seconds a man who is 70 years, 17 days, and 12 hours old has lived, and he answered in a minute and a half, '2,210,500,800 seconds.'

Meanwhile, one of the men was working out the answer on paper, and when he finished, he told Fuller that his answer was incorrect. But Fuller quickly responded, 'Top Massa, you forget de leap year'. When the leap year was factored into the calculation, the figure matched Thomas Fuller's answer.

Impressed by Fuller's calculative prowess, Samuel Coates remarked that it was a pity Fuller had no education equal to his genius. But Thomas Fuller responded, 'No Massa, it is best that I had no learning, for many learned men be great fools!'

Albert Einstein, Charles Hatfield, and Thomas Fuller, however, weren't the only ones with ingenium. In fact, some people with ingenium walk on the surface of the earth with us without being noticed, whereas others are noticed, except that they aren't in the limelight.

Before Higher Education was Established

Centuries before University of Karueein (859 AD) was founded, civilisation was already in the making. This is evident in the early inventions and scientific breakthroughs that still have modern relevance.

For example, Euclid of Alexandria (mid-4th century BC), the father of geometry, formulated the Euclidean geometry, which still has relevance in modern mathematics; Archimedes (287–212 BC), among other things, invented the Archimedes screw: a device that moves water uphill and it's still widely used in rural Egypt to raise water from a lower irrigation ditch to a higher one; Aristarchus of Samos (c. 310–c. 230 BC), an ancient Greek astronomer and mathematician, was the first person to conceive and present the heliocentric model, which holds that the sun is at the centre of the known universe, with the earth circling around the sun once a year and rotating about its axis once a day.

Pythagoras of Samos (570–495 BC) invented the Pythagoras theorem around 530 BC, and it's still relevant in modern mathematics. The list goes on.

As far back as the 5th century BCE, Indian physician Sushruta knew of diabetes and referred to it as *honey-like urine*. To describe the disease, he pointed out that the urine of diabetics was sticky to the touch and sweet enough to attract ants. He was emphatic that the disease primarily affected people who ate a lot of rice, sweets, and cereals.

During the era of classical antiquity (8 BC–9 AD), engineers constructed architectural marvels that continue to fascinate modern engineers. They're collectively known as the Seven Wonders of The Ancient World and are:

- Great Pyramid of Giza, Egypt.
- Hanging Gardens of Babylon, Iraq.
- Statue of Zeus at Olympia, Greece.
- Temple of Artemis at Ephesus, Turkey.
- Mausoleum at Halicarnassus, Turkey.
- Colossus of Rhodes, Greece.
- Lighthouse of Alexandria, Egypt.

The Great Pyramid of Giza, constructed between 2584 and 2561 BCE for the Egyptian Pharaoh Khufu, was the tallest edifice in the world for almost 4,000 years and a testament to human ingenuity and engineering. Having been a subject of ongoing investigation for centuries, exactly how it was built remains a mystery, with people claiming everything from extraterrestrials to an advanced and unknown civilisation as the true source of its creation.

It is so imposing that people even believe aliens were involved in its construction. Meanwhile, the pyramids' architecture still amazes modern engineers. Let's examine its features: The pyramid is 756 feet long on each side and 481 feet high. It is composed of 2.3 million stones (weighing nearly 3 tonnes each, for a total mass of 6.5 million tonnes) and was built by 4,000 workers in 20 years, using manual labour, sledges on tracks, and other simple machines, to say the least. Yet, even with modern heavy-duty machinery, it'll be daunting to construct the Great Pyramid of Giza today. First, modern building materials don't have an expected lifespan anywhere near 4000 years, and the construction process will consume so much energy and produce high carbon emissions. Moreover, new passages are still being discovered, adding to the baffling mystery of its architecture.

The Hanging Garden of Babylon was planted by King Nebuchadnezzar II (between 605 and 562 BCE) as a self-watering plane of exotic biodiversity, reaching over 75 feet high through a series of climbing terraces. According to the ancient writer Diodorus Siculus, Nebuchadnezzar's wife, Amytis of Media, missed the beautiful mountains with their blooming flowers in her homeland, so Nebuchadnezzar planted the spectacular Hanging Gardens for her as a gift to make up for her homeland mountains.

The Statue of Zeus at Olympia was a 40 feet high statue sculpted in the 5th century BCE by the great Greek sculptor, Phidias, to enthral worshippers who visited the Temple of Zeus at Olympia. The statue depicted Zeus on his throne, clad in a robe made of hammered gold over his ivory skin.

The Temple of Artemis at Ephesus took 120 years to be completed in 550 BCE. According to all accounts, the temple was so magnificent and was once said to be the largest temple and building in antiquity.

By Zee Prime at cs Wikipedia, CC BY-SA 3.0, https://commons.wikimedia.org/w/index.php?curid=6347027

The Lighthouse of Alexandria rose from the square base of a middle octagon, sectioned up to a circular top, and stood close to 440 feet as the third tallest man-made structure. It was constructed between 284 and 246 BCE and was commissioned by Ptolemy I Soter. Travellers who visited the spectacular lighthouse reported, at the time, that words weren't enough to describe its beauty. Its light in the day was the sun's reflection; at night, it was a bonfire, which could be seen 35 miles offshore.

The Mausoleum at Halicarnassus was built in c. 351 BCE as the final resting place of the Persian satrap, Mausolus. The tomb stood 135 feet tall and was adorned with fine sculptures. The English word mausoleum was derived from Mausolus.

The Colossus of Rhodes was an imposing monument constructed between 292 and 280 BCE to depict Helios, the patron god of the island of Rhodes, Greece. It stood over 110 feet high on a pedestal, similar to the Statue of Liberty, and overlooked the harbour of Rhodes.

What is more? In addition to the remarkable architectural marvels mentioned earlier, ancient civilisations contributed a plethora of inventions that illustrate human ingenuity. These inventions date back to a time before the establishment of the first university and include the likes of paper, pen, and ink. Such inventions attest to the inherent creativity and resourcefulness of humans across history.

The invention of paper by the ancient Egyptians dates back to as early as 3000 BC. This remarkable invention involved weaving long strips of the pith from the papyrus plant into a strong, thin sheet, which was then weighed down. Additionally, they crafted a writing tool (pen) from cut reeds and blended beeswax and vegetable gum with soot or other organic materials to make ink. These inventions were crucial for the development and dissemination of written language and communication in ancient Egypt and beyond.

It's important to note that these ancient inventions were in use and reproduced for centuries before the establishment of the first university. This fact lends credibility to the effectiveness of self-learning, apprenticeship, and mentorship in acquiring and transmitting knowledge and skills. These methods of education have been instrumental in shaping societies and cultures throughout history, enabling individuals to share their expertise and experience with others in their communities.

CHAPTER TWO

Developing Your Potential

Whatever career path you're considering, your best bet for finding fulfilment is to pursue an interest that is congenial to you. And if you are not sure what that interest might be, you may find it by looking back at your childhood.

Knowing your aptitudes and proclivities is the starting point for your career development. Your next need is an enabling environment; however, deliberate practice and deliberate mentorship are the most effective exercises for proficiency development.

Aptitudes and Proclivities

Our aptitudes and proclivities emerge during childhood and develop further as we grow. For example, a boy child may have an unbridled interest in toy soldiers and weaponry, which he frequently discusses. Give him a variety of playthings in exchange for his toy soldiers and guns, and he won't be appreciative. Ask him to narrate an imaginary story from time to time, and he'll narrate military action again and again.

Such a child is cut out for the military, where he'll find his life's purpose and fulfilment. Any career path other than the military will be a deviation from his calling, and though he may still be accomplished in a different field, such an accomplishment might fall short of fulfilment. Thus, a career that is in harmony with your aptitude and proclivity is the most ideal for your sense of purpose.

But then, some culprits can hinder your inclination. Paradoxically, the education system is one of those culprits, stemming from the limitations of a benighted economy. Otherwise, dispiriting teachers and vetoing parents are to blame.

Benighted Economy

There are as many gifted people in a benighted demography as there are in an enlightened demography who didn't get the opportunity to go to school or have any opportunity for career development. Consequently, they grow ignorant and may never find their life's purpose. In addition, the education system in this benighted demographic is under-resourced and replete with impractical curricula. This situation puts learners, who would otherwise flourish in an enlightened demography, at a disadvantage.

Education System

In his 1983 book, *Frames of Mind*: The Theory of Multiple Intelligences, psychologist Howard Gardner identified eight abilities that indicate multiple intelligences. The table below outlines the various intelligences and their corresponding careers.

Intelligence	**Career**
Musical-rhythmic and harmonic: AKA musicality	Music
Visual-Spatial: aka. spatial intelligence	Artist
Verbal-linguistic: AKA Verbal Intelligence	Communication
Logical-Mathematical: AKA Reason [closely linked to fluid intelligence and general intelligence (*g* factor)]	Research
Bodily-kinaesthetic	Sports
Interpersonal: AKA Social skills	Politics
Intrapersonal: AKA Introspection	Management
Naturalistic	Naturalist

Unfortunately, the mainstream education system is particularly inclined towards Logical-mathematical Intelligence. So, it favours academically gifted students while downplaying other potentials that aren't relevant to academics, though they are worthwhile. This is one of the major flaws of the education system.

Dispiriting Teachers

With the prevalence of success stories of luminaries and business magnates who were average in school, dropouts who became business tycoons, and dunces who grew to be global icons, it comes as a surprise that some teachers still look down on their non-performing students and belittle their aspirations instead of motivating them. This attitude can demoralise students and leave them with low self-esteem.

Vetoing Parents

During his childhood, Ralph would dismantle his toys and put the parts back. He would also cut cardboard and design cars or any gadget out of them. On top of that, he was precocious and grew up with a penchant for mechanics and electronics. But when he completed high school and wanted to study engineering at the university, his father objected and insisted that he study medicine.

A contention between father and son ensued; in the end, his father's will prevailed, and seven years later, Ralph became a medical doctor. His father was proud of him, but Ralph was indifferent. He, however, practised as a doctor, though half-heartedly, and he would cast aspersions on his father's name whenever he encountered an occupational challenge.

Alfred Nobel was also precocious and excelled in chemistry and literature. He showed interest in explosives at an early age and learnt about their principles from his inventor father, Immanuel Nobel.

But writing was Alfred's primary interest, which didn't appeal to Immanuel Nobel. He wanted Alfred to follow in his footsteps as an inventor. So, he made him travel to have his training in chemical engineering, expecting that while he was away from home, he wouldn't get the time to pursue his writing interest.

But contrary to his father's expectations, Alfred did not devote himself entirely to chemical engineering. At his leisure, he read voraciously and learnt to be a writer. He became versatile through his reading habit and wrote plays, novels, and poetry. He also became an accomplished chemical engineer, notable for inventing dynamite and holding over 355 patents.

In addition, he published a tragedy by the title *Nemesis* (1896) and left behind a voluminous collection of letters, a handful of poems, some early drafts of analytical novels titled *I ljusate Afrika* (In Brightest Africa, 1861) and an outline of a satirical comedy titled, *The Patent Bacillus* (1896).

Finally, he instituted the Nobel Peace Prize to be awarded annually to individuals who confer the most significant benefit on mankind in physics, chemistry, medical science or physiology, literature, and peace.

Lord Randolph, however, backpedalled from the veto fray. Even as a politician, he didn't peddle influence to get Winston Churchill admitted to law school, though he had wanted to see him become a lawyer.

First, he admitted to Winston's academic shortfall and knew he couldn't qualify for Cambridge University to study law. He also knew that young Winston Churchill loved playing with toy soldiers when he was a child and had seen him spending hours arranging his toys in a battle formation. It was obvious Winston had an inclination for the military, so Lord Randolph enrolled him in the Royal Military College, after failing two entrance exams and passing on his third attempt.

Lord Randolph's interest in Winston at the Royal Military College was to see him become an officer in the infantry, but due to his borderline pass mark in the entrance exams, Winston missed the infantry and had the cavalry instead.

Years ago, at Harrow School, Winston wrote poetry and letters that were published in the school magazine. He also excelled in history studies, even as he performed poorly in other subjects. His aptitude in English and proclivity for history, therefore, were his foundation in oratory and writing.

Years later, while he was in the Army, he wrote two books on his experiences: *The Story of the Malakand Field Force* (1898) and *The River War* (1899). He wrote 43 books, totalling 72 volumes, which earned him the Nobel Prize for Literature in 1953.

Following a stint in the military, Winston Churchill worked as a war correspondent, reporting on the Boer War in South Africa, and was taken prisoner by the Boers. But he escaped and travelled almost 300 miles to the Portuguese territory in Mozambique.

Having also experienced combat during the 1898 Battle of Omdurman in Sudan, he led Britain from the brink of defeat to victory in WWII. Apparently, Winston Churchill's non-performance in school couldn't hold him back as he drew on his childhood proclivities, aptitude, and military experience to become one of the most influential politicians the world had ever seen.

Understand: However benighted the economy of your country, the poor education system you studied in, the dispiriting teachers who belittled your aspirations, or the vetoing parents who didn't support your primary career interest, you can still work your way to success.

Setting goals is imperative for achieving this. If you're in college, don't wait until you complete; you can still pursue your primary career interest alongside your formal studies. Because except for the strictly full-time academic programmes, there are many courses you can study on the sideline. Thanks to the proliferation of books and open learning, which has enabled self-learning and career development opportunities like never before.

Case in Point: Derrick, like Ralph, was forced by his father to study medicine against his interest in coding. So, he went on to study medicine, but on every semester vacation, he learnt coding and kept at it even after he had completed medical school. When he became versed in coding, he established himself as a developer while he practised as a physician. Thus, unlike Ralph, Derrick circumvented his father's veto and fulfilled his childhood aspiration.

Smile at the naysayers

There are two types of people who will tell you that you cannot make a difference in this world: those who are afraid to try and those who are afraid you will succeed. – Ray Goforth.

Until you're accomplished and successful, the people around you will doubt your potential to achieve something phenomenal and belittle your aspirations. When they do, don't take it personally; just smile at them!

The naysayers

Parents are the most culpable in the naysayers' scheme of things. Teachers are next. But your friends and colleagues can't impose their will on you. They may, however, attempt to sow doubt in you in order to make you feel less capable.

Parents

First, let's try to understand our parents: they're protective of us and always seek to be our safety net. They become anxious when they see us ploughing from their bosom into uncertainty and would discourage us out of fear. For instance, when American actor Alec Baldwin told his parents he would be an actor, they screamed, wept, and freaked out. But he became a successful actor anyway!

For most of us, our parents wish to see us taking the safest route in life. Thus, by making good grades in college, getting into intellectual professions, and climbing the career ladder, hoping that we'll reach the pinnacle and prosper. They feel we're safer this way rather than leaving us to wander through uncertainty. To them, uncertainty includes athletics, entrepreneurial risk, and uncharted waters. They perceive these routes to be slippery, and to protect us, they say nay.

However, if Florence Nightingale had listened to what her parents wanted her to become rather than what she wanted to be, perhaps her name would've been lost in oblivion.

Her father was a wealthy landowner, and her mother was a socialite who wanted Florence to conform to the Victorian standard for a woman: i.e., to settle down in marriage and have children. Hence, they discouraged her from becoming a nurse. Moreover, in those days, the nursing profession was lowbrow and undignified, with an air of promiscuity. But Florence defied her parents, enrolled in nursing training at age 30, and later became the founder and iconic figure of modern nursing.

David Brinkley's penchant for reading stimulated his interest in storytelling and journalism, but this was much to his mother's distaste. He once gave her a story he had written, and when she glanced through it, she threw the paper at his face and blurted out at him: 'Why are you wasting your time on such foolishness?' This remark became a scar on David's mind and took a long time to heal. Nonetheless, David grew to become an iconic newscaster for NBC and ABC in a career that spanned 54 years (from 1943 to 1997).

Miles Davis' father wanted him to be a dentist, and his mother wanted him to play the violin, but Miles himself had a penchant for the trumpet. The future nine-time Grammy winner might have turned out, perhaps as an ordinary man, if he had listened to his parents. But he went ahead with his love for trumpets and created iconic sounds that greatly influenced jazz and other genres. His accomplishment, thus, was phenomenal!

These stories of parental naysay-proven-wrong are many, counting the successes of historical figures, public figures, and people we personally know whose parents disagreed with their choice of career. This is why you must believe in yourself, and it's only then that you won't be distracted by naysayers.

Teachers

Our teachers are predisposed to either validate or invalidate our aspirations, depending on the grades we score in our examinations. And if we score excellent grades, we get their absolute validation.

Case in Point: Ellie Hylton scored straight A's, with no A minuses, in every semester examination she took during her undergraduate years, including courses she didn't particularly like. Take the popular introduction to economics course at Harvard, which her father also took during his undergraduate years and attested to how tricky the final exam questions could be, but Ellie scored 100 percent.

Earlier, she intended to become a medical doctor until she realised that she didn't like biochemistry or spending time in the science lab. Yet she aced the biochemistry class with a 99% score.

She became interested in topics concerning social inequality and realised that sociologists asked all of the world's questions. So she opted for a sociology major and relished the research opportunities therein.

She graduated with the highest GPA in 2013 and was eulogised as the Number One student. As far as anyone knows, she's the first African-American to achieve this ground-breaking record in Harvard's history.

Her thesis was titled *Bridging the Gap: Social Integration and Academic Achievement in the Desegregated Public High School.* Having perused Ellie's thesis, Professor Waters (Harvard) recommended the highest-grade possible summa cum laude for her, which made her the winner of the Sophia Freund Prize, established in 1964 to be awarded to the highest-ranking student graduating summa cum laude with the highest GPA—4.0.

Professor Waters acknowledged: 'There has been a lot of literature on social alienation and academic performance, but never the two.' He added, 'Ellie was original because she focussed on the relationship between both alienation and performance, and she concluded that students are still able to perform and flourish despite the feeling of social isolation.'

Ellie was inducted into an elite list of graduates elected to *Phi Beta Kappa,* the US's oldest and most prestigious academic honours society. *Phi Beta Kappa* are Greek initials meaning, 'Love of learning is the guide of life.'

If you were a high performer like Ellie Hylton, you would've gone through your education without any teacher doubting your aspirations. Tell them you'll move the moon to the sun's place, and they'll be like, 'You're smart; you can do it.' But the same validation won't be accorded to you if you're a non-performing student. They'll even doubt your capability to put food on the table.

But the irony of these misjudgements is that many of the prime movers of ancient and modern civilisation, most of the brains behind modern scientific breakthroughs, and many of the business tycoons whose fortunes are the mainstay of burgeoning economies didn't get the grades Ellie Hylton had.

This indicates that what it takes to excel in school is distinct from what it takes to be accomplished and successful in a career. And that the learner who does not perform as well as Ellie Hylton should not be disparaged, but rather encouraged and never given up on.

John Gurdon placed last (out of 250 boys) in the biology class and any other science subject at Eton College. A schoolmaster once wrote in his report: 'I believe he has ideas about becoming a scientist. On his present showing, this is quite ridiculous; if he can't learn simple biological facts, he would have no chance of doing the work of a specialist, and it would be a sheer waste of time, both on his part and of those who have to teach him.'

John Gurdon, nevertheless, grew to become a developmental biologist, best known for his pioneering research in nuclear transplantation and cloning. He received numerous awards throughout his career, including the 1985 Royal Medal, the 2003 Copley Medal, and the 2009 Albert Lasker Basic Medical Research Award, which he shared with Yamanaka.

He was made a fellow of the Royal Society in 1971 and a foreign associate of the US National Academy of Sciences in 1980. He was knighted in 1995 and won the Nobel Prize for Physiology and Medicine in 2012 for discovering that mature cells can be converted to stem cells.

Shakira began writing and composing music when she was only eight years old. She thrilled everyone with her dance moves and earned the moniker, belly dancer. However, her voice didn't sound like she was cut out for singing. As a result, her music teacher told her she couldn't sing, and didn't accept her into the school choir. Her classmates even told her she sang like a goat.

Yet, these naysayers couldn't deter her from becoming the Queen of Latin Music. In a 2018 report by Forbes, Shakira was mentioned as the first female Latin artist to have sold the most albums in history, having earned three Grammy Awards under her belt.

When albert Einstein graduated from Zurich Polytechnic in 1900, his plan was to start a doctoral programme and work as an assistant to a professor at a university. He had obtained a diploma; a recommendation from professors under whom a candidate had studied was a prerequisite for job placement. But Einstein's request for a recommendation letter was spurned by his professors.

His final grades were average, and his notoriety in class had earned him the animosity of his professors. He had also skipped classes, and on days he attended classes, he would rebel at any opportunity.

So, no professor was willing to give him a recommendation or reference letter. Apparently, his supervisor (Professor Weber) had besmirched him among the faculty, and he was the only one in his class who had no job placement after graduation.

Einstein's father, Hermann Einstein, was worried and wrote a letter to Professor Wilhelm Ostwald:

Esteemed Herr Professor!

Please forgive a father who is so bold as to turn to you, esteemed Herr Professor, in the interest of his son.

I shall start by telling you that my son Albert is 22 years old, that he studied at the Zurich Polytechbikum for four years, and that he passed his diploma examinations in mathematics and physics with flying colours last summer. Since then, he has been trying unsuccessfully to obtain a position as an Assistant, which would enable him to continue his education in theoretical and experimental physics. All those in position to give a judgement in the matter praise his talents; in any case, I can assure you that he is extraordinarily studious and diligent and clings with great love to his science.

My son, therefore, feels profoundly unhappy with his present lack of position, and his idea that he has gone off the tracks with his career and is now out of touch gets more and more entrenched each day. In addition, he is oppressed by the thought that he is a burden on us, people of modest means.

Since it is you, highly honoured Herr Professor, whom I have taken the liberty of turning to with the humble request to read his paper published in the Annalen fur Physik and to write him, if possible, a few words of encouragement, so that he might recover his joy in living and working.

If, in addition, you could secure him an Assistant's position for now or the next autumn, my gratitude would know no bounds.

I beg you once again to forgive me for my impudence in writing to you, and I am also taking the liberty of mentioning that my son does not know anything about my unusual step.

I remain, highly esteemed Herr
Professor.
Yours devoted
Hermann Einstein

The letter landed on Professor Wilhelm Ostwald's desk, and he read it but ignored Hermann Einstein's plea. As for Professor Weber, he had developed such a dislike for Albert Einstein that when no other physics or math graduate was available to be his assistant, he hired two engineering students instead and shunned Albert Einstein.

Earlier in 1895, Einstein's teacher wrote in Einstein's school report, 'He will never amount to anything.' Nonetheless, Einstein grew to be an esteemed professor, a Nobel laureate, and the most eminent scientist of his era.

In 1965, while studying for a bachelor's degree in economics at Yale University, the future founder of FedEx—Frederick Smith—wrote a term paper for Economics 43A. In the paper, Smith outlined the logistical challenges facing the pioneering firms in the information technology industry.

He wrote: 'Most airfreight shippers relied on passenger route systems, but this didn't make economic sense for urgent shipments.' He further proposed a pertinent system that would allow the timely delivery of medicines, computer parts, and electronics. Smith's 'outlandish' thesis didn't make sense to his supervisor, Professor Challis A. Hall, and he awarded him a low grade.

Six years later, following a stint in the military, Smith bought a controlling interest in Arkansas Aviation Sales, located in Arkansas. In his new firm, he saw how difficult it was to get packages and other airfreight delivered within a day or two. With his lowly graded term paper in mind, Smith sought a better way to do express delivery, and the idea for Federal Express was born.

In his early years, Winston Churchill (1874–1965), who would later win a Nobel Peace Prize, was said to be unmotivated, wilfully troublesome, and a dunce by his teachers.

After performing poorly in his first two schools, he enrolled at Harrow School in 1888 with abysmal entrance exam scores that placed him at the bottom of his class. Except for the two subjects he loved, English and history,

Winston had no interest in studying any other subject, and his general performance was appalling. This dimmed his prospects of entering the university.

After two failed attempts at gaining admission to the Royal Military College, Sandhurst, Winston Churchill passed on his third attempt with a score that qualified him for the cavalry rather than the infantry. Lord Randolph Churchill, his father, however, had hoped for an infantry career for Winston Churchill, so he was deeply disappointed.

Winston Churchill had thought for years that his father had discovered a military genius in him, despite the fact that the military was not a preferred career choice for a highborn at the time, until he was told that his father had chosen the military for him only because he (Winston Churchill) wasn't clever enough to enter law school.

Despite his poor school performance, however, Winston Churchill grew to become the British prime minister from 1940 to 1945 and again from 1951 to 1955. Before then, he was an army officer, a journalist, and an orator. In 1953, he was awarded the Nobel Prize for Literature for his endearing authorship and was knighted by Queen Elizabeth II.

Friends

Friends' naysaying could be because they unconsciously project their inadequacies and insecurities on you. It could also be that they're regressive thinkers. Regressive thinkers believe that great things can only be achieved by great people, and they simply cannot see that you can do something phenomenal while you're an ordinary person. Moreover, for what they can't do, have never heard of, or haven't conceived, they don't expect that you can do it.

Envy and jealousy may also play a role; people often cannot bear the thought of being left behind by those they began life with, whereas those ahead may be unhappy that those they left behind will catch up with them.

This is a complexity of human nature, and you shouldn't take it personally. Instead, you should cease and desist from discussing your aspirations with friends who show no interest in your life goals.

Understand: Whenever you conceive an idea, there's a tendency that you'll want to discuss it with one or a few relatives and friends, expecting their validation. But until you have already attained greatness, most people will always doubt your potential, which implies that their response to your sense of purpose will often not be what you want to hear.

This therefore renders the validation you seek unnecessary. Instead, after you have conceived an idea, your next step is to find out how you can achieve it and then devote yourself to the process. The more silent you are about the process, the better.

Making an appointment with a career/life coach or finding a mentor at this juncture is a priceless opportunity. But this wouldn't necessarily deflect naysayers because, at some point, they'll notice that you're up to something and would attempt to detract you from your purpose. As I've already stated, when they do that, smile at them!

The Mentor Factor

Although his father, Piero da Vinci, was a wealthy notary, Leonardo da Vinci was barred from attending university or practising any noble profession. This was because he was born out of wedlock, and for that matter, the only education he could have as an illegitimate child was an informal elementary education, which was limited to reading, writing, and arithmetic. So during his childhood, he was mainly left to himself, and when he had nothing to do at home, he went strolling in the forest to see the landscape, the olive groves, the waterfalls, the wild boars, the flowers, the insects, and the birds.

One day, he sneaked into his father's office, pulled out a paper (rare in that era), and went to the forest to sketch the biodiversity around him. He hadn't been schooled in the arts, nor had he ever observed the making of an artwork, yet he sketched so meticulously. This was how his artistic aptitude was first noticed.

When he turned 14, his father apprenticed him to Andrea del Verrocchio, the leading Florentine painter and sculptor. Andrea del Verrocchio was also specialised in chemistry, metallurgy, mechanics, and engineering. This means that he was a well-rounded artist, and he mentored his apprentices accordingly.

As an apprentice, Leonardo da Vinci applied himself to the subjects and learnt as much as possible. But he realised along the way that he was different from his co-apprentices. For example, unlike them, he did not follow Verrocchio's procedure in its entirety to arrive at his final work; instead, he preferred to add his own uniqueness to bring his arts to life.

One day, Andrea del Verrocchio tasked him to paint an angel, which he (Andrea del Verrocchio) had already designed. To avoid imitating his mentor so as to make his painting realistic, Leonardo da Vinci painted a flowerbed in the foreground, but instead of the usual look of a plant in his immediate surroundings, he painted the forest at Vinci from his childhood memory, and it was meticulous. To paint the angel's face, he visited a church and gazed at several people's faces until he fixed on a particular man whose face looked angelic. He scanned the man's lips, cheeks, eyebrows, and eyelashes and absorbed every detail of his facial expression.

Back in the studio, Leonardo da Vinci tested several colour schemes until he found one that would emit an angelic radiance. His next task was the wings. As usual, he ignored Verrocchio's design and bought some birds from the marketplace. He then spent some days observing the birds' wings and noticed how their feathers overlapped and were tucked into their bodies. He also observed the shades of their colour as they could be perceived from near and far.

With these vivid details in his mind, he painted a masterpiece of an angel that would wow Verrocchio for life.

When he had finished painting the angel, a light-bulb moment dawned on him: what if humans could fly? He pondered! That's how Leonardo da Vinci's mind worked; one successful project inspired his next idea, and he spent several hours each day studying everything he could know about birds to the extent that he became obsessed with them.

This ultimately led to his conceptualisation of flying machines, but he couldn't design them due to the limited technological know-how of metallurgy in the Renaissance. Despite this, he is credited with inventing the parachute and helicopter.

By 1472, when Leonardo da Vinci had turned 20, he was qualified to be a master and was inducted into the *Guild of Saint Luke*. Following his induction, his father set him up for his own enterprise, but he had become so attached to Verrocchio that he continued to live and work with him.

Leonardo da Vinci trained under Verrocchio for a total of ten years. During that time, he became well versed in painting, sculpting and diverse mechanical skills.

From 1478, however, Leonardo da Vinci was on his own, and he received his first independent commission to paint an altarpiece for the chapel of St. Bernard in the *Palazzo Vecchio*.

Though only 15 of his works survive, they're the most quintessential paintings. The most popular is the Mona Lisa (1503–19), whereas The Last Supper (1495–98) is the most reproduced artwork.

Mona Lisa

The Last Supper

Years after Leonardo da Vinci's passing, his notebooks were collected and found to contain sketches and technological concepts that were centuries ahead of the Renaissance. He was also acknowledged for conceptualising armoured fighting vehicles, concentrated solar power, adding machines, and the double hull.

Explication

The social order of the Renaissance era rendered the birth of Leonardo da Vinci illegitimate and therefore attempted to repress him by limiting his education. But, as I've been emphatic from the beginning of this book, human ingenuity is inherent and can be effectuated with or without higher education. Furthermore, the foundation of life's achievement is a sound mind in a healthy body, driven by a sense of purpose. And with his sense of purpose, Leonardo da Vinci beat the status quo that should've rendered him a nonentity.

After identifying his artistic aptitude, the next task was to develop his potential. He didn't have the right to formal education, but having a mentor was even more important. Fortunately, he had the most accomplished artist as his mentor. And after years of apprenticing under him, he emerged as a polymath and the most outstanding artist the world had ever known.

Leonardo da Vinci's career development pathway attests to how effective apprenticeship and mentoring can be. It also applies to all fields, though it is more common in technical or vocational occupations and is underutilized in intellectual professions.

Would Leonardo da Vinci's accomplishment be as lustrous as it was if he had sidestepped his aptitude for arts and trained in a different field? Would he have emerged so capable? What if he had gone to the university?

The Salesman Turned Fashion designer

Ellis was a 22-year-old salesman when I began coaching him. He had decided on a lifelong career in fashion, and unlike most people his age who had completed Senior High School, he wasn't fixated on getting a degree but developing proficiency.

At first, he wanted to study at the university. So he visited the academic office of a university and discussed his needs with a representative. He also requested to see the curriculum, and to his disappointment, he found that what was meant to be a major in fashion design was laden with extraneous courses, including quantitative studies, philosophy, and African studies.

With a wry face, he asked the representative why it was so, and the representative told him those courses were required for the degree. Ellis further requested to have an interaction with the students and was led to a class of some winsome coquettes who warmly welcomed him. He interacted briefly with some of them and took their phone numbers before he left.

The next day, he called one of the students to inquire about her learning experience. At first, she said it was all well, but she suddenly began to lament her regret over her inability to make garments, even though she was in her final year. She disclosed to Ellis that the programme was 95% academic; the remaining 5% were practical sessions, but those practical sessions only scratched the surface.

More to Ellis' disappointment, she revealed to him that several students had dropped out and enrolled in vocational schools instead, adding that, in an entire semester, each student made only one garment, totalling eight, for the four-year degree programme.

The last straw was when she told Ellis that not all of the clothes they wore in the university's fashion show were made by the students but with the help of professional fashion designers from their localities.

I told Ellis to ask the same question of the other students. He did, and their responses were similar, except that some of them didn't mind the impracticality of their studies. For them, their primary interest was getting degrees to seek jobs with; proficiency development wasn't on their mind.

Ellis made a second and a third inquiry at two other universities, and their testimonials didn't vary much from what he had from the first university. But he knew exactly what he wanted to do. He wanted to learn and acquire fashion design skills, and upon completion, he intended to set up an enterprise that would include a workroom for apprenticeship. He was sure that a degree didn't matter in his plan, but he neither downplayed it nor discouraged his friends who took the university path. His goal was very personal to him.

After reflecting on the students' testimonials, Ellis changed his mind about enrolling in the university and asked for the most skilled fashion designer who took apprentices. When he found him, he apprenticed under him and related well to the practicality of his mentoring.

In the beginning, Ellis was slow, as though he merely had a passion for making garments without aptitude. Nonetheless, he persisted, staying behind each day to practise. And unlike the university, there were no quantitative studies to regurgitate and nothing about philosophy to learn in fashion design. So, every moment he spent learning or practising improved his proficiency.

I also encouraged him to reskill in computer-aided design (CAD) technology and troubleshooting sewing machines, which he did on the sideline. Again, unlike the university, where students were assessed mainly by written exams, in the vocational studio, apprentices were assessed by tasks and demonstrations. Therefore, the highest mark was awarded to the apprentice who designed and made the most elegant garments in the shortest possible time. Ellis became nifty and nimble as a result of this model.

The most advantageous part of Ellis' training was that he designed and made many more clothes than he could count in his four-year apprenticeship. There was one other thing he realised; he had noticed some clothes made by the leading brands, and having compared them to his mentor's craft, he found his mentor's proficiency superior, yet his mentor wasn't prominent and was less paid than the leading brands.

I explained to him that proficiency alone isn't enough for career success and that brand building is key! It took him barely a month to imbibe a brand-building book I recommended to him—while he was still an apprentice. And by the time he graduated, he had become extraordinarily capable in fashion design with all its intricacies, including costume designing, brand building, and using computer-aided design (CAD) technology to optimise his design creation.

Three years after Ellis had completed his apprenticeship, while he was running his enterprise, he invited me to instruct him in personal finance, and when he showed me his weekly revenue, I found him way ahead of most graduate employees in the formal sector.

Apparently, a fashion designer's academic background isn't relevant to their customers. Instead, it takes the designer brand that makes the most befitting garments to make the most profit. This applies to all artisans and creatives.

Grades are Good, Aptitudes are Better and Best

Making excellent grades in college will prepare you for some golden opportunities after graduation. Unfortunately, not every student has what it takes to score excellent grades. So, does it mean that the average and non-performers are closed off from success? The answer is a big NO. Because aside from the latter's inability to score excellent grades, they might be fortunate to have talents and passions to draw on.

This is typical of geniuses, whose talents underpin their life purpose, not their school grades. But I must be emphatic that being academically gifted is also a talent to draw on because it underpins the extraordinary performances some students put up. Extraordinary performance, however, could also stem from an ingenium, which enables a student to assimilate knowledge and retain information with the minimum amount of effort.

Kim Peek had that kind of ingenium. He began reading before he was two years old, and he didn't forget anything he read. He also grew to become obsessed with books and committed to lifelong reading. He could accurately recall and recount the content of the 12,000 books he had read, and he demonstrated this capability in school.

Unlike everyone else, Kim Peek read, using his left eye to scan the texts on the left page and his right eye to read the texts on the right page. This enabled him to devour a book within an hour.

Thus, while most collegians have to break their backs to score excellent grades to boost their GPAs, others can score excellent grades 'effortlessly' due to their academic talent or ingenium. And though Kim Peek's ability was extraordinary, we've all had some classmates who have well-demonstrated pockets of academic talent.

On the flip side, this enviable attribute doesn't necessarily engender ingenuity, nor have proven to mint wealth. So, supposing academics is your best foot, then you must draw on your smarts to prospect opportunities that transcend career boost.

In 2021, Martin Hairer, an Austrian-British who lived in a rented apartment and worked at Imperial College London, won a $3 million Breakthrough Prize for presenting a 180-page treatise on stochastic analysis.

Martin Hairer's treatise was groundbreaking, and it mystified his comrades. One of them even said that Hairer's insight must have been passed to him from a more intelligent alien civilisation. In any case, you can imagine the career boost and the smile a $3 million cash prize will beckon!

This makes it necessary for every person to be in tune with their aptitude and passion. The sharp student needs to, the slow student needs to, and both can be successful!

During my years as a teacher, I observed with uneasiness how some of my colleagues disparaged the non-performing pupils and sometimes blurted out unkind words at them. It was even more troubling how some parents felt anxious because their children were non-performers.

But there were two things I always looked out for in non-performing pupils. Do they have aptitude/proclivity? Do they have life goals and a plan to realise those goals? If they answered yes to both questions, I wouldn't worry about their future because I knew they had what it takes to succeed. If they answered no, I didn't get worried either. Because the answer 'no' only meant that they needed some coaching to instil in them a sense of purpose.

And when that is done, they can improve their test scores. But usually, it takes time for slow learners to pick up. For some, it'll be later in their education, and for others, it'll be during their career. Yet, some will still go on in their lives without ever being intellectually sharp, nonetheless, they'll still be accomplished and successful in their careers.

In reality, people are motivated to be the best version of themselves if they work in careers that are congenial to them. This principle applies in our education. Without a taste for a subject, a learner won't have the motivation to study.

In 1888, Winston Churchill was enrolled at the elite Harrow School with poor entrance exam scores. This placed him at the bottom of his class. He later wrote:

> I had hardly ever been asked to learn anything which seemed of the slightest use or interest, or allowed to play any game which was amusing. In retrospect, those years form not only the least agreeable, but also the barren and unhappy period of my life.

Knowing Winston Churchill's poor performance wouldn't get him admitted to Cambridge University, Lord Randolph considered his childhood proclivity for toy soldiers and enrolled him at the British Royal Military College, Sandhurst, hoping that Winston Churchill would become an infantry officer.

But to Lord Randolph's disappointment, Winston's entrance exam score was too low to qualify him for the infantry but for the cavalry. However, during his training in the cavalry, he immersed himself in military subjects and proved his mettle by scoring good marks. That was Winston Churchill's turning point, during which his brilliance was noticed and his sense of purpose dawned on him.

An 18-month practical learning at Sandhurst concluded his formal education, and he graduated 20th out of 130 cadets. Free from teachers and the education system, Winston Churchill applied himself to self-learning, focusing only on his passions.

In 1900, he became a member of the British Parliament and again in 1908, during which he was appointed to the Prime Minister's cabinet as President of the Board of Trade. In 1911, he became the First Lord of the Admiralty (synonymous with the Secretary of State in the US).

Observing how the Nazis were growing belligerent, he prepared Britain for war. He did that by establishing the Royal Naval Air Service, modernised the British fleet, and contributed to the development of the earliest tanks.

In 1917, he was appointed Minister of Munitions and Secretary of State for War and Air from 1918 to 1921. Thereafter, he was made Secretary of State for the Colonies (1921–1922), Chancellor of the Exchequer (1924–1929), and First Lord of the Admiralty (1939–1940). He was elected Prime Minister from 1940 to 1945 and again from 1951 to 1955. In 1953, he was knighted by Queen Elizabeth II and named the recipient of the Nobel Prize in Literature for his 'mastery of historical and biographical description and for brilliant oratory in defending exalted human values'.

Reflecting on how Winston Churchill's teachers perceived him during his school years and all the questions they asked him in class that he couldn't answer, perhaps Albert Einstein was right to have said: 'Most teachers waste their time by asking questions that are intended to discover what a pupil does not know, whereas the true art of questioning is to discover what the pupil does know or is capable of.'

An Enabling Environment Matters Most in the Learning Process

Born on February 12, 1809, to a medical doctor-father, Charles Darwin had no desire to follow in his father's footsteps. His performance in school was drab, and he scored low grades in Latin, Greek, and algebra. His lacklustre performance, however, wasn't because he was slow to learn but rather because classroom learning was too dull for his individuality.

He had an inclination to learn directly from the environment, preferably on his own. And every indication pointed out that he was born a naturalist. Since his childhood, Charles Darwin had shown a keen interest in collecting biological specimens—a hobby his father found repulsive.

In October 1825, his father enrolled him at Edinburgh University to study medicine, but he dropped out after two years because he felt queasy when he saw blood. His father then suggested that he pursue a different degree program in order to qualify for parson training.

So, Charles enrolled at Christ's College in Cambridge, where he studied botany and became a friend to his instructor, Professor Henslow. He studied as much as he could and barely earned a Bachelor of Arts in May 1831. When he graduated, Professor Henslow recommended him for a position as a naturalist aboard the *HMS Beagle*.

The ship, *HMS Beagle*, commanded by Captain Robert Fitzroy, was to take a five-year voyage around the world. Darwin's specific duty was to find evidence of the biblical *Noah's Flood* in South America and the new life that emerged thereafter, as described in the book of Genesis. Darwin was only 22 years old.

From England, the *HMS Beagle* sailed towards the Cape Verde Islands, off Africa's western coast, before she docked at the shore of Brazil. Darwin was enthralled by the intense biodiversity he saw, and a sense of purpose dawned on him.

He began his expedition from there, and as he explored the wild, he observed a struggle for survival among various species almost everywhere: he noticed the march of tiny black ants that stretched over 100 yards and how they devour food on their path. He also caught birds, flies, spiders and crabs, and upon examining them, he noticed that they were different from the species he had known.

He then had to adopt a strategy to organise the specimens he had collected. This presented him with a challenge and excitement, which was how he loved to learn rather than following some abstractions in textbooks.

From the shores of Brazil, the Beagle set sail again, but this time southward along the coast. There, Darwin trekked the Pampas of Argentina with a gaucho escort and collected unusual animal and insect specimens. He also became accustomed to the gaucho's way of life, and before he knew it, he had become adventurous, which was a temperament he lacked before the voyage.

A year into the voyage, on the beach some several miles off Buenos Aires, Darwin chanced upon a cliff with streaks of white matter in its midst. He found the white matter to be fossils, and his curiosity was piqued. He chipped off the rocks and extracted as many fossils as he could. He observed the fossils and found that they were horns and armour of some sort he had never seen. They resembled the remains of a giant armadillo, the enormous teeth of a mastodon and, most unexpectedly, the tooth of a horse.

Darwin knew there were no horses in South America when the Spaniards and Portuguese first arrived. So he began wondering where the horse tooth had come from. Finally, he inferred that many animal species, including horses, had once lived on the land and had gone extinct.

Darwin pondered, 'Could it be that nature had been in a perpetual state of flux and evolving itself'? If so, as it seemed, he deduced that the biblical narrative that the creation of all animals ended on the 6th day is fallacious.

He continued his expedition through the high Andes, looking for rare geological specimens to send back. But at an elevation of 12,000 feet, to his shock, he discovered some fossilised seashells and marine rocks. He was shocked because the altitude was too high, which rendered the environment unconducive for shell animals to thrive. He was also surprised to find marine rocks at such a high elevation.

Where did the seashells and marine rocks come from? Charles Darwin reckoned that the mountain had once been in the Atlantic Ocean, but the recurrence of volcanoes some thousands of years ago had piled up deposits on the mountain to such a high elevation.

Having taken several expeditions in the voyage, Darwin realised that his experience in the South American ecosystem had made him well-grounded.

He could, from then, identify birds by their sounds, the manner they took flight and the markings on their eggs, which he used as information to organise and catalogue his collection.

In September 1835, the Beagle left the Pacific Coast of South America and headed west towards Britain. She docked at the Galápagos, where there was an archipelago that was famous for its wildlife and biodiversity. Darwin was given a week to explore the archipelago. From there, they would be on their way home.

On this expedition, he found the island different from any other wild he had explored: thousands of black marine iguanas swarmed around him, and he observed many more on the beach and in the shallow waters. He also noticed a 500-pound tortoise lumbering about the shore where seals, penguins, and flightless cormorants were also present. What piqued his curiosity was that these creatures were all cold-water organisms, yet they were inhabiting a tropical island.

By the end of the week, he had identified 26 unique species of land birds on that island alone. While he catalogued his collection, he found that the species varied from island to island, though they were only 50 miles apart. For instance, he found that the tortoises' shells had different markings, and their finches had developed different beaks relative to the type of food in their respective habitats.

Back aboard the *Beagle*, he continued to catalogue his collections and counted more than 1,500 different species of animals and plants. He also made remarkable geological findings during his expeditions and took notes on the effects of earthquakes, erosion, and volcanoes.

While Darwin reflected on his observations, a light-bulb moment dawned on him, and a theory, so revolutionary in its essence, took form in his mind.

This was what he reckoned from his expeditions: the Galápagos Islands, similar to the Andes, had gradually been formed out of the sea due to several volcanic eruptions. Initially, there was no life there until birds visited and dispersed seeds, which brought about plant life. Various animals including lizards, insects, and tortoises also came from the sea to live on the island.

Over thousands of years, the animal populations adapted to the food and predators they lived with, causing them to change their shape and appearance. It was a survival of the fittest; the animals that couldn't adapt became extinct, and their fossil remains were what he chanced upon in Buenos Aires.

Finally, he inferred that the living creatures he found were those that had ever so slowly evolved to their present form, and perhaps, they were not created according to the widespread biblical narrative in the book of Genesis. Proving this theory became Darwin's life's work.

In October 1836, the *Beagle* arrived in England, and Darwin, now 27 years old, wrote:

> The voyage of the *Beagle* has been by far the most important event in my life and has determined my whole career. Everything about which I thought or read was made to bear directly on what I had seen or was likely to see, and this habit of mind was continued during the five years of the voyage. I feel sure that it was this training which has enabled me to do whatever I have done in science. – The life and letters of Charles Darwin, 1887.

Although Charles Darwin's theory of evolution doesn't attribute the existence of biodiversity to a creator but rather to evolution, it fails to explain how the first life emerged. Otherwise, the theory is plausible!

Darwin eventually formulated a persuasive account of the changes in biological life, which he called evolution by natural selection. This made him an icon worth learning about in school.

Explication

In his early years, Charles Darwin didn't have much interest in schoolwork, and he would rather engage himself tirelessly in the outdoors, like hunting, roaming the countryside to observe rare breeds of beetles, and collecting flowers and mineral specimens. But, according to his father, his outdoor activities would not amount to a career. He grew impatient, and one day, he flared up at him: 'You care for nothing but shooting, dogs, and rat-catching, and you will be a disgrace to yourself and all your family.' These words would echo in Darwin's mind for a long time.

But unlike Lord Randolph, who considered Winston Churchill's childhood proclivity for toy soldiers and enrolled him in the Royal Military College, Dr. R.W. Darwin's first attempt was to make Charles Darwin a medical doctor. His second attempt was to make him a parson—both of which were incongruous with Charles Darwin's aptitude and proclivity.

Conversely, if Charles Darwin had relented to his father's will, he would've managed to graduate medical school and settle as a doctor, but it was unlikely he would've become the icon he was. This is because his love of nature was so strong that any other career would've resulted in job dissatisfaction and career alienation.

But when he finally found himself in an enabling environment, in the wild, his naturalist forte dawned on him. It also turned out that his early years struggle with learning Latin, Greek, and algebra distressed him for no gain and made him come off as though he was a dunce.

How many Darwins, Churchills, and Einsteins are there who fell short of their full potential due to the one-size-fits-all education system that stifled their ingenuities and dissipated their aptitudes and proclivities?

Wouldn't they have been promising from the onset if they had had their education and training in a more enabling learning environment that suited their individualities?

In his autobiography, *My Early Life*, Winston Churchill recounts his experience at the elite Harrow School:

> I had scarcely passed my twelfth birthday when I entered the inhospitable regions of examinations, through which for the next seven years I was destined to journey. These examinations were a great trial for me. The subjects which were dearest to the examiners were almost invariably those I fancied least. I would have liked to have been examined in history, poetry and writing essays. The examiners, on the other hand, were partial to Latin and Mathematics. And their will prevailed. Moreover, the questions which they asked on both these subjects were almost invariably those to which I was unable to suggest a satisfactory answer. I should have liked to be asked to say what I knew. They always tried to ask what I did not know. When I would have willingly displayed my knowledge, they sought to expose my ignorance. This sort of treatment had only one result. I did not do well in examinations.

Churchill further recounted his experience with a form master at St. James's Preparatory School 'where flogging was a feature of the curriculum and kindness and sympathy were conspicuously lacking':

> I was taken into a Form Room and told to sit at a desk. All the other boys were out of doors, and I was alone with the Form Master. He produced a thin greeny-brown covered book filled with words in different types of print.
>
> 'You have never done any Latin before, have you?' he said.
>
> 'No, sir.'
>
> 'This is a Latin grammar.' He opened it at a well-thumbed page. 'You must learn this,' he said, pointing to a number of words in a

frame of lines.' I will come back in half an hour and see what you know.'

Behold me then on a gloomy evening, with an aching heart, seated in front of the First Declension.

Mensa	a table
Mensa	O table
Mensam	a table
Mensae	of a table
Mensae	to or for a table
Mensa	by, with or from a table

What on earth does it mean? Where was the sense in it? It seemed absolute rigmarole to me. However, there was one thing I could always do: I could learn by heart. And I thereupon proceeded, as far as my private sorrows would allow, to memorise the acrostic-looking task which had been set before me. In due course, the Master returned.

'Have you learnt it?' he asked.
I think I can say it, sir,' I replied; and I gabbled it off.
He seemed so satisfied with this that I was emboldened to ask a question.
'What does it mean, sir?'
'It means what it says. Mensa, a table. Mensa is a noun of the First Declension. There are five declensions. You have learnt the singular of the First Declension.
'But, 'I repeated, 'what does it mean?'
'Mensa means a table,' he answered.
'Then why does mensa also mean O table,' I enquired, 'and what does O table mean?'
'Mensa, O table, is the vocative case,' he replied.
'But why O table?' I persisted in genuine curiosity.
'O table – you would use that in addressing a table, in invoking a table.' And then seeing he was not carrying me with him, 'You would use it in speaking to a table.'
('But I never do,' I blurted out in honest amazement.)
'If you are impertinent, you will be punished and punished, let me tell you, very severely,' was his conclusive rejoinder.

> Such was my first introduction to the classics from which I have been told, many of our cleverest men have derived so much solace and profit.

Churchill further narrated:

> My teachers saw me at once backward and precocious, reading books beyond my years yet at the bottom of the Form...Where my reason, imagination or interest were not engaged, I would not or could not learn. In all the 12 years I was at school, no one ever succeeded in making me write a Latin verse or learn Greek...
> Being so long in the lowest form, I gained immense advantage over the cleverer boys. They all went on to learn Latin and Greek and splendid things like that. But I was taught English. We were considered such dunces that we could learn only English. Mr Somervell-a delightful man, to whom my debt is great-was charged with the duty of teaching the stupidest boys the most disregarded thing-namely, to write mere English...Thus, I got into my bones the essential structure of ordinary British sentence-which is a noble thing. And when in years my schoolfellows who had won prizes and distinction for writing such beautiful Latin poetry and pithy Greek epigrams had come down again to common English, to earn their living or earn their way, I did not feel myself at any disadvantage.

One thing is clear here: the one-size-fits-all curriculum is a fundamental problem of the education system. When a high-potential learner is presented with studies that are at variance with their inclination, they get bored and decouple from those studies. They may even quit.

When Albert Einstein was in elementary school at the Luitpold Gymnasium in Munich, Germany, the future laureate became bored with the Prussian-style education system, which he felt was kiboshing his impetus and ingenuity. Hence, he dropped out!

The only thing that interferes with my learning is my education. – Albert Einstein.

Light-bulb Moment

In 1884, while lying on his sickbed, five-year-old Albert Einstein received a gift from his father. It was his first time seeing a magnetic compass, and he began playing with it and turning it around to trick its northern-pointing needle into changing its direction. But however hard he tried, the needle kept to the north. He became curious as to why the needle didn't change direction and wondered if there were some invisible forces at play.

In 1891, when Einstein was 12 years old, he chanced on a geometry book from which he taught himself algebra, calculus, and geometry. He later referred to the book as 'sacred little geometry book.'

For the rest of his life, Albert Einstein's work was inspired by the invisible forces he conceived from the compass and the pith of the geometry book. His curiosity about the hidden forces of the compass engendered in him a thinking pattern that stimulated his thought experiments (meaning that he conducted his scientific experiments in his mind).

After earning a diploma, Einstein was the only graduate in his class who had no job placement. Professor Weber had said bad things about him to the other professors, so when Einstein asked for a letter of recommendation, no one gave him one.

Due to this situation, he couldn't get a teaching post for two straight years and had to settle for a low-paid job teaching children at home. He later wrote: 'I would have found a job long ago if Weber had not played a dishonest game with me.'

In 1902, however, on the recommendation of his friend's father, Einstein had his first official job as a clerk in the Swiss Patent Office in Bern. At the patent office, he quickly reviewed and processed patent applications, so that he was left with enough time to explore his scientific interests.

While he worked, he mused over questions such as, 'What would happen if you raced alongside a beam of light?' At the polytechnic, he studied Maxwell's equations, which explain the nature of light, but Einstein found that the speed of light is constant regardless of how fast one races along with it. This phenomenon was unknown to James Clerk Maxwell himself, and it also violated Newton's law of motion because there was no absolute velocity in Isaac Newton's theory. With this hindsight, Einstein formulated the principle of relativity, which states that the speed of light is constant in any inertia frame.

In 1905, when he was 26 and still working in the Swiss Patent Office, he published four papers in the journal Annalen der Physik that would alter the course of modern physics and our understanding of the universe:

1. *On a Heuristic Viewpoint Concerning the Production and Transformation of Light*: In this paper, Einstein used quantum theory of light to explain the photoelectric effect: if light occurs in tiny packets (later referred to as photons), then it should precisely knock out electrons in a metal.
2. *On the Movement of Small Particles Suspended in Stationary Liquids Required by the Molecular-Kinetic Theory of Heat*: In this paper, Einstein offered the first experimental proof of the existence of atoms. By analysing the motion of tiny particles suspended in still water, called Brownian motion, he could calculate the size of the jostling atoms and Avogadro's number.
3. *On the Electrodynamics of Moving Bodies*: In this paper, Einstein laid out the mathematical theory of special relativity.
4. *Does the Inertia of a Body Depend Upon Its Energy Content?* This paper came forth as an afterthought, showing how relativity theory led to the world's most famous equation, $E = mc^2$. This provided the first mechanism to explain the energy source of the sun and other stars.

That year, which became known as his miracle year, Albert Einstein submitted a paper for his doctorate. Initially, these papers were ignored by the physics intelligentsia until they came to the attention of Max Planck, the founder of quantum theory and the most influential physicist of the time. Following Planck's meritorious comments on Einstein's papers, other scientists became interested and conducted experiments to verify his points. They found Einstein's findings to be accurate!

Word spread, and Einstein became the talk of the town, particularly in academia and among the intelligentsia. He began receiving invitations to lecture at international conferences and became an influential figure in the science community. Even then, he wasn't a standout scientist but one of the elites. However, his standout status began to take shape in 1911 after he published a paper that modified Newton's theory of gravity.

In his paper: *On the Influence of Gravitation on the Propagation of Light*, Einstein explained that great masses were able to bend light. Although Newton had already pointed this out, he couldn't explain the mystery of gravity's action at a distance. A few years later, Einstein calculated a curvature that was double what was predicted by Newton's calculation.

Now, the intelligentsia had heard Einstein and wanted to verify his finding. Erwin Finlay-Freundlich, a German astronomer and one of Einstein's collaborators, posited that if Einstein was right about his finding, then it should be possible to detect the deflection of the starlight that reaches the earth after travelling past the enormous mass of the sun.

However, due to the intense brightness of the sun on a typical day, this deflection cannot be seen. Finlay-Freundlich came to the conclusion that if this deflection happens at all, it can only be seen during an eclipse.

Fortunately, a solar eclipse was imminent, and Frank Dyson, the then UK Astronomer Royal, proposed sending an expedition to ascertain the curvature of light as expounded by Einstein. Two expeditions were sent: one sailed to the Island of Principe, off the West African coast, and the other went to Sobral in northern Brazil.

Both scientists were to observe and capture images of the solar eclipse of May 29, 1919. They presented their results at a joint meeting between the Royal Science and the Royal Astronomical Science on November 6, 1919. Their verdict was unequivocal, and Einstein's theory of gravity was validated that day. It also meant that Einstein's theory had overthrown the 230-year-old Newtonian model.

Einstein's finding was so profound that it was given resonance by the media. He began receiving invitations to academic positions from prestigious universities. Subsequently, he received the 1921 Nobel Prize in Physics. From there, he became a celebrity scientist and a global icon whose name, Einstein, remains a byword for genius.

This was the same Albert Einstein who was disparaged by his college professors and had earlier been told by his schoolmaster: 'You will not amount to anything.'

Explication

Everyone, at some point, experiences a lightbulb moment. It could be a sudden idea for an invention, a solution to a problem, or an answer to a puzzle. It's nature's gift to us, regardless of our faith, race, and educational attainment, and it comes with transformative power to fulfil our life purpose. Yet, few people heed these lightbulb moments and accord them the needed attention.

When Einstein first had a compass at age five, he never ceased to be fascinated by it. This made him think about the hidden forces that made it work the way it did, which kept his mind active for the rest of his life. With this cognitive ability, he could describe events in the universe without using his eyes or scientific apparatus. Thus, he worked the entire scientific method in his mind to arrive at his verifiable findings.

In 1878, when the Wright family was living in Iowa, in the US, Milton Wright brought home a toy helicopter made of paper, bamboo, and cork with a rubber band to twirl its rotor. Wilbur and Orville Wright, who were eleven and seven, played with the toy helicopter until it broke, and they rebuilt it on their own. Twenty-five years later, they invented the first piloted airplane.

It is interesting to note that the Wright brothers had no prior aeronautic experience and never went to college. Wilbur only completed high school but never received his diploma due to their parents' impromptu relocation from Indiana to Ohio in 1884. Orville, on the other hand, designed and built a printing press with Wilbur's help in 1889. When he was done setting up the press, he dropped out of high school to manage it.

After successfully inventing and flying the plane, the Wright brothers attributed their success to their childhood toy helicopter, which had piqued their interest from the start.

Wilbur had wanted to attend Yale when he completed high school, but he lost motivation after he lost his front teeth while playing an ice-skating game with his playmates. He would be stuck at home for the next few years and study a lot in his father's library.

After Orville designed and built his first printing press, the Wright brothers ventured into publishing and the manufacture and repair of bicycles. It was during this period that their interest in flight began to manifest, but they didn't act on it until six years later, when they saw pictures of German gliders in a newspaper. These pictures inspired them to invent the airplane.

They began their research on aerodynamics at their local library, and they read, took notes, and assimilated every bit of information. In May 1899, they wrote to the Smithsonian Institution to ask for access to books on aeronautics:

> The Smithsonian Institution, Washington:
>
> Dear Sirs:
>
> "I am an enthusiast, but not a crank in the sense that I have some pet theories as to the proper construction of a flying machine. I wish to avail myself of all that is already known and then if possible add my mite to help on the future worker who will attain final success."
>
> Wilbur Wright

When they were granted access, the Wright brothers immersed themselves in aeronautics and studied voraciously. Meanwhile, other engineers were also trying to invent the airplane, but they went too slowly, focusing instead on man-carrying gliders.

On the contrary, the Wright brothers didn't take a gradual evolutionary approach with their project. They began by designing an airplane instead of wasting time designing gliders, as their competitors did.

First, they found the things that made it possible to fly and put them into three main groups: wings, a way to keep the plane balanced and in control, and a way to move forward.

To design their first airplane, they revisited their wind tunnel data and the lift and drag equations. For the plane to bear the weight of an engine, propellers, and additional structural reinforcement, they had to increase the wing area to more than 500 ft^2. Taking into account 200 pounds for the propulsion system and an estimated 625 pounds for the plane with a pilot, they figured out the power, thrust, and speed requirements. An eight-horsepower engine that could produce 90 pounds of thrust was chosen so that the plane could fly at least 23 miles per hour.

By 1903, the Wright brothers had completed their project with the invention of the first piloted airplane. They are still considered one of the most influential geniuses of all time, owing to the novelty of their flying invention and how it awed the world.

Understand: A regressive mindset often makes people find others to blame for their inadequacies. Some say: 'My parents didn't send me to the university.' Others say: 'The system doesn't work in this country.' Yet, in the 21st century, we have more resources and incentives than everything that was available to the Wright brothers in 1903.

They had the potential to do something, which any other human has; they had a sense of purpose, which only a functioning brain can conceive of; and finally, they studied books; books on any topic are even more abundant, improved, and widespread today than they could ever be in 1903. However, none of these incentives or their aggregate surpasses the accessibility and versatility of the internet, through which we have search engines, open access (OA), open learning, social media, e-commerce, and artificial intelligence (AI). None of these were available in 1903.

In the internet era, the above-mentioned resources put us at a thousand-fold advantage over the Wright brothers, whose accomplishments, nonetheless, exemplify the aphorism: 'The foundation of life's achievement is a sound mind in a healthy body, driven by a sense of purpose.'

So, considering that their achievement was before the internet era and devoid of academic attainment, it becomes inexcusable for anyone to attribute their unproductivity to not having had the opportunity to study in a university, and if you have been to university, you have no excuse at all to be unproductive.

Eureka Moment

At a certain depth of our consciousness, while we reflect on our problems and become desperate for understanding, our thinking transcends into musing. When we peak in our musing, a synergy of our aptitudes, proclivities, knowledge, and experience transmits an impulse from our unconscious mind to our subconsciousness, then to our conscious minds. At this juncture, known as the eureka moment, the understanding we seek dawns on us and we experience an enlightenment.

Conscious Phenomenon

Around 212 BCE, King Hiero of Syracuse gave some gold to a goldsmith to make a crown for him. After a few days, the goldsmith brought the finished crown to Hiero, but for some reason, Hiero suspected that the goldsmith had pulled a fast one on him. So, he weighed the crown against the mass of the gold he gave to the goldsmith, and the scale was balanced. Yet he still wasn't satisfied and wanted another way to ascertain his suspicion. He then remembered Archimedes.

Archimedes was a genius and the most acclaimed engineer of classical antiquity. However, the puzzle Hiero presented to him was really hard, and moreover, there wasn't any technology he could've used.

One day, he went to a public bath, and upon entering the water-filled tub, his mass displaced a certain volume of the water. A light-bulb moment dawned on him, then he jumped out of the tub and ran naked through the street, shouting, 'Eureka! Eureka! Eureka…' which means, 'I've found it.'

What did Archimedes find? Volumes of different metals of the same mass vary. For instance, the mass of iron and gold might both be five grams, but their volumes are never the same. So, when each one is put in separate containers full of water, the iron will displace more water than the gold.

Archimedes knew this principle and set out to ascertain if Hiero was right in his suspicion. So he took two bowls, filled each with water to the brim, and placed each separately in two large vessels (A and B). He then took a lump of gold of the same mass as the crown and gently dropped it in the bowl of water in vessel A. Next, he took the crown and placed it gently in the bowl of water in vessel B. He observed the difference in overflow in the two vessels and saw that the crown had displaced more water than the lump of gold.

This was an indication that the crown was alloyed. Otherwise, the crown and the lump of gold would've displaced the same volume of water. It also meant that the goldsmith had stolen some of the gold that Hiero gave him to make the crown. Archimedes reported his findings to Hiero, and the goldsmith was summoned. When he was interrogated, he confessed to stealing some of the gold. Problem solved!

Subconscious Phenomenon

Unlike Archimedes, who experienced his eureka moment while fully conscious, some other achievers and extraordinary achievers experienced their epiphanies in their dreams.

Madam C.J. Walker

Born in 1867 to formerly enslaved couples, Sarah Breedlove was orphaned at age seven and widowed at age 22. She had earlier learnt about hair care from her brothers, who were barbers, and also during the period she sold hair care products as a commission agent.

So when she began experiencing baldness in her youth, she knew some hair care formulas she could use, but none worked. Desperation set in, and one night, a hefty man appeared in her dream and gave her some ingredients to concoct to treat her balding scalp.

Sarah Breedlove sought out those ingredients and learned that some were available only in Africa. She sent for them, and when she received all the ingredients, she concocted her hair care formula as she was directed in the dream and tested it on herself. The result was jaw-dropping; she also tried it on her friends, and it worked! In a few weeks, her hair was growing faster than she had imagined.

Realising the economic prospect of her formulation, she began selling her products door to door in the black community and gained traction with the brand, *Wonderful Hair Grower*. From then, she worked even harder to develop other hair formulations: *Glossine Hair Oil*, *Temple Grower*, and *Tetter Salve* for scalp psoriasis.

She also designed a hot steel comb with teeth spaced far apart, to be used by black women to straighten, press, and easily style their thick hair. The sales and endorsements of her products grew by leaps and bounds, necessitating her resignation from the laundry work.

In 1906, she married a man named Charles Joseph Walker, a Denver newspaperman whose journalistic background was instrumental to Sarah's branding and marketing strategy. Sarah Breedlove's marriage was short-lived, but it provided her and her company with a new professional name—the Madam C.J. Walker Company.

By 1908, she had established a school in Pittsburgh called Lelia College, where she trained black hairstylists and beauticians in the Walker System of Hair and Beauty Culture. She also toured places near and far to market and promote her products.

In 1910, she moved her headquarters to Indianapolis, where she built a new factory to manufacture new hair solutions and cosmetic brands. She also established a new centre for her sales force, research and production laboratories, and another beauty school.

Madam C.J. Walker gradually built a conglomerate in the way that most American businesses do. She made the products in her plant, hired a large sales force to sell them, and established beauty shops and schools to promote her products.

Madam C.J. Walker, with her elite sales force, soon outpaced her competitors. By 1919, she had 25,000 active Walker sales agents, and her behemoth empowered many women who would've otherwise been consigned to jobs as maids, cooks, laundresses, and farmhands. But they became financially independent, bought their own houses, and supported their children's education.

She became the first richest woman in the US and went on record as the first female self-made millionaire. She was overjoyed with her success, and in her address at the National Negro Business League, she stated, 'I have enabled many coloured women to abandon the washtub for a more pleasant and profitable occupation... the girls and women of our race must not be afraid to take hold of a business enterprise.'

Madam C.J. Walker was unschooled, and her only exposure to chemistry was in 1905, when she worked as a cook for a pharmacist and would sometimes sneak a peek at his work.

> I had to make my own living and my own opportunity! But I made it! Don't sit down and wait for opportunities to come. Get up and make them. – Madam C.J Walker.

Elias Howe

Born on July 9, 1819, Elias Howe had a proclivity for machines and started his career in the early part of 1835 as a machinist apprentice in a textile factory in Lowell, Massachusetts. Two years later, he moved to Cambridge, Massachusetts, where he apprenticed as a mechanic. But contrary to urban myth, Howe wasn't the first person to conceive the idea of a sewing machine.

In fact, by the latter part of the 18th century, some engineers had already patented their designs. However, Howe's sewing machine design was a remarkable innovation among the earliest designs. This earned him credit as the inventor of the modern sewing machine.

While inventing the sewing machine, he reached the point where he had to perforate a tiny hole to make the eye of the needle, but unsure of the exact spot for the hole, he did trial and error until he was exhausted and frustrated.

Then one night, he dreamt he had been ordered to invent a sewing machine for a savage king under a 24-hour ultimatum, or else he would be executed. Just as he was experiencing it in real life, also in his dream, Elias Howe was faced with the conundrum of finding a suitable spot for the eye of the needle. The 24-hour deadline had passed, and Howe had been seized and bound by the executioners for failing to figure out where the needle's eye would be in order to complete the invention.

On their way to his execution, he saw a hole near the oddr of the executioners' spears. Eureka! He conceived the solution instantly and began begging the executioners for more time to complete his task. It was at this point that he snapped out of the dream. It was 4:00 am, and he immediately bounced up from his bed and went to his workshop. He worked tirelessly for the next five hours, until he rudely modelled a needle with an eye at its point. He refined his work in the following days until he completed his invention of the sewing machine.

How to Manage Eureka Moment

Whether experienced in full consciousness or in a dream, an eureka moment is worthwhile and must be managed properly. By principle, you should never trust your memory with eureka; no matter how vivid the details in your mind, they can be easily forgotten and never be recollected. So whenever you experience it, you must write it down immediately. Remember: 'The shortest pencil is longer than the longest memory.'

Otto Loewi

Otto Loewi, however, was fortunate to have experienced an unlikely repeat of his eureka dream. The second time around, he wrote down the details of the dream immediately after he woke up, and proceeded to work on it.

Born of Jewish ancestry in Germany, in 1873, Otto Loewi had a taste for the humanities and wanted to major in art history. But his wealthy merchant father opposed his interest in the humanities and made him enrol in medical school.

So, he gained admission to the University of Strasbourg's medical school, where he skipped many classes to attend lectures in the humanities. He barely passed his final year examination and had to stay a year behind for remedial studies to complete his degree in medicine in 1896.

His first job was as an assistant at the city hospital in Frankfurt. Otto Loewi found the work frustrating as he couldn't find an efficacious medicine for treating patients with tuberculosis and pneumonia.

Feeling dispirited by his frustration, he abandoned the clinical practice and took a research position in the laboratory of a prominent German pharmacologist named Hans Meyer. In the next six years, Otto Loewi researched the metabolism and nutrition of glucose and found that the human body can synthesise protein from amino acids. This was a major scientific breakthrough!

In another study, he examined the effect of drugs on biological systems and found that small doses of cocaine caused a direct stimulation of either the sympathetic nerve or exogenous epinephrine. In 1908, he became a professor of pharmacology at the University of Graz in Austria, where he was famed as a lively lecturer. He also served briefly as dean of the medical faculty.

On the night before Easter Sunday in 1920, Otto Loewi woke up from a dream, scrawled some notes on a piece of paper, and went back to sleep. At daybreak, he was surprised he couldn't read his own scrawl because it was illegible, and he spent the rest of the day in a futile attempt to recollect the dream. However, the next night, while he was asleep, the dream came to him again, and it was about an epochal experiment.

This time, when he woke up, he immediately wrote down the details of the dream in legible handwriting and proceeded to the laboratory to conduct the experiment he had dreamt about. He completed the experiment by the end of Easter Monday.

This was the experiment: for 70 years, it had been known that vagus nerve stimulation causes the heart to slow. To conduct his experiment, Loewi placed a beating frog's heart in saline water with its vagus nerve still attached. The saline in the bath was allowed to flow into a second bath containing a second beating-frog's-heart but without an attached vagus nerve. When the vagus nerve of the first setup was stimulated, the heart slowed as expected, and in a latent period, the second heart—without the vagus attached—also slowed.

Otto Loewi inferred that a soluble chemical, which he called vagusstoff, had transmitted the nerve stimulus to the second heart, thereby indicating that the process of neurotransmission is chemical, not electrical, as had been widely believed for decades. His finding won him the Nobel Prize in Medicine. Later analysis of vagusstoff revealed it to be acetylcholine.

In his final years, Dr. Otto Loewi returned to his childhood proclivity: his love for the arts—literature, music, human fellowship, mountain climbing, and biological science. He died at the age of 89 on December 25, 1961.

Caution

Be mindful that you don't mistake a figment of your imagination for a light-bulb moment or eureka. In 1991, when visitors were at the zoological garden at the University of Ibadan, Nigeria, Prophet Daniel Abodunrin emerged in a red robe with his Bible tucked in his armpit. He had gone to the zoo to remake the biblical scene of Daniel in the Lion's Den. According to the Bible, Daniel was thrown into the lions' den, but the lions' mouths were shut by the angels of God, so they couldn't harm him.

On that fateful day in 1991, Prophet Daniel Abodunrin asked the zoo workers to allow him entry into the lions' exhibit to demonstrate the power of God that protected the biblical Daniel in the lions' den.

Initially, they denied him access, but he pestered and dramatised until the zoo workers relented. Some other visitors even pleaded with him to abandon his demonstration, while others looked on quietly to see the drama unfold.

Prophet Daniel Abodunrin confidently entered the lions' exhibit while praying in tongues. At first, the lions blenched at the sudden appearance of a human in their exhibit, then they pounced on and devoured him, leaving only his blood-soaked robe and his Bible.

A similar incident nearly happened in November 2004 when a 46-year-old man identified as Chen visited the Taipei Zoo in Taiwan and jumped into the lions' enclosure, shouting at two lions, 'Jesus will save you.' The lions snarled at first, then charged at Chen, ripping off his jacket. He fell back on a stone ridge, and the lions pounced on him, biting him in the arm. They then crouched in readiness to maul him, but were quickly fended off by the zoo guards. Chen then picked up his jacket, climbed out of the enclosure, and was attended to by paramedics.

The fate of Prophet Daniel Abodunrin and Chen has befallen several people who said they were spiritual and could hear God talking to them, only to turn out after an unfortunate debacle that they had mental issues and that the supposed voice they claim to have spoken to them wasn't God's, neither a lightbulb moment nor eureka, but a fevered imagination.

CHAPTER THREE

Career Elitism

There's no other way to attain outstanding career proficiency other than rigorous training and persistent practice.

Training and Practice

Success stories of the ordinary-turned extraordinary abound on social media and should be a source of inspiration. Yet, people still believe that one must be born gifted to attain elitism in any field. In any case, there's a reason for this misconception.

Born on January 18, 1984, Michael Kearney began talking at four months. When he was six months old, he said to his paediatrician, 'I have a left ear infection.' He could read when he was eight months old and he imbibed the elementary school curriculum by the age of four. Around that time, he was tested with a multiple-choice diagnostic test for the John Hopkins precocious maths programme. Though it was his first attempt, and hadn't studied specifically for the programme, he aced the test. He entered college at the age of six, graduated at age 10 and obtained a master's degree in chemistry when he was 14 years old.

Saul Kripke taught himself ancient Hebrew by the age of six. He read the entire collection of Shakespeare by the age of nine and mastered the works of Réne Descartes and other complex mathematical problems before he completed elementary school. He became a philosopher by the age of 12 and was invited to apply for a teaching post at Harvard when he was in high school.

During that period, he began working on the semantics of modal logic and published a groundbreaking paper, A Completeness Theorem for Modal Logic, at the age of 19, when he was a freshman at Harvard. Kripke later said, 'I wish I could have skipped college. I got to know some interesting people, but I can't say I learned anything. I probably would have learned it all anyway, just reading on my own.'

Gregory R. Smith entered college at the age of 10 and was nominated for the Nobel Peace Prize for the first time when he was 12 years old.

Dong Qichang passed the prefectural civil aviation exam at the age of 12; Tiger Woods won the Optimist International Junior Tournament for the first time when he was eight years old.

Terrence Tao was the youngest participant in the International Mathematical Olympiad; he competed for the first time in 1986 when he was 10 years old and won a bronze medal. He competed again in 1987 and 1988 and won silver and gold medals, respectively. He was said to be the brightest person of his age worldwide.

Pablo Picasso's artistic aptitude was first noticed when he was 10 years old, and he grew to become the most influential artist of the 20th century. He produced his first masterpiece, *The Old Guitarist*, between late 1903 and early 1904, when he was only 13 years old. The Old Guitarist is on display at the Art Institute of Chicago.

The list of prodigies goes on and on, and if you've followed the life stories of prodigies-turned-extraordinary, as were Pablo Picasso et al., you too might have drifted into the misconception that elitism can only be innate. After all, the people mentioned above were prodigies, and other than being gifted, one cannot be convinced that they trained extraordinarily to attain elitism.

On the contrary, not all prodigies grow to be extraordinary achievers. In fact, in most cases, they're surpassed by non-prodigies. This calls to mind the accomplishments of Albert Einstein, Winston Churchill, Charles Darwin, the Wright brothers, et cetera, whose lives' work I've discussed at length, and there was no indication that they were gifted children.

Charles Darwin even admitted that he was a very ordinary boy, rather below the common standard in intellect. He added: 'I have no great quickness of apprehension…my power to follow a long and purely abstract train of thought is very limited.'

So, aside from drawing on one's talent, how else can people attain career elitism? How is it also possible that non-gifted people are able to surpass gifted people in proficiency?

Practice Makes Perfect

Albert Einstein

At the age of five, when Albert Einstein first encountered the magnetic compass, he immediately conceived the idea that some invisible forces made it work the way it did. For the next 20 years, trying to understand those invisible forces became his primary thinking and lifelong thought process. The cumulative hours of his thought processes eventually developed his brainpower. Hence, he could conduct high-powered physics experiments and conceive invisible happenings in the cosmos entirely in his brain. This is why his name became a byword for genius!

Charles Darwin

Before the voyage of the *HMS Beagle*, Darwin had practised specimen collection as a hobby. Little did anyone, including himself, know that his practice would culminate in extraordinary career proficiency, making his voyage with the *Beagle* a transformative and worthwhile experience.

King David

During the Battle of Elah, between the Israelites and the Philistines, the army of Israel had a standoff with the army of Philistines in the valley of Elah. Goliath, the musclebound champion of the Philistine army, comes out twice a day between the lines and calls for a duel. For 40 days, no one in the army of Israel had the nerve to accept the duel.

David, a shepherd boy without combat experience, was sent by his father with food to his brothers on the battlefield. When he arrived, Goliath was ranting about a duel as usual. And though he had gone to the battlefield unprepared but 'armed' with only a shepherd's staff and a sling, he accepted the duel and took five stones for a face-off with the fully armour-clad, nine-and-a-half-foot-tall giant.

Goliath noticed David, and perceiving him as an underdog, he underestimated him. He advanced to attack, and as David ran to meet him, he reached into his shepherd's bag, took out a stone, and hurled it with his sling. The stone hit Goliath in the forehead and sank in, causing him to stumble and fall face down. David advanced on Goliath's fallen body, drew his sword from its sheath, and decapitated him.

News about David's glorious triumph made the rounds and made him worthy of royalty. His victory, however, did not come on a silver platter, as the story implies. He had practised his attack techniques for years and was well versed in duels with beasts that were slick and more ferocious than humans. Goliath's stature, therefore, couldn't have intimidated him.

For more than 10 years as a shepherd, David had practised sling throwing as his hobby in the wilderness. He could aim at both close and distant targets, throw without missing, and hit hard enough to jar his targets. At that level of proficiency, the sling was thus a lethal weapon in his hand, and with it, he had fended off bears and lions from his flock.

This experience, over time, nurtured his bravery to the extent that when a lion or bear swooped in and carried off a sheep from his flock, he gave chase and struck the beast to rescue the sheep from its mouth. And when the wild beast turned on him, he caught it by its hair and clubbed it to death.

Deliberate Practice

Winston Churchill

Winston Churchill became a great orator and was eulogised as the all-time best. His oratory skill, however, had no correlation with his aptitude. In fact, he was born somewhat disadvantaged for public speaking.

He suffered speech impairment at an early age and had difficulty pronouncing the letter s. He spoke in a monotonous tone, his voice was bland, and his stammer made matters worse. But he understood the influence written and spoken words could have on an audience, and knowing where he was headed in life, he was determined to master oratory.

As a child, Churchill often witnessed live parliamentary proceedings and observed them with all seriousness. He would sit quietly and imbibe his father's speeches, then reread them meticulously till he could recite them by heart. Churchill further studied the speeches of Olivia Cromwell, William Gladstone, and William Pitt.

At age 21, he travelled to the US and met with the then New York Congressman, Bourke Cockran, whom he admired for being affable. He would later describe him as a remarkable statesman, due to the manner in which he spoke.

When Churchill asked the congressman for his advice on how to enthral an audience of thousands with a speech, the congressman told him to speak as if he were an organ and use strong words and utter them with clarity in a wave-like rhythm. Churchill called Congressman Bourke Cockran his 'mentor' and could quote from speeches he gave 60 years earlier.

Inspired by his father's political career, Winston Churchill desired to be a statesman but was worried about his speech impairment. Once, he consulted a throat specialist, who detected no defect upon examining him. The specialist then told young Churchill: 'Only practice and perseverance will help you.' These words reverberated in his mind for years.

From then on, Churchill practised the art of public speaking with diligence and devotion. He rehearsed words, particularly those that began with the letter s. On the street, he recited the sentence: 'The Spanish ships I cannot see since they are not in sight.'

While he was making the effort to overcome his stammer, his stammering attenuated and eventually dissipated. Years later, in his speech, he said: 'Never give in! Never give in! Never give in except to convictions of honour and good sense.'

Churchill wrote an article about oratory called 'The Scaffolding of Rhetoric' when he was 23. In it, he says that oratory gives a man the power of a great king, but that the orator must feel the emotion himself before he can make the audience feel it.

From his maiden public speech to his last, Churchill prepared thoroughly for his speeches and he was as meticulous in his 70s as he was in his 20s. To him, a speech, both in substance and form, had to be a work of art.

On how he prepared his speeches, he once said: 'I take the very greatest pains with style and composition. I do not compose quickly. Everything is worked out by hard labour and frequent polishing. I intend to polish till it glitters...'

In all these cases, it took Winston Churchill's deliberate practice to become an outstanding orator without a shred of oratory aptitude in his DNA.

Kobe Bryant

There wasn't any basketball move Kobe Bryant couldn't do at his best; he could dribble, pass, shoot, dunk, rebound, and defend. His beginning, however, didn't look like he was cut out for basketball.

In the summer of 1991, he joined the camp of some young basketball players and played against them, but they outmanoeuvred him on every front, and he couldn't score a point. He felt demoralised after the match and questioned if basketball was his thing. Subsequently, Kobe Bryant chanced on some literature about Michael Jordan, the all-time best basketball player, and learnt that Michael Jordan was removed from his high school basketball team because he couldn't match up with the best players.

According to the tale, Michael Jordan didn't quit but immersed himself in deliberate practice and eventually outperformed everyone. Kobe Bryant was so moved by this story that he started a tough training routine and worked harder than his peers.

At high school, he got to the gym at 5:00 a.m. and stayed until 7:00 p.m. When official training was over, he stayed behind and goaded other players to a duel for up to 100 points.

His arduous training routine in high school turned him into an elite player. He became so good that only six years after he had failed to score a single point at the basketball camp in the summer of 1991, he was adjudged the 13th overall best in the NBA.

Kobe Bryant's success story is a modern testament to how practice beats talent and that deliberate practice is the only pathway to attaining elitism. It demands at least a 10,000-hour duration of practice, which can span up to 10 years, and not even a gifted person can skip the 10,000-hour rule to attain career elitism.

Deliberate Mentoring

The Polgars

Laszlo Polgar, a Hungarian educational psychologist and a chess teacher, studied the biographies of hundreds of intellectual achievers, and realised that they all had an early start and specialisation.

Laszlo believed that the current educational system produces mediocrity, and was confident that he could turn any healthy child into a prodigy. He had already authored the book *Bring Up Genius*, and he needed a wife to complement his plan.

Laszlo could've penned a breathtaking love letter to Klara, a Ukrainian foreign language teacher who he had a crush on. But instead, he wrote a marriage proposal with a detailed pedagogical experiment: Laszlo had long been inclined to carry out this experiment on his future children. He believed that if education begins by the third birthday and specialisation begins by the sixth birthday, every child has the potential to become a genius in any field.

Klara received the letter and read it quietly with a smile; Polgar's idea had sunk in. She fell in love, and they married and had three daughters: Susan, Sofia, and Judit.

Initially, the Polgar parents were unsure of the discipline in which to train their future children; formal schooling, however, was clearly out of their consideration. Finally, they settled on homeschooling.

In 1973, when Susan was barely four years old, she chanced on a chess set while scrambling through a cabinet and stopped to gaze at the chess pieces. Her mother saw how interested she was in the figurines, and by the end of the day, both parents agreed to teach her how to play chess.

Laszlo began training Susan in chess for an hourly session per day and progressed to several hours. In 1974, when he was in the middle of a chess lesson with Susan, a call came in: Klara had given birth to Sofia. After 21 months, Judit was born.

When Sofia and Judit were old enough, they showed interest in Susan's chess lessons, and soon, their father enrolled them. Laszlo and Klara also schooled their three girls in English, German, and high-level mathematics. The three sisters became multilingual.

Aside from their practice with their father, they had a personal devotion to chess, and their level of immersion was profound. One late night, Laszlo found Sofia in the bathroom with the chessboard on her knees and implored her to go and sleep.

Susan picked up chess so fast and won her first competition in 1973, when she was four years old. By the age of 15, she was ranked among the elite players in the world and went on to best several adult opponents when she was 16 years old. Her string of victories landed her on the front page of the New York Times.

Meanwhile, Sofia and Judit were racking up wins in their league. In 1984, when the two sisters were nine and seven, they competed in two blindfold chess games against two masters and won.

In 1991, when Susan was 21 years old, she earned the Grandmaster title as the first woman. Judit became a Grandmaster at the age of 15 and was the youngest person in the world to earn the title. Sofia also earned the Woman Grandmaster title.

By every indication, Laszlo Polgar's pedagogical experiment to make geniuses of his daughters was successful.

When I look at the life stories of geniuses, I found the same thing...they all started at a very young age and studied intensively. – Laszlo Polgar.

Explication

Nobody remembers how we learned our mother tongue, but what matters is that we can communicate fluently in it. We also understood our mother tongue effortlessly, not because it was easy to learn but because we were children. On the contrary, it takes much effort and commitment for adults to learn a language.

Let's take, for instance, the English language as a variable for any skill; for a child to learn to speak it, they don't need to know what phrasal verbs, adverbial clauses, and coordinating conjunctions are. The child only has to mingle with English speakers, and they will understand and speak the language.

This boils down to the elasticity of a child's brain as compared to an adult, and why childhood is the best period to be mentored. The Spartan's knew about this thousands of years ago.

By 346–336 BC (more than 100 years after the Battle of Thermopylae), Phillip II of Macedon had brought peace to Greece by ending his decade-long conflict for supremacy with Athens. He was also the de facto leader of Greece because he had a large kingdom, a strong army, and a lot of money.

Having already subjugated several key Greek city-states, Philip II turned to Sparta and sent them a message: 'You are advised to submit without further delay, for if I bring my army into your land, I will destroy your farms, slay your people, and raze your city.' The Spartans replied to Philip II with just one word, 'If.'

In the Macedonians' ensuing campaign, neither Philip II nor his successor, Alexander the Great, dared Sparta.

Sparta was a small Greek city-state and obviously incomparable to Macedon in terms of economy, population, technology, and military size. Unlike the other Greek city-states, the Spartans didn't even have walls around their city. So how could one word, 'If,' deter Philip II from waging war against an 'underdog' Sparta?

Build a Formidable Reputation

Earlier, in 491 BCE, Darius I, King of Persia, sent envoys to Greece to coerce the various city-states to submit to Persia's authority. The Athenians turned the Persian envoys down; the Spartans were vexed with the Persian envoys over their impudence and shoved them into a deep pit.

Eleven years later, Darius I's son and successor, Xerxes, was even more determined to continue his father's plan to conquer Greece and punish Sparta in particular.

Xerxes had grown more powerful and led a multitude of armies; once upon a time, on a march past the *Echedoros River*, it was said that his soldiers proceeded to drink the river dry. With an army so vast, a coalition of the entire Greek armed forces was still an underdog against the Persian army, let alone only a 300-strong handful of Spartan soldiers.

The Battle of Thermopylae

By 480 BCE, Xerxes had set out to annihilate all of Greece. He intended to seize Northern Greece first, then turn his offensive toward the south. At Thermopylae, Xerxes met the resistance of a coalition of 7000 Greek infantrymen, comprising Thebans, Corinthians, Philias, Mycenaeans, Acadians, Thespians, and, of course, the 300 Spartans, led by King Leonidas I.

Though the Persians numbered anywhere from 70,000 to 300,000, they suffered heavy losses in the narrow pass of Thermopylae, where they were funnelled into a gap so that only their frontline could clash against the Greek shields while the rest of their troops could only scramble from behind their men in front.

That was what Leonidas had hoped for, and it played out well in his hands. He believed that once they held their ground, no enemy force could break their line. The Greeks held the line for two days, slashing through the Persians and trampling thousands of their dead.

While the war ensued, the Greeks were betrayed by their countryman, Ephialtes. He had switched to the Persians' side and shown Xerxes a goat path around Thermopylae where they could outflank the Greeks.

Xerxes then dispatched his archers along the goat path, led by Ephialtes himself. When Leonidas saw that they were being outflanked, he ordered the coalition forces to withdraw while he remained with his Spartan troops to guard their withdrawal.

It was their last stand: the Spartans charged with far greater ferocity at the advancing Persians from the east. By then, the Persian archers along the goat path had taken their stand at the flank and shot their arrows down at the Spartans.

The Spartans couldn't fend off the swarm-like arrows that were said to have blotted out the sun. Leonidas lay slain with his troops, but the Spartans' heroism made the rounds and their reputation soared.

Among the ancient Greek city-states, the Spartans were the most badass and an epitome of valour. In Sparta, from the day a male child began to walk, he was 'baptised in the fire of combat.' At age seven, the male children were taken from their mothers and sent to the Agoge: a modern-day boot camp.

At the Agoge, they were trained and made to compete in combat manoeuvres and strategies. They graduated when they turned 12 years old and were regarded as youth, at which point their training was intensified. They were made to walk barefoot to develop greater agility and athleticism. They were also given a single cloak called Phoinikis to wear, regardless of the weather condition. This exercise was designed to toughen them mentally and also help them thrive in any weather during combat.

And indeed, in real-life combat, Spartans were unperturbed by the extremes of any weather condition. They were given small amounts of rations each day in order to get used to hunger; if they wanted more food, they had to steal. If they were caught stealing, they were punished severely, not because they stole, but because they couldn't manoeuvre well enough and got caught.

By the time the Spartans turned 20 years old, each trainee had morphed into an elite warrior and was drafted into the army. But they continued to live in the barracks and weren't allowed to marry until they turned 30. To choose a wife, they were encouraged to select women whose physiques were likely to yield bouncy progeny.

With the Spartans, combat was more comfortable than training, and their mental toughness was incredible.

The Spartans were legendary for their superior fighting abilities; they went to war with only a small number of men. They were raised to be warriors, so they had unmatched bravery and fighting skills. They also had a lot of confidence and never felt afraid.

Unlike their neighbouring city-states, which built formidable walls for protection, the Spartans built no walls around their city. When a visitor questioned Agesilaus II, King of Sparta (c. 444–360 BCE), about the lack of walls around his city, he pointed to his troops and responded, 'These are Sparta's walls.'

The Spartans were also cocky. When the King of Macedon, Demetrius I, received ambassadors in his court, he noticed only one Spartan ambassador. He felt disrespected and snapped: 'What? Have the Lacedemonians (Spartans) sent no more but one ambassador?' The Spartan responded: 'One ambassador to one king.'

For hundreds of years before Philip II became king of Macedon and the de facto leader of Greece, these stories made up Sparta's reputation.

So, if you're wondering why Philip II and his son Alexander the Great were put off by the Spartans' response, 'If,' here's why: they were aware of the Spartans' history and valour, and they knew that fighting Sparta would cost them more than it was worth.

Key Takeaway: To build a formidable reputation, enter contests, win victories, chalk up successes, cover milestones, make gains, and let your success stories be told. The hype will inevitably follow, making you appear larger than life. But don't fake it; otherwise, you'll be exposed and disgraced, as Eliseo Gil was in *The Veleia Affair*.

The Veleia Affair

In 1994, Eliseo Gil and his wife secured €3.7 million in funding from the regional public train companies through their private archaeology firm. The fund's purpose was for Eliseo Gil to lead an archaeological investigation in the ancient Roman city of Iruña-Veleia in the Basque region of northern Spain.

In 2006, he made progress and said that he had found pottery pieces and other things from the third century A.D. Gil's discovery wowed the archaeological world and made headlines in the Spanish press. The hype followed. One of the news headlines was: 'A discovery of this magnitude comes along once every two generations.'

The sherds had some remarkable graffiti scratched on them. One was a depiction of the Calvary scene, making the find one of the oldest images of Christ's crucifixion. Eliseo Gil thereby became an overnight celebrity.

The other finds were animal bones with the name of the Egyptian queen, Nefertiti, engraved on them. Some of the sherds also had hieroglyphics and Latin inscriptions, while others had ancient texts in the Basque language.

What these finds could've meant for the ancient Roman city, Veleia, was that the ancient Basque text on the sherds would've elicited both archaeological and cultural hysteria. Because although the origin of the Basque language remains inconclusive, the 2.3 million residents of Veleia consider themselves more Basque than Spanish.

Gil's finds were about to herald a revolution in the city's understanding of the Mediterranean region. And, having lauded the veracity and authenticity of his discoveries, Eliseo Gil basked in the glory of the publicity he was receiving until other scholars weighed in!

At first, some experts in ancient history approved of Gil's finds. He also asked Joaquin Gorrochategui, a professor of Indo-European linguistics at UPV and an expert in ancient Basque, to assess the inscriptions on the artefacts.

Joaquin Gorrochategui became suspicious of the inscriptions, observing that they seemed too modern for a third-century find. He also noticed that the

Latin inscriptions had an odd grammar; however, he had seen only a handful of the finds and couldn't say much about his suspicion.

So he went to the Lava Archaeological Museum to see what else was there. To his shock, he found the inscriptions ENIIAS, ANQVISIIS ET VENVS FILI on a sherd and snapped: 'This can't be. For one thing, there's a comma, which is modern. And 'Eneas' should be written 'Aenae' and 'Venus' should be 'Veneris.'

Joaquin Gorrochategui further explained: 'I had doubts about the Basque inscriptions, but it was harder to confirm because of the scanty information we have on ancient Basque. But Latin is a different story. In the end, what explained everything was that they were fakes.'

Other experts, including participants of an internet forum, also weighed in. For instance, in 2008, one participant pointed out that the graph in the Veleai patina report, which supposedly proves that the inscriptions were made before the sherds were buried, was 'a manipulated copy of a sample graph advertised on the internet by the German scientific instrumentation company, FAST ComTec. The measure time, real-time, and live time of the sample acquisition in the Veleia report compiled for Eliseo Gil were identical to those of the FAST ComTec graph. Both graphs also had the same acquisition date, October 31, 1990.

Another participant wrote to the German company, FAST ComTec, concerning Gil's graph, and was sent a reply that reads: 'I agree that the picture of that [graph] was copied from our datasheet...this [graph] is not a real measurement but just a clumsy copy.'

One other issue that cropped up was that there was little evidence that the artefacts had indeed come from the excavation site. Moreover, Eliseo Gil had refused to show his original field notes, excavation photographs, and the results from the laboratories that authenticated the finds.

The final straw was the letters RIP for 'Requiescat in Pace,' inscribed on the cross in the crucifixion scene on a sherd, which contravenes the resurrection and divinity of Christ.

A fact-finding commission comprised of Eliseo Gil and other experts was constituted to probe the Veleia project. A few hours after their final meeting, the Álava government suspended Gil's project permit and all activities on the project site.

In the end, the totality of the evidence gathered pointed out that Eliseo Gil had contrived the finds. He was subsequently arrested for fraud, prosecuted, and found guilty.

From a compelling headline in June 2006 that read: 'A discovery of this magnitude comes along once every two generations,' in June 2020, the Olive Press reported Eliseo Gil's tumbling reputation with the headline: 'Spanish

Archaeologist Sentenced to More than Two Years in Prison for Faking Finds that Would 'Rewrite History.'

You are not too Young to Be an Extraordinary Achiever

'*Behind every young child who believes in himself is a parent who believed first.*'—Mathew Jacobson

---

You're not too young to be a great achiever. So just when you deem yourself able and ready to execute your idea, go ahead and do it. The younger you are, the sooner you'll be noticed, the faster your reputation will spread, and the more likely you'll be immortalised. So, show up early!

Ideally, there's no better place to train for a career other than within the career itself, as proficiency is better developed on the job than in the classroom. This is why professionals who didn't do well in school can still catch up, match up with high job performers, or even come off as the best on the job.

Finally, deliberate mentoring at a young age allows for early career advancement and elitism. Laszlo Polgar has proven this, whereas the Spartans' early military training is even more telling.

Jesse Martin

At the age of 14, Jesse Martin and his brother joined their father on a two-month adventure voyage, sailing a 14-foot catamaran from Cairns to Cape York. Jesse Martin learnt navigation on this sail, and his desire for circumnavigation was born.

When they returned home, he began seeking sponsorship for a solo circumnavigation as the youngest person to ever do so, but his request was refused due to his age and inexperience. In the next three years, Jesse embarked on a five-week kayaking expedition in Papua New Guinea. He also joined a yacht crew and sailed from Belize to Tahiti with them for three months. When he got back home, he was sure he could do his planned solo circumnavigation.

He put school on hold, and for most of 1998, he tried again to get sponsorship for his solo circumnavigation, but it didn't happen until his mother mortgaged their house and purchased a yacht for him. Word spread about the yacht purchase and made the rounds, thereby attracting sponsorship from four companies.

In December 1998, when Jesse was only 17, he departed Melbourne in his yacht, Lionheart, to sail around the world. He spent 11 months at sea, and his encounters included narrowly escaping a collision with a tanker, being hit by a whale in the South Atlantic Sea, and taking a severe knock from a heavy sea.

When he was near Africa's Cape of New Hope, a Force 10 storm threatened to dismantle the Lionheart. This made him quiver at the threats of the sea, but he kept his composure and penned down all his encounters, which he later developed into a book titled *Lionheart:* 'A Journey of the Human Spirit.' The book was subsequently adapted into a documentary.

Jesse Martin returned on October 31, 1999, at the age of 18, to meet a rousing welcome from some 20,000 well-wishers.

In 2000, he was named the Young Victorian of the Year and was awarded the Medal of the Order of Australia. Jesse would later attribute his accomplishments to his parents. In his address, he said of them: 'I was made to believe I could do anything.'

Bill Gates

Bill Gates became interested in computer programming at the age of 13 while he was at Lakeside School in Seattle. During that period, an IT company in Seattle offered to provide computer time for students. Gates was kindled with delight and marvelled at what a computer could do. He spent much of his free time practising with a teletype terminal that his school had provided and wrote a tic-tac-toe programme in BASIC computer language that allowed users to play (game) against the computer.

In 1970, Gates went into business with his friend, Paul Allen. Together, they developed 'Traf-o-data', a computer programme that monitored traffic patterns in Seattle, and earned a whopping $20,000.00. Gates was only 15 years old.

Starting at age 13, with unrelenting practice, Bill Gates and Paul Allen built the world's largest software business, Microsoft. In 1994, at age 38, he became the wealthiest man in the US, with a $9.35 billion fortune.

The above narratives are only a few among several success stories that point out the fact that youngsters might be capable. And it would be regressive to dismiss a young person for what they have shown up for simply because they are not older.

CHAPTER FOUR

Occupational Intelligence

Safeguard your Achilles Heel

History has imparted invaluable lessons that caution us against placing absolute trust in others when it comes to our Achilles heel. The timeless tale of Samson and Delilah serves as a poignant example, and repeating such a mistake, even if one is unaware of its far-reaching consequences, would undoubtedly be regarded as an act of foolishness.

In the Iliad, Achilles, a renowned warrior in the Trojan War, possessed an extraordinary invulnerability to physical harm. This extraordinary invulnerability was bestowed upon him when his mother, the sea nymph Thetis, immersed him in the river Styx, rendering him invincible. Regrettably, as Thetis held Achilles by his heel during the immersion, his heel therefore remained his sole point of weakness.

The tale goes that during a pivotal battle in the Trojan War, Paris, the prince of Troy, under the guidance of the god Apollo, aimed an arrow at Achilles, accurately striking him in the heel and eventually bringing about his death.

Achilles heel is therefore used metaphorically to symbolise a vulnerability within an individual or entity. Despite possessing immense strength, remarkable abilities, or unparalleled competence, this vulnerability can be exploited to bring about their downfall.

In a career context, the term "Achilles heel" can indeed apply to professional or workplace vulnerabilities that, if exploited, can lead to the downfall of an individual or organisation. These vulnerabilities may encompass sensitive information, actions, or sources that, whether legitimate or not, should be safeguarded against disclosure. The following examples are illustrative of the issues I have read about or assisted clients in successfully resolving:

1. Anna misrepresented her qualifications on her CV, claiming to be a skilled graphic designer, which ultimately helped her secure a job as a communication specialist. Over the course of three years, Anna managed to avoid any major issues, primarily because a significant portion of her

responsibilities involved writing and editing, with minimal involvement in graphic design.

Conveniently, she outsourced the graphic design task to a friend who worked for a different company. Anna kept this outsourcing arrangement a secret, impressing the general manager with her productivity and her ability to excel in multiple areas such as writing, editing, and graphic design. However, Anna made an error in judgment by confiding in her closest friend at work and divulging the truth about her CV fabrication and the outsourced graphic design work, explicitly requesting that it remain a secret. Unfortunately, the information began to spread as rumours swirled, each person adding their own speculations until it reached the general manager's ears that Anna had been outsourcing tasks to a competitor.

Naturally, the general manager was incensed and profoundly disappointed in Anna, not only for lying on her CV but also for her lack of discretion in outsourcing vital corporate responsibilities to a rival company. This implied that Anna might have been compromising sensitive internal information by leaking it to the competition.

Although the general manager contemplated terminating Anna's employment due to her transgressions, he recognised her exceptional writing skills and unparalleled productivity. So he decided to demote her instead of dismissing her outright. However, in a moment of heated emotion, Anna chose to resign to salvage her reputation. Regrettably, this impulsive decision had consequences, as she faced significant difficulty securing her next job. Ultimately, Anna did find employment, albeit not in a managerial capacity as she had previously held but rather in a staff-level role.

2. Edward Seward, known for his habit of giving lottery tickets as tips, handed Tonda Lynn Dickerson, a divorcee in her twenties, a lottery ticket after she served him at the restaurant. This was a customary gesture from Seward, as he often gifted lottery tickets to friends, relatives, and even waitstaff.

   Unexpectedly, Tonda's tipped ticket turned out to be a jackpot winner, granting her a substantial sum of $10 million. Her colleagues at the restaurant were overjoyed for her, but they harboured expectations that she would share her newfound wealth with them. However, much to their disappointment, Tonda had no intention of doling out any portion of her winnings to them. Consequentially, they sued her, alleging that an agreement existed between Tonda and themselves, stipulating that she would share her lottery windfall if she emerged a winner.

Furthermore, Edward Seward, the man who gifted Tonda the lottery ticket, also sued, claiming that Tonda had promised to buy him a pickup truck if she won the lottery. Following an arduous legal battle, Tonda emerged triumphant, successfully defending herself and winning both cases. Unfortunately, Tonda's troubles were far from over. Her ex-husband, Stacy Martin, whom she had been divorced from for several years, embarked on a disturbing course of action, attempting to kidnap her. In a desperate act of self-defence, Tonda shot Martin in the right side of his chest, inadvertently saving herself from harm. Fortunately, Stacy Martin survived the ordeal, but the incident added yet another traumatic chapter to Tonda's life.

Subsequently, Tonda found herself entangled in a dispute with the Internal Revenue Service (IRS). The IRS insisted on imposing a gift tax of $1 million on the portion of Tonda's $10 million lottery win that she had gifted to her family. Refusing to back down, Tonda took the IRS to court, determined to challenge their demand. In a significant legal victory, she emerged successful once more, winning her case against the IRS.

3. Dyson was known for his unassuming nature and dedication to his work, maintaining harmonious relationships with his boss and colleagues. Despite not possessing extraordinary talent, he mysteriously enjoyed certain privileges that left the rest of the staff and executives puzzled. Little did they know that Dyson was actually the CEO's undercover informant, entrusted with the task of observing and reporting on daily occurrences within the company.

   Each day, he diligently stayed behind work hours to compile a detailed report, which he would discreetly send to the CEO. This covert arrangement remained a well-kept secret for several years, with nobody suspecting Dyson as the source behind the CEO's uncanny knowledge of even the most trivial happenings. However, a turning point arrived when Dyson developed an unusual fondness for a newly hired colleague of remarkable beauty. In an unfortunate twist of fate, she accidentally cracked her laptop screen while working on an urgent assignment. Displaying an uncharacteristic act of kindness, Dyson decided to lend her his laptop, leaving it in her care for a significant portion of the workday. Unbeknownst to him, this seemingly innocuous gesture would lead to his downfall.

News of Dyson's daily reports to the CEO spread like wildfire, and copies of these reports quickly went viral among the employees. The revelation instantly created a palpable distance between Dyson and his coworkers, who now viewed him with suspicion.

The news reached the CEO, who regarded Dyson's decision to lend his laptop as a foolish lack of discretion, considering it was his Achilles heel. As a consequence, the CEO made the regrettable decision to terminate Dyson's employment, citing his indiscretion as the reason behind this drastic action.

Explication and Rowback

Some truths are meant to remain concealed, especially if they expose our deepest vulnerabilities. In such instances, it becomes paramount to protect them at all costs, as revealing them would be like sealing one's own death warrant—a self-destructive act that unfolds inevitably.

Surprisingly, Anna, Tonda, and Dyson seemed unaware of the crucial importance of discretion when it comes to their Achilles heel.

This lack of awareness resulted in a significant blunder that deprived them of valuable opportunities and peace of mind. Nevertheless, had they exercised caution and kept their secrets hidden, they could have spared themselves the ensuing conflicts and challenges.

1. Anna made a grave mistake by discussing her falsified CV and unethical outsourcing of graphic design tasks with someone. She should have refrained from disclosing such sensitive information to anyone. Apart from succumbing to the temptation of impressing someone with her intellect and strategic thinking, her disclosure served no strategic purpose and, in fact, proved to be unwise.

   By revealing these details, Anna failed to consider the potential consequences and the lack of benefits they would bring. Instead of finding validation or satisfaction, she inadvertently put herself at risk. It is crucial to recognise that sharing such information without a clear purpose can lead to negative outcomes and damage one's reputation or professional standing.

   In hindsight, Anna should have exercised restraint and refrained from divulging these secrets. Keeping such matters confidential would have been a wiser choice, sparing her unnecessary complications and safeguarding her professional interests.

2. Envy can easily be ignited among friends, and even more so among work colleagues who are in constant, overt or covert competition for top positions or lucrative opportunities. Therefore, it is prudent to exercise discretion when it comes to windfalls related to work. In the case of Tonda Lynn Dickerson, considering the circumstances surrounding her

acquisition of the lottery ticket, it proved to be a mistake for her to disclose her win to anyone unless she was prepared to fairly share it with 'those involved.'

Alternatively, Tonda could have discreetly distributed a portion of her winnings as anonymous gifts to her colleagues, without revealing the source, on the condition that she could ensure her kind gesture would not raise suspicion. nevertheless, the wisest course of action for her would have been to keep the information about receiving the lottery ticket, let alone winning it, entirely to herself.

By avoiding any mention of the ticket and its subsequent winnings, Tonda would have protected herself from potential envy or conflicts within her professional circle. Sometimes it is best to guard one's good fortune silently, without arousing unnecessary attention or risking the delicate dynamics of workplace relationships.

3. Due to the confidential nature of Dyson's assignments involving his laptop, it was imperative that he never entrusted it to anyone, regardless of any circumstances that may have risen.

To safeguard your Achilles heel effectively, it is crucial to refrain from entrusting it to anyone or discussing its existence. Unlike the events depicted in Homer's Iliad, in reality, unless you explicitly disclose or display your Achilles heel, not even the gods themselves can be aware of it.

Always bear in mind that your Achilles heel represents your vulnerability, and its protection is paramount in shielding yourself from potential exploitation or harm. Practising discretion, relying on your instincts, and being cognizant of the potential risks of divulging sensitive information are essential. There's no option to this caution.

Do Due Diligence

Common sense dictates that before we pass judgement on a case, we must hear both sides; before we review a book, we must read everything therein; before we sign any document, we must read every sentence and understand it.

The list goes on and on, yet it's common to find that people contravene these elementary principles and land in controversies they could've avoided.

Shockingly, notable people who should've known better have been culpable for not being thorough. The causes of their culpability vary; fundamentally, it could stem from misguided trust, laxity, or incompetence.

Misguided Trust

There'll come a time in your professional life when someone has to act on your behalf or represent you. It's only natural that you'll pick someone you trust for this purpose, expecting that they'll act in good faith. But there's a reason you should attentively follow whatever is being done on your behalf. For instance, a contract may be written for you, but be sure to read it thoroughly and understand every sentence before you sign it or authorise someone to sign on your behalf.

The reason is that people can be funny and plainly mischievous in a manner you cannot wrap your head around. As a result, you must avoid misguided trust.

In 1997, The Gap (clothing company) hired LL Cool J to perform in a commercial for its line of easy-fit jeans. In the 30 seconds of recording for The Gap, while wearing The Gap's jeans and a T-shirt but a FUBU hat, LL Cool J name-dropped FUBU (another clothing company) in his rap, saying, 'For us, By us.' The Gap didn't notice LL Cool J had pulled a prank on them until some months later.

In retrospect, perhaps the thought of pulling the prank wouldn't have crossed LL Cool J's mind if The Gap had asked him to submit the rap lyrics to them for review before shooting the commercial. And although LL Cool J's prank didn't hurt The Gap, it benefited FUBU immensely.

He was the man of the hour, and his reach at the time had no bounds. So, it wasn't a surprise that FUBU's sales soared and reached their peak the following year, grossing more than $350 million in sales.

Laxity

There have been times when a professional wasn't thorough with their work, which led to damage. In fact, no one is unerring in this regard due to our fallibility as humans, and yes, experts can also be fallible. Nonetheless, it comes with a price, from reputational risk to legal liabilities, and the cost can be severe.

Kim Kardashian West's Robbery

On October 3, 2016, when Kim Kardashian West's bodyguard was accompanying her sisters at a nightclub, five masked men—dressed as police officers—stormed into her Paris hotel room, grabbed her, and led her through the hallway. They taped her hands, mouth, and legs together and bound her with plastic cables before they robbed her of an estimated $10 million worth of jewellery.

According to the terms of her agreement with her insurer, she was compensated $6.1 million, but they in turn sued her bodyguard for reimbursement. According to the insurer's suit, the bodyguard wasn't present to protect Kardashian at the time of the heist. They also pointed out significant security lapses the bodyguard failed to address, which included a missing or broken lock on the hotel's courtyard gate, a concierge with no security training, a lack of security cameras, and a broken intercom on the door that separated the concierge's desk from the courtyard. According to the lawsuit, those lapses made it conducive for the heist.

In any event, Kim Kardashian West's bodyguard had an assuring professional résumé. His clients were high-profile and included A-list celebrities. In fact, his credentials would make you compare his guardianship to the swift kicks and jabs of Jason Bourne. However, he was blamed for the robbery because he didn't inspect the security credentials of the hotel before their check-in. In the end, the Wests let him go.

Global Blueprint Excellence Award

On August 29, 2020, Ghanaians woke up to a viral video of the vice chancellor of University of Ghana giving a speech at an event dubbed *Global Blueprint Excellence Award*, purportedly in collaboration with the Kofi Annan Foundation and the United Nations:

> … It's because of us at the University of Ghana, where we would call the Home of Mr Kofi Annan. Because this is the only institution where Mr Kofi Annan worked as a Ghanaian, truly leading this great University to greater heights. If that is the case, then we have an obligation; if this country is to grow, then we must make sure that our democracy also matures. So, we're looking at a democracy that is 'you-centred' but also bordered on decency, and when I talk about decency, I talk about language. The language of democracy is extremely important. You don't build democracy based on insults; you build democracy based on courtesies and respect for one another.

The video clip showed the event organiser, a certain Dr. Kwame Owusu Fordjour (now known as Dr. UN), putting stoles around the neck of the esteemed Vice-Chancellor, whereas other clips showed him presenting 'plaques' to some high-profile personalities in the entertainment, political, academic, and media landscapes.

The next Monday, August 31, 2020, Dr Fordjour visited the studio of Angel FM and presented a citation in the category of *Development Programme of Africa* under the '7th Global Leadership Service to Humanity Award' to the host of the studio's Morning Show, Captain Smart, and touted the citation as 'the most prestigious award in the world from the highest office.'

While the award event was trending, a whistleblower blew the cover off the event organiser. This caused a buzz on social media and drew people to take a second look at the event. It then came to light that the award scheme was a sham. Apparently, 'Dr.' Kwame Owusu Fordjour was a fake.

A recollection of the seriousness with which the esteemed Vice-Chancellor delivered his speech evoked an apologetic sentiment, whereas the passion with which Captain Smart and his co-host received the citation from Dr. UN made people burst into uncontrollable laughter.

Another look at the excitement with which some of the awardees flaunted their 'UN plaques' on social media didn't help curb the laughter. Notable among them was Rapper Sarkodie! He should've been present at the prestigious VGMA event that night, but he had shunned it and attended what he thought would be his next-level prestige, only for him to be pranked by Dr. UN.

But nothing could be more hilarious than the fact that the award plaques Dr. UN presented to his victims were cocktail shakers, underplates, low-cost citation frames, and medallions emblazoned with the inscription, 'UN Kofi Annan Excellence Awards.'

It's strange, however, that the A-list rapper Sarkodie didn't notice that the 'plaque' he had happily received was a cocktail shaker, and went on to flaunt it the next day with a tweet:

> A great honor to receive the 7th Global Leadership Service to Humanity Award...RIP To a great son of the Land Mr Kofi Annan… Your legacy is still alive.

To some people, the hysteria surrounding the prank was comic relief in a gloomy year of coronavirus; others opined that the prank was legendary. Yet, some people expressed their disappointment in the awardees for their failure to do due diligence after receiving the invitations, thereby falling flat for Dr. UN's mischief. A week after the event, the United Nations office in Ghana tweeted:

The @UNinGhana has no affiliation with the Blueprint Global Challenge Awards, nor with the organizers. We advise the general public to access genuine info. by visiting the relevant @UN websites…

Explication

The orchestrator of the Global Blueprint Excellence Award, Kwame Owusu Fordjour, aka Dr. UN, had observed that people have a thirst for recognition in their careers, even if they're undeserving. He was sure his targets would be conceited and wouldn't be attentive to the details of his invitation if he tantalised them with awards. He wanted to be famous overnight, and he thought that if he could outwit notable personalities, he would make waves and be given resonance by the media.

So, he targeted prominent government officials, vice chancellors, A-list celebrities, business moguls, religious figures, traditional rulers, et cetera. Though he was unknown, Dr. UN knew that if he could come off as the herald of iconic brands such as the United Nations and its former Secretary-General, Mr. Kofi Annan, he would appear larger than life and be able to woo his targets.

So, he orchestrated the dubious ticketed award event and tied it to the United Nations and the Kofi Annan Foundation. He sent out his invitations with these iconic brands on them, being certain that his invitees wouldn't verify the event. And just as he had anticipated, none of them took the trouble to verify their invitation and ended up making a laughing stock of themselves.

A few days later, when the dust of the awards hysteria had settled, a rumour began to spread: it was being speculated that aside from the ticket sales to the event, Dr. UN had also swindled the awardees out of a substantial sum of money for the awards he gave them. But the rumour died out quickly as none of the awardees came forward to comment, lest it be found to be true and stoke a second wave of public mockery.

Key Takeaway

Whenever you have to deal with someone you don't know or a scheme that is alien to you, ask for the person's particulars or the details of the scheme, and then verify. A simple internet search can save you a tort.

Due Diligence can be Inculcated

Due diligence can be inculcated in the heedless person and reinforced in the cautious person. It can be done through self-development or in-service training. This is crucial because no matter how mindful we are, we can make mistakes simply because we're humans.

That's the reason I wouldn't readily fire an employee who comes up short on attentiveness for the first time or commits a one-off tort. I would rather give them room for correction and let them benefit from their lesson. For example, the benefit of a mistake that does not result in irreversible loss is that it provides an opportunity to learn and gain experience. For this reason, it's worth giving people a second chance, even a bodyguard, and I would've kept Kim's bodyguard.

In 2016, Melania Trump was derided for her plagiarism-dented speech at the Republican National Convention in Cleveland. Her speechwriter was faulted for the gaffe, and she offered to bow out for the embarrassment she had caused, but Candidate Donald Trump declined her resignation, and said: 'You know, people make mistakes.'

Hopefully, she has learnt to write with caution and would likely check for plagiarism in her subsequent speech writing.

So yes, everyone is prone to an occupational blunder or an occasional failure. However, recognise when a mistake is a disguised mischief or a sign of incompetence. In that case, giving someone a second chance is akin to playing Russian roulette with yourself.

Know Your Limitation

Some people are conceited and overrate themselves. As repulsive as this habit is, it stems from a cognitive bias known in psychology as the Dunning-Kruger effect. We've also known people who lobbied for certain roles while touting themselves as the best fit for the job and promising sunshine and rainbows, but when given the nod, they came off as incompetent and delivered doom and gloom.

The Dunning-Kruger effect also explains why some people overestimate their own influence. The outcome of this misjudgement can be delusive and ridiculous. This brings to mind a parliamentary hopeful I knew. No one perceived a leader in him, but the man fancied himself larger than life and boasted that he would easily unseat the incumbent in the upcoming general elections.

The elections were held, and when the votes were counted, he pulled zero votes at the polling station where he voted. This made him wonder what became of his own vote, but his constituents, who knew him to be a confused man, weren't surprised that he didn't vote for himself.

In any case, lessons from the past should teach us to tread cautiously in fields we're novices in and areas we're aliens to, lest we come off as inept in a futile attempt to look smart. The repercussions can be stressful to a public figure, much more so to a political leader, as in the case of what seemed to have been an attempt to end the political career of a former US vice president.

Dan Quayle's Misspelling

In 1992, while serving as vice president and running mate of President George H. W. Bush, Dan Quayle accepted an invitation to moderate a spelling bee. As the spelling bee ensued, a participant spelt the word 'potato,' but Quayle objected and announced that the participant had misspelt the word, suggesting the wrong spelling, 'P-O-T-A-T-O-E,' instead.

Dan Quayle's misspelling turned into a hysteria; a heated national dialogue followed, and derision was hurled at him left, right, and centre from his political opponents. As though the derision wasn't enough, his allies even called for his replacement as running mate. Quayle later described his misspelling as 'a defining moment of the worst imaginable kind.'

Though he explained that the word was misspelt on his cue card, his name had already been brought into disrepute, and he probably still wishes he had declined the invitation to moderate the spelling bee.

Einstein Didn't Know it All

In May 1952, Johanna Mankiewicz, a 14-year-old high school sophomore at the Westlake School for Girls in Los Angeles, needed help with her geometry homework. Having been familiar with celebrities in her upbringing, she sought out a celebrity scientist to help her, and only one name came to mind: Albert Einstein. She then wrote to him:

> I realise that you are a very busy man, but you are the only person we know who could supply us with the answer.' What is the length of the common external tangents of two circles of radii 8 inches and 2 inches? She added, 'I think you will agree it is the hardest thing!

Unknown to little Johanna, Einstein corresponded with children and ordinary people if he felt their inquiry was sincere. So, having received and read Johanna's postcard, Einstein turned to the back and scribbled the answer:

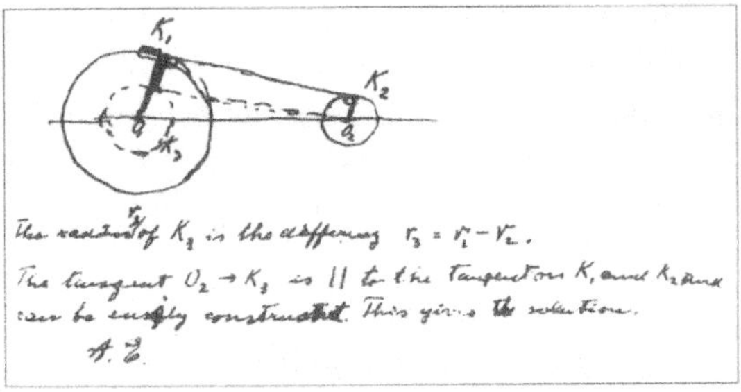

The radius r_3 of K_3 is the differenz $r_3 = r_1 - r_2$.
The tangent $O_2 \rightarrow K_3$ is // to the tangent on k_1 and k_2 and can be easily constructed. This gives the solution.
A.E

The answer above confounded Johanna to the core, as she expected a standard geometry problem to be answered by Pythagoras' theorem. But she couldn't find the required length, nor could she explain how Pythagoras' theorem was used.

Given Johanna's celebrity environment, reporters learnt of her correspondence with Einstein, and the media weighed in. Initially, the press focussed on Einstein's willingness to assist a teenager with her schoolwork. This was featured in at least 82 newspapers in the US. But afterwards, the media went hard on Einstein:

On May 17, 1952, the LA Times headlined, 'Einstein flunks out as geometry teacher.' The editorial implied that although Johanna appreciated Einstein's response, she didn't understand the answer.

While the homework hysteria dragged out, a Los Angeles dentist called Leon Benkoff, who had a side interest in leisure math, weighed in. He explained that something was off about Einstein's answer: 'Well, I looked at the postcard sketch pictured in the newspaper, and Einstein wasn't right either. He answered a different problem; he described how to construct a tangent to a circle, but the problem was to compute the length of the tangent.'

A reporter's visit to Leon Benkoff's house landed him on the front page of the Mirror the next day. The headline read, 'Einstein fails in math but still has a Nobel Prize.' Leon Benkoff soon became famed in the city as 'the man who corrected Einstein.'

Explication

You should be aware of what you know and don't know, what you can do best, and what you can't do at all. Without this awareness, you'll jump into unfamiliar terrain and find yourself wanting. It happened to Albert Einstein; it happened to Dan Quayle.

Fortunately, you and I have their experiences to learn from, and as a matter of fact, they weren't ever going to repeat their mistake.

Dan Quayle would subsequently avoid discussions he wasn't prepared for. As for Albert Einstein, Helen Temple, the principal of the Westlake School for Girls, cautioned him after the geometry homework gaffe, 'Great scientists should be bothered with only great problems.'

Subsequently, when Einstein was asked what the speed of sound was, he responded, 'I do not carry such information in my mind since it is readily available in textbooks.'

Had he attempted to answer and flunked out, another brouhaha would've ensued, and the media would've been much unkinder to him than his previous gaffe. Thankfully, he seemed to have internalised the caution given to him by Helen Temple and has since been conscious of his limitations.

On November 9, 1952, Chaim Weizmann, the first president of Israel, died, and the search for his successor took centre stage. The Israeli government, led by Prime Minister David Ben-Gurion, decided to offer the position of Israeli president to 73-year-old Albert Einstein, who was then living in Princeton, New Jersey, USA.

On November 17, 1952, the Israeli Ambassador to the US, Abba Eban, wrote a letter to the renowned scientist:

> EMBASSY OF ISRAEL
> WASHINGTON, D.C.
>
> Dear Professor Einstein:
>
> The bearer of this letter is Mr David Goitein of Jerusalem who is now serving as Minister at our Embassy in Washington. He is

> bringing you the question which Prime Minister Ben Gurion asked me to convey to you, namely, whether you would accept the Presidency of Israel if it were offered to you by a vote of the Knesset. Acceptance would entail moving to Israel and taking its citizenship. The Prime Minister assures me that in such circumstances complete facility and freedom to pursue your great scientific work would be afforded by a government and people who are fully conscious of the supreme significance of your labors. Mr. Goitein will be able to give you any information that you may desire on the implications of the Prime Minister's question. Whatever your inclination or decision maybe, I should be deeply grateful for an opportunity to speak with you again within the next day or two at any place convenient for you. I understand the anxieties and doubts which you expressed to me this evening. On the other hand, whatever your answer, I am anxious for you to feel that the Prime Minister's question embodies the deepest respect which the Jewish people can repose in any of its sons. To this element of personal regard, we add the sentiment that Israel is a small State in its physical dimensions, but can rise to the level of greatness in the measure that it exemplifies the most elevated spiritual and intellectual traditions which the Jewish people have established through its best minds and hearts both in antiquity and modern times. Our first President, as you know, taught us to see our destiny in these great perspectives, as you yourself have often exhorted us to do. Therefore, whatever your response to this question, I hope you will think generously of those who have asked it, and will commend the high purposes and motives which prompted them to think of you at this solemn hour in our people's history.
>
> With cordial personal wishes,
>
> Abba Eban

Einstein replied:

> I feel deeply moved by the offer of our state Israel, though also sad and ashamed that it is impossible for me to accept this offer. Since all my life, I have been dealing with the world of objects. I have neither the natural ability nor the experience necessary to deal with human beings and to carry out official functions. For these reasons, I do not

feel able to fulfil the requirements of this great task, even where my advanced age does not limit my strength to an increasing extent.

This situation is indeed extremely sad for me because my relation to the Jewish people has become my strongest human attachment ever since I reached complete awareness of our precarious position among the nations.

After we have lost in recent days the man who, among adverse and tragic circumstances, bore on his shoulders for many years the whole burden of leadership of our striving for independence from without, I wish from all my heart that a man be found who by his life's work and his personality may dare to assume this difficult and responsible task.

Yours respectfully,
Professor Albert Einstein
Princeton, N.J.

Getting Around Your Limitation

Avoiding an opportunity because of your limitations is understandable. But under some circumstances, you must get around your limitations and take those opportunities. There are two things you can do: either reskill or outsource.

Reskill

In 2020, when the coronavirus was raging and companies were laying off, Humphrey, a 34-year-old office assistant, lost his job and fell into dire straits. He had a degree in biology, but he wanted to work as an accountant because he was passionate about working with numbers. However, due to his pressing need for a new job and the fact that studying accounting would take some time, I advised him to study bookkeeping, which would take a lesser period of time to complete, and after getting a bookkeeping job, he could proceed to study accounting.

In one of my coaching sessions with Humphrey, I informed him of a bookkeeping job opening. And though he didn't have the qualification, I asked him to apply for the job and use the waiting period to reskill. I then wrote his cover letter and CV, with which he sent the application; I also gave him some tutorial videos on bookkeeping to start reskilling.

For two months, he put in three sessions per day; the first two sessions were for learning, and the third session was for practising what he had learnt. Finally, Humphrey's much-awaited call for a job interview came in; by then, he could confidently tell me bookkeeping was a piece of cake. I couldn't be sure of his claim, but I could tell from his confidence that he had reskilled.

Two days before his job interview, I referred him to an accountant friend to assess his readiness for the job. My friend assessed him as I had requested and sent me assuring feedback on Humphrey's readiness. So, it didn't surprise me that Humphrey aced the interview and started working as a bookkeeper, later as an accounting student.

Outsource

In 2016, Ghanaians and Kenyans castigated the Ghanaian government for the error-ridden 59th Independence Day anniversary brochure distributed at the Independence Day ceremony in Accra. The blunder subjected the Presidency to derision, and it was embarrassing.

The acting director of the Information Services Department took responsibility for the gaffe and issued a misdated apology letter—March 10, 2016, instead of March 7, 2016. In the apology letter, he tacitly apportioned blame by explaining that he gave the draft of the brochure to 'someone' to proofread. However, the wrong date on the apology letter didn't augur well for him as a successive blunder, and he was fired!

Obviously, the acting director couldn't write well and wasn't attentive to details. This was his limitation, and he ought to have assigned the brochure preparation to a competent editor or communication specialist instead of giving the draft to 'someone' to proofread.

Mistakes of this sort stem from mediocrity and occur when people are given jobs they haven't trained for. The repercussions are a vicious cycle of blunders that can lead to disaster and embarrassment.

Find your Ideal Career

Experience with my first client

Henry was a level 400 undergraduate, studying a programme he didn't like. He was confused and unhappy, seeing an uncertain career path ahead of him. Most of his seniors who had graduated were struggling to find jobs, primarily because they studied a low demand academic programme, and they didn't know what to do. As a matter of fact, I had never seen or heard of any job opening seeking an applicant in his field of study. Apparently, his entire university education was academic, devoid of career development.

He needed a career advisor to talk to, and his mother referred him to me. As a career coach, I had a duty to help him chart a career path and see him become as accomplished as he could be. My first task was to assess him in order to determine his:

- Proclivity
- Aptitude
- Flair
- Fascination

After assessing him and making him retrospect his childhood interests, I observed a pattern. I made further inquiries from his childhood playmates and schoolmates and saw a consistency.

Henry loved selling and had contacts of diverse suppliers. Mention anything you want, and he'll readily offer to supply you. He was also good at persuasion and was very aware of this potential. Furthermore, he talked endlessly about the merchandise he had sold to his friends and teachers since junior high school. Hence, I noted commerce as his proclivity.

To determine his aptitude, I found that he was the go-to person for mobile phone and laptop problems. During my coaching sessions with him, I was amazed by his adeptness with keyboard tricks and shortcuts and how abreast he was with the trends in computing. Mention anything you want to do on the internet, and he'll recommend the right website or app to you.

He also did a minimal internet search. If he wanted any information on the internet, he typed the URL of the website directly in the address bar and pushed the enter key. He seemed to have a directory of URLs in his mind. I asked him how he had learnt all that, and he responded, 'I don't even know.' Indeed, he had never been schooled or mentored in computing. From my observation, I could tell that had an aptitude for computing.

My third task was to identify his flair. I asked him if he had any. He responded, 'Not that I know of.' I couldn't also deduce his flair immediately, so he suggested that I brush the flair aspect aside so that we could concentrate on his proclivity and aptitude. But I had to remind him of the economic realities we faced in Accra: 'one job isn't enough; a side hustle is a must, and a second side hustle isn't bad. That's the reason why, aside from being a career and life coach, I'm also a start-up consultant, a biography and memoir writer and an editorial consultant.'

Telling him about my skill set struck a chord with him, and he agreed I should proceed to identify his flair. I revisited the self-assessment I earlier did with him but found nothing I could pinpoint as his flair. I asked for his semester examination result; his grades were average. I then reflected on the conversations I've been having with him, and ahaa... I figured out that he was articulate in both verbal and written communication.

Being a professional editor, I couldn't remember seeing a *typo* or *grammo* in any of the long emails he had sent me. In addition, his writing was tight, assertive, and factual. There and then, I found his flair and suggested to him that he consider a career pathway in communication. His mother wasn't surprised and told me Henry's junior high school English teacher had earlier told her Henry could write so well.

It came down to what fascinated him the most, which wasn't job-related. He replied, 'Landscape.' 'When I see a landscape, I don't blink; I love it in its physicality or as a graphic image.' I then advised him to put a landscape wallpaper in his study and to go sightseeing during his vacation.

But what connection could his fascination have with his career development process?

As often as he sees the landscape wallpaper on his wall or when he goes sightseeing, the sight of a landscape can inspire him with an idea for a creative project.

James Cameron had been fascinated with shipwrecks since he was a child. While he was researching submersible systems for the production of the film *The Abyss*, he encountered Robert Ballard, a National Geographic explorer-in-residence and the crew leader that discovered the Titanic wreckage.

From that encounter, the idea of the Titanic story took shape in James Cameron's mind, and he proceeded to make the Titanic film. With a budget of $200 million, the Titanic was the most expensive film ever made at the time. It was also the first film to make more than a billion dollars, and when the 3D version came out, it became the first movie in history to make more than $2 billion.

Amazed by how a simple fascination could inspire a meritorious project, Henry made a phone call and ordered landscape wallpapers to be delivered to him.

At this juncture, he knew the career path on which he would most likely find fulfilment and fortune. They were commerce, computing, communication, and marketing. With a smile and a thumbs up, Henry and his mother concurred. But this was only the beginning of Henry's career development process, and he was happy to see a clear career path ahead of him.

Experience with my second client

As a fresh graduate, Nick had formed a project team for an e-commerce business. He had only managed to develop a website of some sort, but where to get funding was his challenge. I researched the startup capital of the thriving e-commerce companies, and considering the figures I came by, I wasn't sure Nick would get that amount of funding from an investor in Accra.

His three-member project team was novice, and he hadn't reached any milestone to attract an investor. But he had fire in his belly, which was inspired by the success stories of e-commerce behemoths in the US and China.

I admired Nick's enthusiasm, but I had to remind him that investors don't fund projects at the idea stage in our part of the world. They would first want to see any progress he had made on his own. This meant that he needed a standard e-commerce website up and running to show to a potential investor.

However, he couldn't afford it, so I advised him to upskill and develop his proficiency in the skill set required for launching and managing an e-commerce website. He had come to me for startup consultation, but career coaching was at play here!

The basic technical skills for launching an e-commerce website are coding (web and mobile app development), Google Analytics, graphic design, and digital marketing. It would take him some time to learn and master these skills, depending on his focus and speed, but once he learns them, he would be able to do the major task by himself and save cost and time. 'Is it possible for me to learn to do all that?' Nick asked me. 'Yes'! I responded. (More of this in chapter seven)

Now, where was he going to learn? He already had a degree in computer science, which hasn't been very practically helpful to him. However, there were free and affordable online courses he could buy or a boot camp he could attend. But he was too extroverted for the boredom of online studies. The boot camp would be okay for him, so he enrolled and trained in coding, Google Analytics, graphic design, and digital marketing.

It took Nick three years to upskill and reskill. By then, his old project team had dissolved, and at the boot camp, he built a network of professional developers. Two years after the boot camp, though Nick hadn't developed an e-commerce platform, he had become a hotshot developer and earned a substantial income from his skill set.

Experience with my third client

As a career/life coach, I've held sessions with graduates who were oblivious to their potential, and had it not been for the timely career advice I gave them, they would've ploughed into dead-end jobs. I've also coached professionals who were considering resigning from their workplace to work for different organisations, but after I assessed their situations, I found that changing their workplace wasn't the solution to their problem unless they changed their careers entirely.

My sessions with undergraduates were even more interesting. One of them was Derrick, a level 400 business administration student. He had performed tremendously well in levels 100 and 200, but he hadn't been doing well since level 300, and he risked missing out on scholarship opportunities if he didn't graduate with a good GPA. Well, he didn't care!

His godfather, a retired British headmaster who paid for his education, referred him to me. He asked me to help him get to the bottom of Derrick's non-performance and put him back on track.

I soon found out that Derrick's non-performance was a result of his religion. He had been introduced to a church by a group of soul winners, and his new pastor had made him believe that the second coming of Jesus was imminent and that everything else in the world was vanity. So, to prepare for the rapture, he had to master the Bible. He had been made to believe that Christ would appoint him among the saints to judge the rest of mankind and even angels, as stated in 1 Corinthians 6:1–3.

Derrick began intermittent fasting and prayer after internalising that belief, and he frequently attended classes hungry. The consequence was that there was nothing taught that sank in on the days he was fasting. And when he returned from lectures, he spent most of his time studying the Bible and other Christian literature rather than his course notes. He believed that was how to please God, and had it not been because he didn't want to upset his parents, he would've dropped out.

Nothing else mattered to him aside from the second coming of Jesus. Worse, the emergence of COVID-19 reinforced his belief that the coming of Jesus was more imminent than before. He owed a school fee—not because he wasn't given it but because he gave it out as an offertory to his church.

I had several coaching sessions with Derrick. I had to tackle his situation as a life coach before I could turn his purpose toward career development. He was the most challenging client I ever had because he had been indoctrinated and was well-read in the things his brainwashers had made him believe. I also realised that his non-performance wasn't because he was slow-witted, and had he applied the same studiousness to his coursework as he did to his religious work, he would've graduated with a first-class degree.

By March 2020, the COVID-19 panic had heightened, and President Nana Akuffo-Addo announced a lockdown and a temporary ban on all gatherings. Derrick's pastor urged him and the rest of his congregation to ignore the president's 'satanic ban' on churches, claiming that COVID-19 would perish in Jesus' blood. He even told them to disregard wearing face masks so as to prove that the blood of Jesus was their real protection.

Derrick called and sought out my advice on whether he should adhere to the president's ban or join his church for a clandestine fellowship. I knew he had already made up his mind that he would defy the president's ban. Nonetheless, I saw in his defiance an opportunity to open his eyes. I told him his pastor wouldn't allow his family to attend any of the clandestine meetings because he wanted to protect them from the coronavirus.

Just as I predicted, in all of the clandestine fellowships they held during the lockdown, no family member of the pastor showed up, not even his wife, who had always been by his side.

And even as the COVID-19 lockdown threatened people's livelihoods, it was during the clandestine fellowships that the pastor made the congregation pay offertory the most, while assuring them that God would return their kindness by protecting them and their families from COVID-19.

A month after the lockdown was eased, Derrick's pastor called and asked Derrick to help his son process his university admission form to study medicine in Europe. Immediately after the call, Derrick came to his senses and began wondering: if the second coming of Jesus was imminent, why would the person preaching it want his son to travel abroad for a world-class education? Again, if COVID-19 would succumb to the blood of Jesus, why didn't the person preaching it allow his family to attend the clandestine church fellowship? If it was an act of godliness to sacrifice his school fees for the church, why did the very person who fed him those ideas pay more expensive fees for his son to study in Europe?

Regarding COVID-19 in Ghana, Derrick saw the data published by the Ghana Health Service and realised that the prevalence of the disease was low. Moreover, most Ghanaians didn't catch the coronavirus, including his relatives and friends who don't even attend church. He also realised that he didn't contract the virus because he never came into close contact with anyone who had it and not because the offertory he paid to the church protected him. He was even shocked to see Archbishop Nicholas Duncan-Williams wearing double-face masks at President Rawlings' funeral—all the more so when the archbishop said he wore the double-face masks at the funeral out of common sense.

After giving it some thought, Derrick gave up his newfound faith and set some realistic goals for his life. He vowed to never again let himself be brainwashed and manipulated.

Know Your Worth

As a professional, your friends and associates will, from time to time, invite you to partake in some work they're doing. Other times, they'll ask for your expert advice on a project they're working on. As casual as these calls might be, their recurrence indicate that they recognise your expertise.

But it's only when they involve you in a paid project, give you a referral, or recommend you for a profitable deal that you can be sure they value your worth. In any case, until you recognise your own worth and put a price on your proficiency, you'll be a magnet for freeloaders, opportunists, and exploiters.

None of these adjectives describes Jamie Uys, but the point here is that people will be inclined to pay you less than you deserve if you don't know your worth, and you're to blame, not them.

Before Jamie Uys discovered N!xau Toma, N!xau knew only the indigenous culture of the Bushmen tribe in Namibia. He, however, shot to worldwide fame after he was cast as the lead actor in the 1980 film The Gods Must Be Crazy, which grossed $60 million. Yet, Jamie Uys paid him only $300.00.

When the film's fans criticised Jamie Uys for not relocating N!xau from the bush, he retorted that N!xau was born to act and that all Bushmen are natural actors. Jamie Uys's response indicates that he picked N!xau Toma on merit, having noticed his proficiency in acting, but because N!xau Toma didn't know his worth nor have a price on his proficiency, he paid him next to nothing—regardless of how much profit his contribution brought to the project.

This kind of inequity isn't about how things are done in filmmaking, but that's how things play out in life, and it would be meted out to you if you didn't know your worth or have a price on your proficiency. Meanwhile, you might be unmatched in skill, yet others of lesser proficiency but more confident, branded, and prominent will be the ones making the most profit in your industry.

If you find yourself in this situation, what you can do to turn things around is to show your capability at the next opportunity. It doesn't matter if you do it on social media or traditional media, but be sure to put something out there as often as possible for people to see how good you are at what you do. Be dramatic if necessary.

The more dramatic your performance, the higher your chances of being noticed and enthralling an audience. You will then be recognised and desired. This was how David transformed himself from shepherd to king.

Around 1020 BC, the army of Israel was camped on one side of a hill, whereas the Philistine army was on the opposite side. They had a simple term for a duel: if an Israelite kills Goliath, the Philistines will submit to Israel, and if Goliath kills an Israelite challenger, Israel will submit to the Philistines.

For forty days, Goliath came forth every morning in his armour and called for a duel with an Israelite challenger. But there wasn't an Israelite to accept his challenge. His formidable reputation as a champion swordsman was well known to the Israelites, and his gigantic stature scared all of them.

Now, David, a young shepherd, had been sent by his father with food to his three brothers on the battlefield. When he arrived at the Valley of Elah and was asking his brothers how they were faring, Goliath came forth with his usual rants.

David heard him and asked the soldiers, 'What will be done for the man who kills this Philistine and removes this disgrace from Israel?' They answered, 'The King will give him great wealth, exempt his family from taxes in Israel, and give him his daughter's hand in marriage.' When David heard their response, he moved to a different group of soldiers and inquired again about what would be done for the man who killed Goliath; he was given the same answer.

Having confirmed the prize for the duel, David accepted the challenge from Goliath, struck him in the forehead with a sling throw, and decapitated him.

Explication

The commonality between David and N!xau Toma was that both men were proficient in their expertise before the public witnessed their capabilities. For David, it was sling throwing; for N!xau Toma, it was acting. The difference between them, however, was that David knew his worth and had a price on his skill, so he wouldn't settle for less, whereas N!xau Toma knew nothing about his worth.

Most skilled but lowkey creative professionals I know would back down when they noticed branded personalities and mammoth corporations on the turf. This is because they associate brand with popularity and prominence with competence. The former might be true, but the latter isn't always the case.

When I started out as a newbie editor, I had a call from a lecturer who wanted me to edit his manuscript. But one of his colleagues told him not to allow me because I had only a first degree, and then referred him to a veteran academic editor with a PhD.

Fortunately, I heard of the attempt to stymie my bidding, and I immediately sent samples of my work to the lecturer, drawing his attention to the fact that the job to be done was a creative work, not an academic post; moreover, proficiency and ingenuity emanate from the brain, not from degrees. I also told him the only way he could judge who edits better was not to compare which of us had the highest educational attainment but to allow the veteran editor with a PhD and myself to work on a piece of his manuscript separately.

He agreed and emailed me a half-page of his manuscript. I edited, proofread, and emailed it back to him with my price. He responded promptly and intimated that my price was much higher than the veteran editor's quote. However, he emailed me the entire manuscript the next day and made full payment for me to edit his manuscript.

He has since been a loyal client of Zenith Editing and sends us all his writing assignments for editing and proofreading. Had I backed down when I heard there was a PhD holder on the turf, I would've lost a reputation and the cash that came with the opportunity. I'm glad I contested and won.

Before David killed Goliath and became prominent in Israel, he was a nonentity, yet his proficiency with sling throwing was ace, and his gallantry was legendary. He had taken down lions and bears that threatened him in the wilderness, and he had hit targets with slings without missing. His exploits, thus, were his worth, which he had up his sleeve.

While none of the experienced Israelite combatants had the nerve to stand up to Goliath, David perceived Goliath's call for a duel as the most opportune moment of his life to prove his mettle. Two kings and their armies were present to witness the duel. David was smaller, and Goliath was nine-and-a-half feet giant.

If David bests Goliath, he will enthral two nations. His victory would make the rounds and earn him a far-reaching reputation. However, his prize would be infinitesimal compared to the colossal gain his king would make from his win. In reverse, losing the duel meant that he would be dead. Therefore, it was only prudent that he knew what he was risking his life for.

In the end, he received the reward promised to the person who killed Goliath. He later acceded to the throne of Israel.

Understand: Whenever you're invited to join a project, even if it's at your bidding, it's because you're needed, not because they want to help you. You should factor in your proficiency, your input, the scarcity of your expertise, and your exposure to risk when negotiating your pay.

Do you remember the space shuttle that blasted in mid-air and killed everyone on board? What of the submarine that went missing underwater with its crew and was never found? How about the numerous mine collapses that trapped miners underground forever?

In filming Resident Evil: The Final Chapter, Hollywood stunt performer Olivia Jackson was hired as actress Milla Jovovich's body double. Unfortunately, what could've been a breakthrough for Olivia Jackson ended in a horrific accident on set that left her in a two-week coma with an amputated arm. Nonetheless, the film grossed over $300 million internationally and amounted to $1 billion for the entire Resident Evil franchise.

Michael Jackson's hair caught fire while filming a commercial for Pepsi, resulting in a severe burn to his scalp. In filming Titanic, several actors caught cold, flu, and kidney infection due to the prolonged hours they spent in cold water. Kate Winslet had her share of it and decided she wouldn't work with director James Cameron again unless there was much more money in it for her.

Secure your Pay

Promises are no longer held sacred in modern times as they were in the ancient era, so it can be a grave mistake if you don't convert a promise into a contract before you commit to someone's gainful interest. In June 1884, Thomas Edison hired Nikola Tesla and promised him a $50,000 reward if he improved upon his direct current (DC) generation plant.

A few months later, Tesla accomplished the task and reported to Edison, expecting his $50,000.00 pay. But according to Tesla, Edison reneged and said to him, 'When you become a fully-fledged American, you will appreciate an American joke.' Pained by Edison's duplicity, Tesla quit working with Edison and left without a penny from the gain he had made for him.

Fortunately, today, it's much easier to hold people to their word, lest they decide to renege after they've gotten what they wanted from you. A simple email from you restating their promise and seeking their authorisation to proceed with their request will convert a promise into a contract. If they reply to the email in the affirmative, the contract then becomes legally binding. Otherwise, you should take any promise with a pinch of salt.

Track Record is Golden

John Sculley joined Apple Inc. in 1983 without much knowledge of the tech industry. But he had already established his reputation as a marketing bigwig and had a track record of introducing the Pepsi Challenge initiative, which brought immense success to PepsiCo by out-earning its competitors.

So, when Apple Inc. needed an executive to overturn the dwindling fortunes of Apple I, Steve Jobs considered John Sculley for the job and asked him, 'Do you want to spend the rest of your life selling sugared water, or do you want a chance to change the world?' John Sculley couldn't resist Steve Jobs' appeal, and he left PepsiCo to join Apple Inc. as CEO on April 8, 1983.

In May 1987, Sculley was named Silicon Valley's highest-paid executive, with an annual salary of $10.2 million. Under his leadership, sales soared from $800 million to $8 billion, thereby justifying his high income.

So, it doesn't matter if you're new in an industry or whether you're low-key. If you'll ever be invited to take on a new challenge, it will be because you have a track record, especially with your most successful initiatives. So if you haven't yet taken any initiative in your work, do so now. Post them on your website, put them on your CV, and mention them at interviews. They're your keys to opportunities and are more important than your academic credentials.

During the Battle of Elah, though there was no officer or soldier among the army of Israel to stand up to Goliath, it still doesn't mean that David was given an easy pass to duel with Goliath. He wasn't a trained soldier, nor was he known for swordsmanship; hence, King Saul nearly denied him the duel.

He told David, 'You can't go out against this Philistine and fight him; you are only a young man, and he has been a warrior from his youth.' But David, having perceived the duel as a life-changing opportunity, didn't relent; he told the king about his daredevil exploits to convince him that he was more than qualified for the task. 'I keep my father's sheep in the wilderness. When a lion or bear came and carried off a sheep from the flock, I went after it, struck it, and rescued the sheep from its mouth. When it turned on me, I seized it by its hair, struck it, and killed it. I have killed both the lion and the bear.'

It was only after David had told his exploits to King Saul that he was allowed to duel with Goliath.

So, having a track record is crucial, and despite N!xau Toma's aptitude for acting, he didn't have one, which was more the reason why Jamie Uys didn't value him the first time. However, for the film's sequel, N!xau Toma had learnt of his worth, and with his meritorious performance in The Gods Must Be Crazy I (1980) as his track record, he insisted on being paid half a million dollars in advance before his appearance on set in The Gods Must Be Crazy II (1989).

Before N!xau Toma died, he relocated to his newly built brick house and owned a car.

Precaution

No matter how prepared you are to take a job, it's important to understand that there are different employers out there with different characters. Some of them are upright; others are crooked. The latter might seem nice from a distance, but get close enough to work with them, and you'll find that they're opportunistic and exploitative; give them your best, and they'll pay you the worst, no matter how much value you add.

One of the ways to recognise them is that they avoid negotiating your pay with you and commit you to working without a contract. Supposing you're a novice, I suggest that you look beyond the pay and set your mind on the learning opportunities on the job. You need that experience to prospect for future opportunities. But if there's nothing to learn there, it's better to quit before long than to stay and be used.

I once coached a client on a job hunt, and after his job interview, the CEO offered him a job without mentioning his pay. And after working for a month, the CEO still didn't give him an appointment letter or a salary. I've observed this pattern with exploitative employers, so I did a background check on the CEO and the position he had offered my client. And just as I had suspected, he was exploitative, and the position also had a high turnover. Besides, the role he had offered my client was menial. So, I advised him to resign and guided him to find another job.

If, however, you're an experienced professional, you must insist on a contract before you commence any work. Because being presented with a contract after you have worked can lead to a misunderstanding or litigation.

Case in point: On July 11, 2021, Nomcebo Zikode tweeted:

> I have not been paid a cent by the label for Jerusalema despite the song's global success. I have been ridiculed, with efforts to marginalise my contribution. The continued love and support from the fans of Jerusalema has been my strength and anchor in this difficult time.
>
> I, as a female artist, can't stay silent anymore; the matter is now with my lawyers.

Open Mic Productions, the record label, admitted that Nomcebo Zikode had not been paid for her part in the Jerusalema song, but said it was because of a contract dispute.

> The featured artist's agreement, which reflected an equal split between the two artists, was drafted last year, November (2020), for both parties to sign. Nomcebo Zikode through her legal team reviewed the contract and proposed for a higher percentage.

The statement revealed that neither of the artists had been paid because Zikode had yet to sign the featured artist agreement. *Jerusalema* was released in November 2019 and became a worldwide hit in 2020.

Rowback

Knowing your worth is one thing; knowing your prudence is quite another. A tactless overprice of your skill at an opportune time of demand may pay immediate dividends. However, a modestly priced but parallel competitor will eventually overtake you. That was the case for the telco OneTouch in the 2000s, until it was surpassed by Spacefon.

When mobile cellular technology first arrived in Ghana, OneTouch and Mobitel charged exorbitant prices for SIM cards, thereby prohibiting the average Ghanaian from subscription unless they could save for months and endure a frustrating queue to purchase a SIM card.

Then Spacefon came in with a customer-centric mass-market approach, touting a similar service with cheaper and easy-to-get SIM cards. They were also the first telco to introduce mass-market utilities, such as SMS, while OneTouch and Mobitel kept to their extortionate prices. Eventually, Spacefon overtook the two telcos, and their subscription grew by leaps and bounds. By 2020, 'Spacefon' had been declared a Significant Market Power (SMP) with a 75% market share.

Don't Overestimate your Worth

At my consultancy (**wa.link/mycareercoach**), I've lost count of the number of times our clients have requested that salary increase letters be written for them. Their reasons were often based on the idea that they had earned more education than what they brought to the job, so they expected their pay to go up automatically.

Interestingly, in most cases that I'm aware of, their employers didn't even acknowledge their requests. The former were peeved with their employers and became discontented with their jobs.

But the trouble didn't end there. My client, Miriam, who had two master's degrees, resigned from her work because she felt her credentials were not valued. So she started working at a different company, but she soon found that she was being outearned by some first-degree holders, whereas her immediate boss didn't even have a degree. She felt discontented again; insubordination set in and led to her dismissal.

The cause of Miriam's troubles came from her mind, stemming from her lifelong misconception that the higher an employee's academic qualification, the higher their worth and entitlement. However, except in some rare cases where it's a policy to automatically adjust employees' salaries according to their academic credentials, a pay raise doesn't happen automatically the way Miriam was thinking, and it isn't everywhere that positions are designated to the person with the highest academic qualification.

Because, for instance, the aim of a business is to make profit, and the most important thing a CEO values in an employee is something that augments the business's profitability. In other words, any academic qualification, even a PhD, that cannot be linked directly or indirectly to an enterprise's profitability will not be valued. This is also why a position may not be offered to the person with the highest academic credentials.

A CEO once told me that he considers a staff's integrity, energy, and competence before he assigns them a managerial role. He said his consideration for academic credentials comes last because he sees no sense in designating a strategic position to the most learned person if they come short of integrity, competence, and energy.

What is your worth? It's the value you bring. In one social enterprise I'm familiar with, the HR manager nagged and whined about being the second in hierarchy, yet he was outearned by a mid-level staff member.

Little did he know the mid-level staff was the bridge to the major donors supporting the enterprise's cause, and she could cut off their funding if she wanted to.

Apparently, she was the lifeblood of the enterprise and had negotiated a higher pay than what the HR manager was earning. Her connections, thus, were her bargaining power, and although she had no degree and her work performance wasn't extraordinary, she had a firm grip on her connections and had been instrumental in forging strategic partnerships for the enterprise.

She was, in essence, a low-key linchpin to the managing director and was needed by the board of directors more than they needed the HR manager. So, in response to the HR manager's annoying grumbling, the MD told him he could resign if he wanted to.

Floyd Mayweather has an unblemished track record in boxing. Having earned an estimated net worth of $1.2 billion over a 21-year career span, he was adjudged the all-time best boxer of the century with a 50–0 win.

In July 2020, he joined a social network, offering to deliver a personalised birthday greeting to anyone for $999.00 a pop. Would you, too, as a boxer, want to be paid that much for offering a personalised birthday greeting on a social network? Then you must be as popular as Floyd Mayweather is and be able to match up with his track record. Otherwise, you would be self-aggrandising and risk making yourself annoying. That was what became of Hollywood action star Jean-Claude Van Damme.

In his prime, Jean-Claude Van Damme was in high demand for a variety of action films, as well as promotions. Also, any project he participated in became a success, and self-aggrandisement set in. When Universal Studios offered him $12 million per film for a three-film deal, he felt the offer was demeaning, comparing it to the higher pay Jim Carrey (a comedy star) was earning. So, he demanded $20 million instead, but Universal Studios turned down his demand and blacklisted him.

If only Jean-Claude Van Damme had understood that more people would choose a comedy movie over an action movie, he wouldn't have found it necessary to compare himself to Jim Carrey and therefore wouldn't have overpriced himself.

Work for Pay, Not for Praise, Not for Pleasure

Nikola Tesla was a futurist and one of the foremost geniuses of his time. Also, as a contemporary of Albert Einstein, he believed himself to be unmatched in intellect—as he could easily pick up languages, memorise entire books, and store logarithmic tables in his mind. In addition, he had the knack for solving mathematical equations in his mind.

He went to the Polytechnic Institute of Graz in Austria to study electrical engineering, where he became known as a top student. However, he didn't finish his studies and dropped out in his third year, so he never got a degree.

After dropping out, he applied himself to his engineering mania and committed himself to inventions. Among his works were the inventions of alternating current (AC), the AC generator, the AC motor, and a method of transmitting power, radio waves, and neon light. His reputation soared, and his fame surpassed that of Thomas Edison, Henry Ford, and Guglielmo Marconi.

But unlike Einstein's esoteric findings, Tesla's AC technology, which produced the type of electricity we use today, had its use in everyday life and was the most valuable invention on the planet. As the inventor of such essential technology, Nikola Tesla stood a chance of becoming the wealthiest man in the world. But due to his lack of business acumen, despite his ingenuity, he died as a pauper, leaving behind bills he owed to several New York hotels he lived in.

Albert Einstein developed the general theory of relativity, which has since been one of the two pillars of modern physics. His life's work, though esoteric, was a contribution to knowledge. As a result, he couldn't have developed his projects into an enterprise or directly cashed in on them. So he sought his gains from the Nobel Prize.

When he and his first wife were negotiating their divorce, they agreed on a settlement. In 1919, Einstein promised Mileva Marić every interest on the money he expected from winning a Nobel Prize, while the principal was kept in trust for their two children. He won the 1922 Nobel Prize in Physics three years later. Winners of the Nobel Prize since 1901 receive an 18-karat gold medal and a cheque for nearly $1 million.

In Albert Einstein's lifetime, his surname became a byword for genius. As proud as he could've been, his children's future couldn't have depended on his accolades. As a result, it was prudent of him to seek to profit from his smarts by aiming for the most prestigious Nobel Prize, which also rewarded him with fortune.

Transgression of your Worth

If you begin by sacrificing yourself to those you love, you will end by hating those to whom you have sacrificed yourself.

– George Bernard Shaw.

Alfred, a 26-year-old MBA graduate, came to me with his two friends for business consultation. He seemed to be the foreperson of the team and had an infectious determination. Though his two friends were older and had technical training, they relied on Alfred's intellect and leadership. It was a Monday morning in November 2017, and we had a fruitful discussion on raising seed capital for their business.

Our next appointment was slated for January 15, 2018, but the two friends came without Alfred. When I inquired of his whereabouts, one of them responded (while smiling), 'Alfred has abandoned us and is now pursuing a wet opportunity.' 'A wet opportunity?' I inquired, intrigued.

But the two friends giggled in response. Unsure of what their giggling meant, I smiled back and welcomed them for the day's business. At the time, I had identified some investors who might be interested in their business idea and written a business plan to send to them. So, we reviewed the business plan and discussed strategies we could use to kickstart the first project.

In 2021, the two friends received seed funding from the investors and launched their business—still without Alfred. Alfred visited me around that time and said he needed a job. When I asked him where he had been, he told me his story:

In 2017, after visiting me with his friends, he met Audrey, a 42-year-old vixen, at a restaurant and struck up a friendship with her. Their friendship progressed quickly, as no day passed without one calling the other. As the end of the year was fast approaching, Alfred accepted Audrey's invitation to attend the December 31st watchnight.

They went to the watchnight service in Audrey's car and parked it a few metres away from the parking lot in the dark. At 12:00 am, the fireworks began, and the sky sparkled with beautiful patterns. Alfred, with his shirt tucked in, and Audrey, with her hair combed into a neat bun, left the euphoric congregation, walking arm in arm towards the car park and into Audrey's car. At 12:45 am, the two emerged from the car park towards the congregation. Audrey's hair was messy then, whereas Alfred's shirt was untucked; he also had his arm around her shoulder, while her arm was tightly around his waist.

By daybreak, the two were calling each other 'babe.' They talked about the fling in the car, and Audrey said it was like never before. They also spoke about her businesses; Audrey had inherited an eatery, grocery store, and boutique. In her submission, Alfred noticed that she was unlearned and inept, though ambitious. He could tell that Audrey's incompetence and mediocrity wouldn't take her far in her ambition. So he decided to help her find her feet.

Initially, Alfred's involvement with Audrey was merely advisory, but when he realised that Audrey struggled to execute the ideas he was giving her, he offered to work with her full time. And having observed how brilliant Alfred was and seeing his extensive connections and business contacts, Audrey gladly embraced him.

As the company's accountant and business advisor, Alfred was determined to give his best to Audrey. Yet he agreed to accept a pittance instead of an actual salary, regardless of the demanding nature of the work. His reason was that the businesses were struggling, and a professional accounting and business advisory fee would further weigh them down.

Meanwhile, Audrey paid herself a full salary with perks. She took GH¢10,000.00, whereas Alfred took only GH¢400.00. For this, Audrey wouldn't miss an opportunity to thank him for his generosity and praise his genius. On top of that, her coquettish mien and Alfred's youthful looks inflamed a libidinous urge for each other. Hence, their sexual escapades were unregretfully excessive!

After a year, Alfred upscaled their operations: he cut out dealers from the supply chain and dealt directly with manufacturers. He also restructured each of the businesses, rebranded them, paid off all debt, and then put them under one company.

For three years, he was still getting by on GH¢400.00, driving Audrey's car, and spending most of his time with her in her house. By 2021, the company was generating steady revenue, and its profit was going through the roof, as Alfred had projected.

Now, Alfred saw it necessary to upgrade to actual salary. So, he called Audrey over to his office and laid the figures to her while apprising her of the company's growth and the more profit to come.

Audrey, upon hearing this, was bubbling up and feeling hot. She took a step back, pushed the door shut and turned the lock. She then unclipped her hair and left it flowing. But while she was unbuckling her belt, Alfred held her off with a gesture and asked her to sit down. She complied and kept ogling him. Uninterested in her provocation, Alfred told her he'll be taking an actual salary henceforth. 'What about your monthly pay? Is it not a salary?' Audrey retorted. 'No, this wasn't what we discussed in the beginning. Chartered accountants and business advisors don't charge GH¢400.00 fee,' Alfred countered.

Audrey then snapped at him, arguing that he ate her food, lived in her house, and never paid a bill (while buckling her belt and putting back her hair clip). She told him point-blank, 'I don't owe you a dime. If you're smart, you should own a business.' She added, 'You've bonked me more than any man, and if I have to quantify the pleasure I've given you, it'll be worth a fortune, and you can never pay.' That night, they slept apart; the next morning, they drove to the office without speaking to each other. At midday, Audrey sent Alfred a text saying that she was expecting a visitor, so he should pack his belongings and leave her house.

Before the close of work, Alfred returned to Audrey's house and packed out. By then, he had snapped out of the infatuation, like a spell on him had been broken. He realised how he had been used by a lowbrow and regretted the wasted years he could've used for something worthwhile. More so for abandoning his two friends he had wanted to launch a business with. Alfred had then turned 30 and had no money in his savings. Pained and vindictive by how things turned out, he told me his story with Audrey.

Explication

The most brilliant student will outperform the rest in the degree and MBA classes as long as he's studious. In the real world, however, an unlearned person can play with your mind and outwit you completely. The reason is that nice-looking rogues abound on the street, and it doesn't even matter if they're beneath your status. As long as they can court your attention, they'll use whatever bait and enticement you can't resist to outwit you.

As you start your career, you must be on the lookout for commitments that can undermine your worth. Whatever kind of person you are, there's something that intrigues you to the core and can make you lower your guard. If that 'something' is identified by manipulators, they can use it to outwit you, regardless of how learned you are and how unlearned they might be. Infatuation is spellbinding; a free lunch could be a false economy. Being overly spiritual will make you less of a thinker and easier to manipulate, and being too religious will make you too gullible.

In December 2015, Alfred received GH¢30,000.00 as his share of his deceased father's pension. It wasn't a secret to his church as most of his friends were his churchmates. Somehow, a prophecy came during a church service, wherein his pastor called for any recent recipient of inherited pension cash. Alfred stepped forward and was prayed for.

The pastor (a prominent one) later told him in camera that he had seen in the spiritual realm that he (Alfred) was destined to become a millionaire the next year. And all he had to do to make the vision come to pass was to sow a seed offering of GH¢30,000.00 in faith and believe that he would soon become a millionaire. Alfred believed and complied.

The year 2015 ended, and fast forward to 2016, Alfred was still getting by on a part-time teaching job. By August 2017, he still wasn't a millionaire and was getting disillusioned. But his pastor came forward with another prophecy. The prophecy was that his millions wouldn't come from his part-time teaching job, but he'd meet his destiny woman by the end of the year, and she'd lavish him with fortune and pleasure. The new prophecy excited Alfred.

So, when Alfred met Audrey, he had a gut feeling he had met the woman of his destiny. He reported to his pastor about her, and the pastor confirmed that he had already seen them in the spiritual realm and that Audrey was the destiny woman he had prophesied about. The rest was what panned out as Alfred's buffoonery!

Understand: It is dangerous to live this life so naive about human nature. Where you expect fairness, you'll be disappointed. The onus is on you to see through people's actions and words in order to defend yourself against their duplicity.

Being streetwise is imperative; otherwise, you'll constantly be played by people. Don't wait till you're a victim before you learn about human nature, and never think that the unfairness that's meted out to unsuspecting people is far off and can't happen to you.

Learn from people's life stories and heed the warnings and cautions they offer, or else what befell them will befall you. Don't also gloss over inimical attitudes and unusual patterns in people's behaviour. When you notice them, ask questions and probe further. If they're being mischievous, their responses won't add up.

While Alfred worked with Audrey, there were instances where he made official expenses from his GH¢400.00 pittance and wanted a reimbursement from the company, but Audrey always refused. On one occasion, she was rude to him when he demanded reimbursement for paying for repair work at Audrey's office. This was a red flag from someone he was making sacrifices for.

It took Alfred too long to realise that Audrey's penny-pinching attitude towards him, vis-à-vis the benefit she was deriving from him, clearly indicated that he was being used and not valued. Her praises for him were all flatteries, and her debauchery with him was intended to keep him enchanted for as long as possible.

Looking back at the wasted four years working for Audrey, Alfred saw his friends, who launched the business without him, making strides in their career and personal lives while he had nothing to show for the 'wet opportunity' he went after. He seemed to be the kind of man of whom it was said, 'Give a weak man consistent sex, good food, cheap entertainment and he'll throw his ambition right out the window.'

Alfred had, thus, learnt the hard way the price people pay when they put other people's interests ahead of their own needs and the regret that often awaits people who sacrifice themselves for others who aren't making sacrifices for themselves.

Correction of Blunder

Whenever you go into business with a love interest, there's a tendency that your affection for them will get in the way. This calls to mind Robert

Greene's quote, 'Friendship and love blind every man to his interest.' This renders both business and intimacy iffy.

Various reasons account for this. For instance, where I grew up, transactional sex and relationships were common, and the opposite sex felt unduly entitled simply because they rolled in the hay with their partners. This made them want to squeeze out as much benefit as they could get from their relationships. It therefore made it inadvisable to go into business with an intimate partner who had that kind of upbringing. Audrey might have been brought up that way. Her cutting retort to Alfred, 'You've bonked me more than any man, and if I have to quantify the pleasure I've given you, it'll be worth a fortune, and you can never pay' was telling, whereas Alfred was blind to his interest.

Now, other than your spouse, you must avoid going into business with someone you're intimate with. But if you have to, then you must tread cautiously. Never treat the business less formally than it should! This way, there wouldn't be any room for one to take the other for granted. But even if one attempts to pull a fast one on the other and the relationship turns sour, the other would still have their business interest intact.

The key is to keep proper documentation on your agreements, legalities, activities, and decisions. It shouldn't matter how small or early the business is; put everything on paper and keep your copy as a curator keeps a relic.

Shakira and Antonio de la Rùa weren't only an item but also business partners. And when their relationship crumbled, their business partnership also tumbled. Antonio de la Rùa sued Shakira for $100 million—an amount he said Shakira owed him for abrogating their business partnership—but without a written contract to buttress his claim, the court dismissed his suit. Had Alfred learnt about this story and taken a cue from the former lovebirds, perhaps he would've tackled his work-romance with tact and avoided the buffoonery he put himself through.

In any case, whenever you're being roped into a deal in which there isn't enough wherewithal to compensate you, you can consider getting on board to sacrifice at the moment to gain in the future.

First, you must assess the future prospects of the deal and decide if it's worth taking a chance on. In 2005, when Facebook was just a startup, they wanted to paint the walls of their first office. Sean Parker, the founding president of Facebook, had been a fan of a graffiti artist called David Choe, whom he called to do the painting.

David Choe invoiced Facebook an amount of $60,000 to decorate the entire building. However, when the job was done and dusted, he walked away without a dime. Apparently, Sean Parker had persuaded him to trade his fee for Facebook stocks. At the time, Facebook was a startup with an uncertain future. But Choe took a chance on Parker's words, and after 10 years, his $60,000 stocks had accrued to $200 million.

Alfred had other options: for a short-term engagement, he should've offered Audrey a deferred payment arrangement. By deferred payment arrangement, Alfred should've calculated his service fee as a chartered accountant and a business advisor over the projected period he would work without pay, put it into a written agreement, and signed with Audrey in order to get paid in the end.

For a long-term business engagement, he should've valued Audrey's businesses, calculated his service fees over the period he would work without pay, and traded the value with Audrey for a stake in the company. Alfred should've done this with an expert before working with Audrey. This way, he would've secured his interest in the company, and their breakup wouldn't have affected his stake.

Last, living with Audrey, driving her car, and eating her food without considering his share of the bill was injudicious and played into Audrey's hands.

Cultivate Self-confidence

Christopher Columbus didn't belong to the aristocracy, but he wouldn't settle for the lowly calling of a commoner or be comfortable as a seaman. So he decided to chart his own path to nobility. He went to sea for the first time at the age of ten and learned sailing by doing. He wasn't a scholar at least not at the beginning of his career.

He first learnt Latin, Portuguese, and Castilian and proceeded to study astronomy, geography, and history, including the works of Claudius Ptolemy, Cardinal Pierre d'Ailly's *Imago Mundi*, *The Travels of Marco Polo*, *The Travels of Sir John Mandeville*, Pliny's *Natural History*, and Pope Pius II's *Historia Rerum Ubique Gestarum*.

He studied these books painstakingly on his own, as was later shown by the hundreds of marginal notations he made in his books. He had also taught himself about the trade winds, which helped him sail across the Atlantic Ocean.

Before then, he proposed to King John II of Portugal that he would sail the Atlantic Ocean in search of an alternative route to the Orient and return after a year. At the time, Europeans knew no direct route to the Orient; the route via Egypt and the Red Sea was closed to them by the Ottoman Empire, as were many land routes.

Per Columbus's proposal, he needed three sturdy ships, a conferment of the rank of Great Admiral of the Ocean, an appointment as the governor of any or all lands he would discover, and one-tenth of all revenue from those lands. His proposal was turned down because the distance he said he would travel, 2,400 miles, was too short. It was assumed that he didn't know the route he wanted to take.

In 1488, Columbus appealed to the Court of Portugal and was invited a second time by King John II, but his presentation was again unsuccessful. He then travelled to Genoa and Venice to seek sponsorship for his navigation, but he had no luck. He had also sent his brother, Bartholomew, to the Court of Henry VII of England to present the *Enterprise of the Indies* proposal to the King, but he was also turned down.

Columbus then travelled to Spain and sent his proposal to the Spanish Crown on the same terms he presented to King John II. The Spanish Crown rejected him twice on the advice of the savants of Spain that Columbus had underestimated his proposed distance to Asia, thereby rendering the *Enterprise of the Indies* implausible.

Finally, in January 1492, after years of lobbying and unsuccessful proposal presentations, Columbus saw the light at the end of the tunnel. At the time, King Ferdinand and Queen Isabella had conquered and taken control of Granada, the last Muslim stronghold on the Iberian Peninsula.

They received Columbus in the Alcázar castle of Córdoba to hear his presentation again, but on the advice of Isabella's confessor, she turned him down. Columbus left, discouraged by the rejections, but King Ferdinand intervened with Isabella on his behalf, and a guard was sent to fetch him.

In April 1492, the Spanish Crown presented the contract, *Capitulations of Santa Fe,* to Christopher Columbus, in which they promised him that if he succeeded in his proposed navigation, he would be bestowed with the rank of Admiral of the Ocean Sea and appointed Viceroy and Governor of all the lands he would claim for Spain. He would also be entitled to 10% of all the revenues from the new lands in perpetuity. In addition, he was given the option of buying one-eighth interest in any commercial venture with the new lands and would receive one-eighth of the profits.

Christopher Columbus led the Santa Maria, the Pinta, and the Nina out of the Spanish port of Palos to find a western sea route to China, India, and the mythical gold and spice islands of Asia.

Explication

As the global economy expands, so does the revenue of conglomerates. The kingpins of these conglomerates are billionaire tycoons and high-net-worth executives who contribute enormous taxes to the economies of their countries.

Names such as John D. Rockefeller, Bill Gates, and Elon Musk come to mind, each having earned the title 'richest man in the world.' Yet none of their endeavours can be singled out as what made the US a rich country.

In 15th century Spain, however, Christopher Columbus could've taken such credit. What was extraordinary about Christopher Columbus? In fact, he didn't have any of the opportunities the billionaires above had; the odds were against him:

- He was not educated: Columbus received no formal education; he learned how to operate a ship through apprenticeship and developed his navigational skills through self-study.
- No family influence: If Columbus had been born into an influential family, he wouldn't have been a ship's boy.
- No political connection: Columbus started out as a commoner without any political connection.

Contrary to what we all expected from our education, only a few people were fortunate to land high-income jobs. The rest have jobs they can only get by with, whereas others struggle to find jobs.

When I interacted with job seekers, those with first degrees said they would've landed jobs if they had master's degrees. Those with master's degrees said they would've landed jobs if they had travelled abroad, and those without degrees said if their parents had connections, they would've landed jobs long ago.

I never disagreed with any of them, but anytime graduates around me bemoaned their struggles with finding jobs, I brought up the story of Christopher Columbus and pointed out to them that Columbus didn't have the education they had. Often, they felt I was questioning their competence, but that wasn't the case.

Before Christopher Columbus became prominent, he wasn't a top-notch navigator. In fact, his navigational prowess was unknown and untested. What made him rise above his limitations was his impeccable self-confidence.

This single trait led him to places where commoners do not go. And in fact, though he was a commoner, he didn't carry himself as one. He had the mind of an elite, carried himself like an aristocrat, and was driven by a sense of purpose.

In modern terms, it can be said that while Christopher Columbus' peers were busily writing job application letters to seek jobs as employees, Columbus was busily writing proposals to kingdoms in order to secure international deals, though he was a commoner and unschooled.

And when one Crown rejected him, he went back to revise his presentation and appeal to them for another hearing, again and again. The most interesting part of Columbus' lobbying was that the idea he was trying to sell to the Crowns wasn't even perceptible to them, but his unyielding self-confidence and tenacity eventually struck a chord with King Ferdinand and won his favour.

Understand: We are observed by the way we carry ourselves. We either exude confidence or timidity. Timidity is a turnoff and doesn't impress anyone, not even the timid. People admire boldness and favour audacity.

If any man fully portrayed the aphorism, 'The foundation of life's achievement is a sound mind in a healthy body, driven by a sense of purpose,' that man was Christopher Columbus. He carried himself so well in his lobbying that no official in the Court of the Spanish Crown could tell that he was a commoner; otherwise, it was unlikely they would've received him properly.

Yet, it was only through his self-confidence that he eventually got what he wanted from the Spanish Crown. His success, therefore, makes it unacceptable for a more educated person to fail.

The best part of Columbus' story was that he didn't disappoint his sponsors. He led four voyages and 'discovered' the various islands in the Caribbean, the Gulf of Mexico, and the South and Central American mainland.

He died in 1506 without realising the scope of his achievements, which included discovering a new world whose resources over the century made Spain the wealthiest and most influential country on earth.

Remake yourself

Richard Montãnez grew up with his parents and ten siblings in a one-bedroom migrant labour camp apartment in Southern California before they later moved to a three-bedroom house. To him, poverty, hunger, and determination were his PhD.

After failing to learn to read and write in school, he dropped out and did a succession of low-paying jobs, including gardening, slaughtering fowl, and washing cars. At the car wash in 1976, his friend informed him that Frito-Lay was hiring. So he picked up a job application form and sent it to his future wife to help him complete it. He submitted the application the same day and was hired there and then.

Unlike any other janitor, Richard Montãnez learnt as much as he could about the company's products and even spent time at the warehouse observing how the machines churned out the snacks. After 10 years of janitorial work, one day, he asked a salesman if he could accompany him on his sales errands. The salesman agreed, and they visited a convenience store in a Latino neighbourhood.

While the salesman was restocking, Richard Montãnez observed that the *Fritos*, *Ruffles*, and *Lays* were all plain. He also noticed a shelf of Mexican spices next to the shelf of chips, and it immediately dawned on him that Frito-Lay had nothing hot and spicy.

A few weeks later, Richard Montãnez stopped at a vendor to buy *elote*: a Mexican street food made of corn sprinkled with chilli powder, lime juice, salt, *cotija*, and *crema fresca*. A light-bulb moment dawned on him while holding the cob, and he began wondering what the taste would be like if he dusted some chilli on *Cheetos*.

One day, during production, a machine malfunctioned in the assembly line, and a batch of Cheetos couldn't be dusted with the usual orange cheese powder. So, Richard Montãnez took some of the plain Cheetos home and dusted them with chilli powder and other secret spices. The taste was yummy! He gave some to his friends—it was finger-licking! Voila! Richard Montãnez has invented a recipe!

Before this invention, he had made a profound observation: the Cheetos were popular in California among Latino customers, and he had deduced that if the taste of the Cheetos could be modified to something Latino, it would soon be a staple food among them and the market would be explosive. That was exactly what he had done; he had modified the taste of the Cheetos with chilli.

Next, he called the CEO of PepsiCo, the holding company of Frito-Lay, and informed him that he had discovered a market for a novel snack. This was good news for the CEO. He responded to Richard Montãnez with delight and gave him two weeks to prepare for a presentation.

Now, the 26-year-old Montãnez only had a fourth-grade education and he couldn't write a business proposal, but he needed a book to prepare for his presentation. So he went with his wife to the library and found a book on marketing strategies, from which he copied an excerpt and studied with the help of his wife.

Two weeks later, Richard Montãnez was in the boardroom with Frito-Lay executives, doing his presentation. An executive interjected, 'How much market share do you think you can get?' Clueless about what market share meant, he opened his hands and responded, 'This market share.'

The boardroom went silent for a while. Suddenly, Roger Enrico stood up with a smile and said, 'Ladies and gentlemen, do you realise we have an opportunity to go after this much market share?' He said that, stretching out his hands too. He then turned to Montãnez and told him, 'Put that mop away; you're coming with us.'

After six months, Frito-Lay began testing Flamin Hot Cheetos in a small Latino market in Los Angeles. Some executives wanted the product to fail; they were well-paid to come up with such innovations and weren't happy that a breakthrough was coming from a janitor. Nonetheless, in 1992, Flamin Hot Cheetos was launched, and it became one of the most successful product launches in the company's history.

Over a 35-year career span, Richard Montãnez rose through the ranks and became the Vice President of Multicultural Sales for PepsiCo America. He was the only four-time recipient of PepsiCo's Chairman's Award: the highest honour bestowed on employees on the merits of their performance and work ethic. He also served on several corporate boards.

Subsequently, Richard Montãnez became a highly sought-after motivational speaker and gave speeches at prestigious corporations and universities, including Walmart and Harvard. He's also into philanthropy and has provided food and educational supplies to hundreds of needy families in the US.

Explication

There are two paths to career progression: schooling and problem-solving. Some corporate professionals pursue schooling primarily to qualify for higher opportunities within their company and also for professional development. Yet, it is not uncommon for them to return to the same type of work they were doing before, using the same methods.

As a career/life coach, I prefer the problem-solving path because it addresses real problems, has economic potential, and can bring about positive change.

The success story of Richard Montãnez illustrates this point. If Richard Montãnez had pursued schooling, he may have earned a degree, but there was no guarantee that he would have achieved success or accomplished his goals.

Let's visit his career trajectory: his education ended in fourth grade, he couldn't read or write, and was hired as a janitor at Frito-Lay. His turning point came at the age of 26, when he took the problem-solving path of career progression by formulating a recipe.

His recipe became successful, and he quickly rose through the ranks to become the Vice President of Multicultural Sales at PepsiCo America. He was also the only four-time recipient of PepsiCo's Chairman's Award and served on several corporate boards.

On the other hand, at age 26, Richard Montãnez could have taken the schooling path of career progression. Now let's consider what his experience might have been like as a 26-year-old fourth-grade school dropout who couldn't read or write, but was determined to turn his life around.

He would have been introduced to literacy and asked to repeat vowels and consonants. Doing such repetitions in a childish manner (as was likely for a beginner) could irritate a teacher, causing them to lose their cool and berate him.

He would also have to learn numeracy in math class, but he may not fully understand concepts like Pythagoras' theorem or the numeric value of pi (π). He would also have learnt to draw and label a cockroach, and may have struggled to understand concepts like the IUPAC name, and how the IUPAC name of sulphuric acid becomes tetraoxosulphate (VI) acid.

After high school, he would enrol in college and take a variety of courses, some of which he may have found frivolous or irrelevant to his career goals. So, if there was a more direct route for Richard Montãnez to progress, why would he have to go through a detour if there was a path he could take to solve an actual problem and earn a fortune?

Around the mid-1980s, Frito-Lay was going through hard time. Its CEO, Roger Enrico, had recorded a video encouraging every worker to act like an owner. Most of the employees ignored this, but Richard Montãnez did not.

As Frito-Lay's CEO, Roger Enrico, sat in his office thinking of how to solve his company's problems, news about Richard Montanez's college graduation might have only made him smile, considering that Richard Montãnez was a janitor. But this news wasn't what Roger Enrico was looking for.

Instead, Richard Montanez's call to him about his new recipe and the market he had found for it was the kind of news he wanted to hear. And once he found merit in Richard Montanez's presentation, he saw bountiful profit on the horizon and could no longer perceive him as a fourth-grade dropout and janitor, but as a genius and a linchpin.

Understand: You will experience a meteoric rise in your career if you succeed in pursuing the greater good of the masses rather than narrowly seeking a personal gain or what will benefit only a few. To achieve this, it's imperative to identify the most essential need of the moment and supply that need.

Desperate times call for desperate measures, and the more desperate a need is, the worthier its supply and the more fortunate the supplier will be.

In 1665, when the bubonic plague reared its ugly head in London, Isaac Newton, who already had an undergraduate degree from Trinity College, retreated to his family's farm at Woolsthorpe Manor, some 60 miles northwest of Cambridge.

Being distant and safe from the epicentre of the ravaging plague, he resumed work on a mathematical problem of determining universal equations involving fluctuating quantities.

By 1666, he had effectively solved the problem with a series of papers on the rules of fluxions, now known as calculus. He also turned his attention to optics to ascertain the notion that every colour on the spectrum was a blend of black and white light.

To conduct his experiment, he perforated a tiny hole in the shutter of his bedroom window, obstructed the incoming beams with a prism, and placed a second prism on the path of the rays refracted by the first prism. The resulting spectrum allowed Newton to measure the angle of each refracted colour.

In his conclusion, he debunked the idea that colours are modifications of white light and proved that white light comprises all colours of the spectrum.

Finally, Isaac Newton discovered, after thinking through inertia principles and how an apple or any object thrown into the air cannot go on indefinitely but will return to the earth, and inferred that the force that pulls down the apple must be the same that attracts the moon to the earth. He further deduced that the moon must also apply the same attractive force towards the earth, but to a lesser degree.

This led to the law of universal gravitation, which says that the forces of attraction are proportional to the product of their masses and inversely proportional to the square of the distance between them.

The deadly plague abated by the spring of 1667, and Newton returned to Cambridge to present the knowledge he had discovered during the quarantine. His scientific breakthrough, though esoteric, gave him a career boost, especially with the publication of his famed paper, the Principia, which states Newton's laws of motion, Newton's law of universal gravitation, and a derivation of Kepler's laws of planetary motion.

It took great effort for Sir Isaac Newton to come to his findings, and his contribution to knowledge is well appreciated. However, in an era of a ravaging epidemic, what would've been more appreciable by the masses was undoubtedly a public health intervention to contain the plague.

Had Newton's work brought such an intervention or contributed to the alleviation of the epidemic, he would've solved a pressing problem and made gains.

For instance, smallpox was a decimating endemic in Berkeley in 18th century England and was the leading cause of death. Like COVID-19, it was no respecter of person, and patients who recovered from it were often left disfigured. The only way to fight smallpox at the time was a primitive form of vaccination called variolation.

In variolation, a healthy person was inoculated with a matter taken from a smallpox patient with a mild condition. The practice was based on the theory that the inoculated person would suffer from a mild illness but would recover and be immune to future infections. Unfortunately, the condition of the inoculated person wasn't always mild. They sometimes progressed to critical conditions and died or infected other people.

But Edward Jenner made a profound observation. He noticed that the people who contracted cowpox recovered without treatment and did not contract smallpox, whether they were intentionally or accidentally exposed to it. He deduced that cowpox didn't only provide immunity against smallpox but could be transmitted from person to person as a deliberate protection mechanism against smallpox.

In May 1796, Edward Jenner took a matter from fresh cowpox lesions on the hand of a dairymaid and inoculated an eight-year-old boy called James Phipps, who had never had smallpox. Phipps became ill with cowpox for nine days and recovered on the 10th day. On July 1, Jenner inoculated Phipps again, but with smallpox matter. Phipps, however, didn't contract smallpox—an indication that he was completely immune.

Jenner concluded his experiment as a discovery of an efficacious vaccine against the ravaging smallpox endemic.

Parliament awarded him £10,000 in 1802 and £20,000 in 1806 for his scientific breakthrough. He also received worldwide recognition and several honours.

Fortunately, being attuned to the problem-solving path of career progression wouldn't hinder others from taking the schooling path, and you should be unapologetic about your choice. Again, for someone like Richard Montãnez, who became accomplished on the problem-solving path of career progression, nothing hinders him from taking the schooling path if he deems it necessary for his career progression.

So, whatever career progression path you find suitable, pursue it and make the most of it. But remember that problem solvers, particularly those who solve the most pressing problems, will be more valued in an enterprise than those who have only their academic credentials to show.

Intelligence is Gem

Never forget that intelligence rules the world, and ignorance carries the burden. Therefore, remove yourself as far as possible from ignorance and seek as far as possible to be intelligent. – Marcus Garvey.

Intelligence, unlike beauty, is the most gratifying human attribute that cannot be debased by philosophy. It is the precursor to success, the answer to every question, and the solution to every problem. Therefore, a lack of intelligence plunges a society into ignorance.

The significance of human intelligence cannot be overstated. When intelligence is displayed, it captivates the observer and elicits favour for the person displaying it. This is the reason for our unconscious bias towards intelligent people, and it is a natural human tendency.

In December 2016, a 24-year-old Oxford medical student stabbed her Cambridge-educated ex-boyfriend with a bread knife during a drug-fuelled quarrel. It was reported that she also pelted a glass, jam jar, and laptop at him. This offence would typically result in a prison sentence, but that did not happen.

Before that, in October 2013, a 23-year-old man punched a 34-year-old victim in the face at a party. Afterwards, he threatened him with a kitchen knife and left him with facial injuries. Although the assailant later wrote an apology letter to the court in an attempt to be shown mercy, he was given a 21-month jail sentence.

In July 2016, a 27-year-old man was given a six-year sentence for kicking a woman in the face and breaking her eye socket. The officers who handled the case stated that the assailant's conviction was an indication that their communities don't countenance domestic offences. Later, in January 2017, a man from Lowestoft was found guilty of stabbing his partner and was given a four-year and three-month prison sentence.

The Oxford medical student's assault on her ex-boyfriend could've been put in the same category as the aforementioned felonies. However, her case was placed in a category that describes great harm but lower culpability, though she had used a weapon and caused an injury. This allowed the judge to temper justice with mercy and spare her.

Explication

During the Oxford medical student's trial, the judge indicated that she wouldn't be jailed because of her extraordinary ability as a medical student aspiring to become a heart surgeon. The judge said:

> It seems to me that if this was a one-off, a complete one-off, to prevent this extraordinary able young woman from not following her long-held desire to enter the profession she wishes to would be a sentence which would be too severe.

In truth, the Oxford medical student was academically gifted and had been tipped to be a laureate in the future. At her college, her name had already appeared in articles published in medical journals, and she had topped her class in a preclinical test that all Oxford medical students take at the end of their third year.

In retrospect, whatever public outrage the judge spun with his clemency towards her, he wouldn't be the first or last overlord to show a soft spot for smart people. Hence, the aphorism, *Intelligence mellows the heart and enthrals the mind* is true in every respect.

Archimedes of Syracuse had a far-reaching reputation as the most ingenious mathematician of classical antiquity; some people eulogise him as the all-time best mathematician.

During the siege of Syracuse (213–212 BC), the Roman proconsul, Marcellus, having learned of Archimedes' scientific works and being in awe of his genius, ordered his soldiers not to harm him.

Ideally, Archimedes should've been Marcellus' prime target in the siege, knowing he was the hotshot behind Syracuse's defence technology. But for someone with such an outstanding brain, Marcellus revered him and asked his soldiers to spare him.

Understand: The ramifications of ignorance shouldn't be underestimated. On the other hand, intelligence is the solution to many of life's problems, and it should be actively sought out. This is why astute leaders prefer to work with learned people. But unfortunately, it turns out that not every learned person is intelligent. Therefore, whenever you have to assign people to strategic roles, you should look beyond their educational attainment and be attentive to their nature.

In 587 BC, King Nebuchadnezzar of Babylon breached the walls of Jerusalem after a long siege and laid waste to the city. He then took the captives along with the spoils of war to Babylon and chose among them the most handsome young men who were well-informed, quick to understand, well-rounded, and well-behaved.

At Babylon, the young men were enrolled in a three-year mentorship programme to familiarise them with the Babylonian system. When they completed their mentorship, they were presented to Nebuchadnezzar for vetting, and he found Daniel, Shadrach, Meshach, and Abednego to be 10 times shrewder than any of his priests and advisors. Subsequently, Nebuchadnezzar inducted the four as courtiers and later appointed Daniel as prime minister and the other three as governors.

The narrative above bears out the fact that the consideration of people's intelligence before they're assigned positions of importance is age-long. But if disregarded, mediocrity and ignorance will come to the fore.

I met Mathew, a 45-year-old entrepreneur who had been running his business for 20 years. When I visited his office and inspected his work, I noticed that his 20-year-old enterprise looked as though it had just started.

Matthew grumbled about his company's slow progress. He questioned why he prays fervently, pays his tithe promptly, attends church regularly, and works hard, yet his work hasn't seen any meaningful development for two decades. He even asked me if I thought his enterprise was being stymied by a hex.

Later that day, I had a meeting with his four managers and realised that their worldview was similar to his. His top manager had never used Google; the second manager didn't have an email address; the third manager had never heard of Donald Trump; and the fourth manager mispronounced malaria as 'naralia' and tattoo as 'cartoo.'

During our conversation, the top manager poked his pinkie in his nose to remove a snot, then popped it into his mouth and swallowed. When our eyes met, he winked at me and grinned.

What was missing in Mathew's enterprise was brainpower. In other words, crass ignorance was conspicuously present, and until he was ready to open up to a realistic worldview and employ smart executives to work with, he would lag behind a bit longer.

Cultivate Intelligence

There is more treasure in books than in all the pirate's loot on Treasure Island –Walt Disney.

Some people are born intelligent. They demonstrate an early aptitude for learning and comprehension, and they progress through their education as high performers, frequently emerging as the best students or among the best.

In the real world, however, intelligence transcends academic performance, and includes having foresight and hindsight, and being a good strategist. In urban life, you must be streetwise, and in your career, you must be well-read and extraordinarily capable at what you do. It's rare to come across one person with all these attributes, but you can cultivate them all.

Centuries ago, philosophers were reputed as knowledge repositories and were relied upon to mentor and impart wisdom to the younger ones. But only the affluent could afford it.

In 343 BCE, King Philip II of Macedon hired Aristotle of Stagira to mentor his 13-year-old son, Alexander. Aristotle taught him for seven years, until Philip died in 336 BCE and Alexander took over as King of Macedon.

Alexander's love for reading is known to have been influenced by Aristotle. He became highly learned and even carried books along on his military campaigns. He was also versed in planning and strategy, and his almost 13-year reign depicted him as the greatest military leader of antiquity, having expanded his empire rapidly to be the greatest at the time and winning every war he fought without ever losing a battle. Thus, his title 'The Great' was not an exaggeration, but rather a fitting description of his genius.

All the while, he corresponded with his former mentor, Aristotle, known at the time as 'The Man Who Knew Everything' or simply as 'The Philosopher.'

Today, we're in an information era where knowledge is more abundant than ever. And they're awash on the internet and well-treated in books. Personally, I follow TED Talks for inspiration and enlightenment, and when I meet smart people, I ask them about the books they've read.

The benefits of reading cannot be overemphasised. As a matter of fact, every great leader I've known or read about was an avid reader. Osagyefo Dr. Kwame Nkrumah loved reading, and his pre-independence Evening News was a way to inculcate the habit of reading in Ghanaians. His purpose for encouraging reading was best captured in the words of United States President, Richard Nixon: 'Reading not only enlarges and challenges the mind; it enlarges and exercises the brain. Today's youth who sit mesmerised by a television screen will not be tomorrow's leaders. TV watching is passive. Reading is active.'

But as much as you strive to gain knowledge and understanding, be mindful of some things that can slow your thinking. In fact, be wary of them. One such thing is superstition.

For instance, in a certain country that was hit by COVID-19, some religious believers turned to the smearing of cow dung and urine on their bodies, despite doctors' advice to the contrary. Was it working for them? No. Did they believe it was working? Yes. That's how superstition affects the brain and makes people think.

Rowback

A tactless show of knowledge in an attempt to impress is nerdy. In the nature of things, people find nerdiness annoying, and if it bruises a superior's ego, they will be unforgiving.

In July 2020, the World Health Organization announced that there was emerging evidence that the coronavirus can be spread by tiny particles suspended in the air. Patrick, a 24-year-old chemistry graduate, was a newly appointed staff member in a marketing agency and was at a meeting with his colleagues when his manager announced that the company would procure face shields for every staff member for GH¢ 40.00.

Everyone welcomed the announcement as the distress of the pandemic loomed, but Patrick retorted. He illustrated the movement of gases and pointed out how flawed the face shield is with all the spaces around it, stressing that it cannot protect wearers against the spread of the virus.

He pulled an authoritative article from an envelope and told the conference (while brandishing the article) that in Switzerland, infections were reported at a hotel in the Graubünden region where several employees and at least one guest tested positive for the virus. And it was found that those infected had been wearing only plastic face shields for protection, whereas those who had worn a face mask weren't infected.

Patrick attempted to pass the article to his manager while making his exposition, but his manager brushed it off and retorted, 'If face shields are ineffective, why are the politicians wearing them? Are you more intelligent than them?' 'The politicians wear face shields because no one has advised them the way I'm advising you now,' Patrick responded. 'I majored in chemistry and I understand how gases move,' he added.

The manager retorted again, 'You are a chemist; you shouldn't be working in a marketing agency.' But Patrick kept reiterating his point by reading the paper in his hand, 'The Swiss authorities hitherto have cautioned that the face shields could create a false sense of security, leading wearers to take unnecessary risk.'

Meanwhile, the rest of the staff sat quietly, turning their heads left and right to listen to each man.

The CEO heard of Patrick's scientific exposition, and it made sense to him. So he cancelled the procurement of the face shield and urged everyone to wear a face mask instead. But two months later, he relented to the manager's pestering. By then, the face shield was widely available, the panic had waned, and the price had been reduced to GH¢3.00.

Too late to procure the face shields for the staff, each of them reported to work wearing one, and the manager expressed his satisfaction that they were protecting themselves from COVID-19. He further announced that he was hiring a marketing graduate to assist the chemist at a marketing agency.

When Patrick heard this, he resigned immediately and did a reflection: his manager's purpose and intent in procuring the face shields was to profiteer, and he had only feigned a heartfelt concern about the staff's safety. And while Patrick's intention was to safeguard his colleagues by sharing what he had learnt with them, he committed a triple cardinal offence: he challenged his boss in front of the staff, made himself appear more intelligent than him, and foiled his plan to profiteer. Any of these would make a superior angry and vindictive.

Injudicious Workplace Romance

Around 1900 BC, Joseph, who was the son of Jacob and a descendant of the Jewish patriarch, Abraham, was sold by his brothers to a slave caravan that was heading towards Egypt. Upon their arrival in Egypt, Joseph was sold again, this time to Potiphar, who intended to use him as a household slave.

Joseph was soon the heartthrob and the most serviceable lad in Potiphar's villa. So, Potiphar put him in charge of everything and gave him unfettered access everywhere. Joseph's only problem was Potiphar's wife. Her libido bubbled whenever she saw him, and she would flirt with him at every opportunity. But Joseph turned a blind eye to her coquetry, making her feel unappreciated.

One day, when the other servants weren't attentive, Potiphar's wife called Joseph to her room, and upon his arrival, she came frolicking with him and wanted to melt in his arms.

Joseph felt the sexual tension, seeing her saucy and on fire. She then reached for his loincloth and drew him to her bed, but Joseph snapped out of her enchantment and pulled back from her bosom. Still holding on to his loincloth, he retreated and fled her presence, leaving his loincloth in her hands.

All alone and disappointed, her mood turned to bitterness, and using Joseph's loincloth as her evidence, she accused him of sexual harassment and had him arrested and incarcerated.

Explication

The narrative above is one of a few where a man avoided an injudicious workplace romance and still got into trouble for it. But by principle, other men have saved their skin by avoiding injudicious workplace romance, as opposed to those who got involved, relished it, and later regretted it. There are two ways to tell if a workplace romance is injudicious:

- You risk getting into trouble for it
- You risk losing an opportunity for it

Nevertheless, many men still get into injudicious workplace romances and bear the brunt. In 2019, a Nigerian soccer player who had signed a three-year contract with a Slovenian second-division club was sacked for impregnating the club's president's daughter—only six months after joining the club. I have also known several people who regretted getting into an injudicious workplace romance:

- Aron had his dream job as an auditor at his dream company, and he was well-paid. His boss fell for him, and they began having an affair. Three years later, his boss, Ann, heard that Aron had taken a female employee to the movie house during the weekend, and it was true. The following Monday, Ann fired the two of them. And it was a big blow for Aron, considering the high dollar income he earned in Accra.
- Daniel was getting too close to Angela, the prettiest lady, who had declined the CEO's advances. When the CEO noticed them, he became envious and invited Daniel to his office. The CEO told Daniel there and then, 'I'm giving you an option to choose between Angela and your job. I would choose my job if I were you.' Daniel kept hanging around with Angela, even tighter than before the CEO

had warned him. He was eventually fired and lost a scholarship opportunity he was due to receive from the company.

- A businessman I know hired Stephen as a weekend home tutor for his son and paid him more than double his salary as a regular teacher. But after three months, he fired Stephen! When I inquired about the cause, the businessman told me his wife mentioned Stephen's name during her orgasmic shiver.

When they thought back on the chances they missed, all three men wished they had kept their romantic adventures out of their jobs.

Be Wary of Honey Traps

The use of a romantic relationship to obtain information from someone for espionage, politics, business, personal, or investigative purposes is known as honey trapping. It involves an initial contact with someone who has certain information or can provide the resource needed by a group or an individual.

The trapper will then attempt to entice the individual into a false relationship in order to gain influence over them and obtain the information or resource from them.

The most ridiculous honey trap story involved a Chinese and a 20-year-old French diplomat who, in 1964, was posted to work as an accountant at the French Embassy in China. His name was Bernard Boursicot.

Bernard Boursicot met the 26-year-old performer, Shi Pei Pu, during a Christmas party at the French Embassy in Peking. Shortly after the party, the two started an affair.

Though Boursicot clearly saw that Shi Pei Pu was a man on the night they met, Shi Pei Pu told him he was a female opera singer but was forced to disguise himself as a man to please his father, who wanted to have a son. Shi Pei Pu therefore convinced Bernard Boursicot that he was a woman, and the two started a sexual relationship that lasted 20 years.

In 1965, Shi Pei Pu became pregnant and later presented Boursicot with a baby boy called Shi Du Du. However, Boursicot returned to France in 1979. From then on, the Chinese Cultural Revolution made it difficult for him to get in touch with Shi Pei Pu until a member of the Chinese secret service offered Boursicot the opportunity to see Shi Pei Pu again if he would leak classified government documents to her.

Boursicot feared that Shi's life would be in danger if he didn't comply. So, he leaked many classified documents belonging to the French government to Shi Pei Pu.

During this period, Boursicot arranged for Shi Pei Pu and their supposed son, Shi Du Du, to be brought to France and live with him as a family. However, on June 30, 1983, Boursicot was arrested by the French authorities. Shortly afterwards, they also arrested Shi Pei Pu, and the two were put on trial for spying for China.

While in custody, Shi Pei Pu confessed that he was a man and had hidden his genitals from Boursicot in order to trick him into thinking he was a woman. He also confessed that Shi Du Du, their supposed son, was bought from a doctor in China.

In the trial that ensued, the prosecution disclosed to Bouriscot that Shi Pei Pu was a man, not a woman. Boursicot didn't believe it until he was made to see Shi Pei Pu's naked body. This made Boursicot a laughing stock and a subject of widespread ridicule in France.

In 1986, after a two-day trial, the two were found guilty of spying against the French government and were handed a six-year prison sentence each. They were, however, pardoned the following year by the French President, François Mitterrand, for what he described as a very 'silly and unimportant case.'

After the pardon, Shi Pei Pu worked as an opera singer in Paris until he died in 2009. When Bernard Bouriscot was told about Shi Pei Pu's death, he responded, 'He did so many things against me that he had no pity for. I think it is stupid to play another game now and say I am sad. The plate is clean now. I am free.'

Honey trapping can also be used to get someone to behave oddly or make them do something unwise. This type of stratagem is intended to blackmail or defame a target. And you must be cautious if you hold a sensitive office, have enemies at your workplace, or you're the good guy who makes the bad guys feel bad or you prevent them from having their way. In that case, they would want to get rid of you and might resort to honey trapping.

In 2019, two university lecturers, one a professor and the other a doctor, were caught on camera frolicking with some ladies who had approached them as students seeking assistance with their assignments. And though it turned out that the ladies weren't even students of the university, but honey trappers, the lecturers were found culpable for their libidinous frolics towards them and were chastised by Ghanaians. This or worse was what the honey trappers and their sponsors wanted to achieve, and the lecturers, unfortunately, fell for it.

Honey trapping has been widely used to ridicule people, humiliate them, or cause their fall from grace. So you must keep it in the back of your mind. This will cause your intuition to warn you to be wary of strangers, especially the unexpected friend-turned-sweetheart.

Some years ago, I met a beautiful young lady who introduced herself as a writer and a wannabe author and said she wanted me to be her editor. It was at a time when I had received a classified report from a high-ranking official to edit and proofread, and my gut instinct told me this beautiful lady was after the document.

She suggested we meet to discuss her book, but the meeting turned into a date, and questions about my work took centre stage. For instance, she wanted to know whether I worked on my projects from a pen drive, desktop, or cloud storage, and which cloud storage I preferred. She even asked whether I kept my laptop in the office or commuted with it. And when I told her I commuted with it, she said she needed my help with a writing assignment, so I should come over to her house with my laptop and stay the night with her.

However, having a classified work in progress on my laptop and knowing about honey trapping, I flagged her as a honey trapper. Maybe she wasn't one, but I got a weird vibe from her and kept my distance.

Know the Flipside of your Career Interest

In 1878, a neurologist called George Miller Beard observed a confounding medical disorder near Moosehead Lake in Maine. He had come to the area after hearing about a strange new behaviour among the local French-Canadian lumberjacks.

Though neither contagious nor pestilent, the disorder afflicted only lumberjacks of French-Canadian descent in Maine. It's known to have affected men, was asymptomatic, and lasted a lifetime. This disorder became known as Jumping Frenchmen of Maine, and the afflicted were called Jumpers.

The condition manifested as an overreaction to unexpected stimuli, which included a jumper dashing himself into fire, pelting whatever they had in their hands, or striking someone without provocation. A jumper would also scream, flail, or jump out of their skin when startled. Other times, they would unintentionally repeat actions and words that were suddenly shouted at them, even if they didn't understand what was said.

George Miller Beard described an incident in which he spoke Latin to a jumper who didn't understand Latin:

> He repeated or echoed the sound of the word as it came to him in a quick sharp voice. At the same time, he jumped or struck or threw or

> raised his shoulders or made some other [aggressive] muscular motion. They could not help repeating the word or sound that came from the person that ordered them…

In another account, George Miller Beard narrates: 'One of the jumpers, while sitting in his chair with a knife in his hand, was told to throw it, and he quickly threw it, so that it stuck on a beam opposite. At the same time, he repeated the order to throw it.'

The English lumberjacks found it funny that the French-Canadian jumpers were sick, so they would often startle them as a way to have fun. In 1880, George Miller Beard recounted:

> Two jumpers standing near each other were told to strike, and they struck each other very forcibly…When the commands were uttered in a quick loud voice, the jumper repeated the order. When told to strike, he strikes, when told to throw it, he throws it whatever he has in his hands…They could not help repeating the word or sound that came from the person that ordered them any more than they could help striking, dropping, throwing, jumping, or starting. All of these phenomena were indeed but parts of the general condition known as jumping… It was not necessary that the sound should come from a human being: any sudden or unexpected noise, as the explosion of a gun or pistol, the falling of a window, or slamming of a door, provided it be unexpected and loud enough would cause these jumpers to exhibit some or one or all of these phenomena… It was dangerous to startle them in any way when they had an axe or knife in their hand. All of the jumpers agree that it tired them to be jumped and they dreaded it, but they were constantly annoyed by their companions.

It wasn't only the English lumberjacks who would startle the jumpers for the fun of it. In the Maine lumber camps, the French-Canadian lumberjacks who didn't have the disorder also startled their kindred jumpers for fun.
Another observer of Jumping Frenchmen of Maine, called Robert Pike, who also spent time in Maine lumber camps, wrote his observation:

> If a jumper was shaving or whistling, or just sitting on a riverbank, and someone came up behind him and suddenly cried, 'Jump into the river!' (or 'into the fire,' if there was a fire), he'd jump in. If someone stepped up behind him and tickled him lightly, he'd jump through the roof… strangely, the [targets] of such mean practical

> jokes never got mad about them. The men would wait until [a cook] was about to place a dish of soup or some other spilly food on the table and then say, 'Drop it!' and down it could come, right down the neck of the nearest man.

The Jumping Frenchmen of Maine disorder is one of the most mysterious medical events in recent history.

Explication

While growing up as boys and girls, each of us had a profound interest in a certain profession. However, most of us didn't consider our suitability for those professions until we went in and experienced recurring occupational turn-offs. It was then that we began to question whether we had made the right career choice.

I've seen a lawyer discouraging his children from lawyering. I've also known a military officer, a specialist doctor, a chartered accountant, and an engineer who discouraged their children from their careers. Interestingly, they were all accomplished, but strangely, they regretted their professions and wished they had taken different career paths.

What could've been their reasons? The education system I experienced didn't and still doesn't recognise a learner's aptitude and proclivity as crucial for their career development, except in academics. This puts many job seekers' consideration for careers that are congruent with their aptitudes out the window. Hence, they settle for jobs that are usually at variance with their aptitudes, but after some years in those jobs, they start to experience career alienation, which manifests as recurring occupational turn-offs.

What is more? We're not all cut out for every occupation, even if we're physically and intellectually capable. This is because the very essence of certain occupations might be at odds with our souls. Such occupations elicit an uneasy emotional response from us, and we can't help it. Had I been a career coach in 1878 and a client of French-Canadian ancestry came to me for advice on working as a lumberjack, I would've dissuaded him against it. Even if it was the only job he could have at the time, I would still discourage him. Why? Because the profession he was aspiring for was essentially dangerous to him, as he could become a jumper. Moreover, there wasn't any amount of pay that could compensate anyone for being a jumper.

When I was a child, the sight of a syringe and needle scared me, and I got chills whenever I saw a wound, blood, or terminally ill patients. However, after completing university, I had my first job as a biomedical scientist in a private hospital. My work was to take blood samples from patients and run a test on them. But while taking a patient's blood for the first time, I saw my hand shaking; the patient also saw it. Yet, I managed to take the blood.

Since then, I have observed my colleagues to see if their hands also shake when they are taking blood samples, and it turned out that I was the only one experiencing that. On a different occasion, while I was taking a patient's blood sample, my hand shook so badly that my whole body shivered. After that day, I began avoiding taking blood samples.

One afternoon, when I was alone in the lab, I reflected on my childhood through my teens. And I remembered that the anxiety I was experiencing on the job wasn't new; it had always been with me. It's my nature, and I hadn't paid heed to it before taking the job. I began to consider the things I was naturally good at in order to forge a new career path, and I listed problem-solving, writing, communication, coaching, and consulting. The next morning, I sent my resignation letter to my boss and never looked back.

Harriet had worked for 14 years in relationship management at a bank. At the age of 39, she was single, had an MBA, and was a senior manager. Money wasn't her problem. Yet she wasn't happy, so she came to me for career advice.

She broke down in tears as she spoke about how unhappy she was with her current job. I then switched the session from career coaching to life coaching. We spoke about her childhood and upbringing, and I found that she was unhappy because she was hankering for a family life and a detective job with the Ghana Police Service. However, she had no boyfriend to plan having a family with and also had no chance to become a detective with the Ghana Police Service because her age exceeded the recruitment age. Thus, having lost interest in her current occupation and missing out on romance, she was experiencing career alienation and boredom, which manifested as a recurring turn-off at work.

Having identified the cause of her unhappiness, I told her it was about time she consciously looked for a partner and switched from her banking profession to a field where investigation was the core competency. I also suggested to her that she consider writing detective stories. This would make up for her lifelong aspiration to be a detective and earn her a fortune if she's able to author a bestseller. But she said she wasn't sure how to go about writing a book, though she'd been thinking up a crime story since her teens.

She also doubted she could write well because she didn't have an English major; more so, she didn't remember scoring an A or B in any English exam she took. I smiled at her misconception and told her she didn't need an English major or a grade of A or B in English to be an author. I then advised her to take to reading detective stories in order to be fired up for detective authorship. She agreed and left cheerfully.

Cynthia and Agartha have been lifelong friends. Cynthia's husband was a successful businessman; Agartha's son had completed national service and was looking for a job. When Agartha heard that Cynthia's husband had a vacancy for a personal assistant, she called Cynthia and implored her to secure the job for her son.

Cynthia's response was, 'My dear Agartha, you know I adore you and won't see your son do what I won't see my own son do. If your son comes to work with my husband, I can guarantee that he'll buy his first car in three months, but my husband cheats friends and foes, sleeps with anything in a skirt, and disrespects women. Any angel that ever did the job you're asking for your son became the devil my husband is, and I will never allow my son to work with him.'

Cynthia had weighed her values against a lucrative job offer in front of Agatha. She chose her values, expecting that her friend would do the same.

A lawyer-friend on LinkedIn told me he discouraged his son from becoming a lawyer because there was a worrying record of depression and suicide among lawyers in his country and that lawyers were 3.6 times more likely to suffer from depression than non-lawyers. Unlike his daughter, whom he had seen through law school, he said his son was too soft-minded and insecure, and he feared that the demands of lawyering would take a toll on his mental health.

This father was determined to make lawyering a family occupation, but he had to painfully spare his son the trouble of putting him through a profession that was incongruent with his temperament. Conversely, Robert Darwin, a wealthy and accomplished medical doctor, wanted to make his son, Charles Darwin, a medical doctor without regard for Charles's aptitude or proclivity.

In 1825, he sent him to Edinburgh University to study medicine, but for the fear of blood, Charles Darwin dropped out in his second year and enrolled at Christ College in Cambridge to study botany.

In his ensuing career, Charles Darwin became the most acclaimed naturalist and one of the most influential figures in modern history. On the other hand, if he had completed medical school and become a doctor, his soul would've still been longing for a naturalist occupation. Second, his fear of blood would have made him feel uncomfortable, which would have caused him to avoid doing some medical procedures.

As a result of these two factors, he couldn't have been fulfilled as a medical doctor; at the same time, he would've missed the opportunity to be a naturalist. His name, therefore, would've sunk into oblivion.

Learn Everything There Is to Know About Your Field: Occupational Disease

In 1998, Gillian Genser set out to sculpt Adam, the first man, and it took her more than 15 years to complete it. Before then, she made a statue of Lilith, the first woman, using only eggshells.

Genser was reputed for using natural materials for her projects, and she had used pulverised blue mussel shells to make the muscle fibres of her Adam sculpture. But before she could complete the entire sculpture, she fell sick, and her health began deteriorating.

It started as headaches and nausea, and despite her numerous doctor's appointments, the exact cause of her debilitating health couldn't be explained. Her symptoms progressed to brain fog, muscle aches, memory loss, helplessness, anxiety, and a loss of appetite. She lost 76 pounds, and her condition aggravated to the point that she lost her left hearing and couldn't recognise people she had known most of her life.

At last, she met a curator of invertebrates on her visit to the Royal Ontario Museum, who informed her that environmental toxins could collect in shells and bones. Subsequent medical tests in 2015 revealed that her condition resulted from heavy metal poisoning. Doctors found that Gillian Genser's body had built up a lot of lead, arsenic, and methyl mercury.

Before the initial investigation into her deteriorating health, the doctors repeatedly asked her if she was handling any toxins, but she always answered, 'No', and even added that she used only natural materials for her work—referring to the pulverised blue mussel shells.

Gillian Genser's condition, however, continued to deteriorate, and she had no hope of recovery. One of her last wishes was to complete her Adam's sculpture, which she named My Beautiful Death. In an interview, she said:

> I keep thinking about him because when I made him, he was made to be a re-expression of what should have been the human-first perception of the ecosystem of the world. It originally began with that terrible statement that man had dominion over all the animals, and I wanted to restate that and say that approach took us to a very bad place. It is very ironic that, of course, this piece, that was representing that first Adam, was so toxic and that he poisoned me.

Understand: Proficiency alone isn't enough to be accomplished in your career. To attain mastery, you must be versed in every facet of your work, including the details of your work materials, the history of your profession, the backgrounds of the pioneers, and who the present and past luminaries are; you must even know about their failures and successes. You must also know your profession's occupational hazards and occupational diseases in order to offset them.

It's uncommon to come across professionals who are well-versed in every facet of their work because most people stop learning when they complete school or training. But if you continue to study and learn while on the job, you'll be amazed by the things you'll know and what you can do. Because continuous learning will reinforce your brainpower and stimulate your creativity and problem-solving skills. This will let you catch up with the industry's old hands and even surpass them.

I have no doubt that Gillian Genser is an accomplished artist. Yet, for many years, she had a misconception about the composition of natural materials. Two reasons account for this misconception: first, we've internalised several widespread beliefs without verifying their factuality.

One of these beliefs is that natural materials are absolutely safe. Like most of us, Gillian Genser also internalised this misconception, whereas most people would argue blindly to defend their misconceptions until they encountered circumstances that challenged the false knowledge they had internalised. Secondly, most of us working in 'relatively safe' environments never really cared about the occupational health and safety concerns related to our work until someone prompted us or something went wrong.

Gillian Genser most likely didn't consider the potential health and safety concerns related to her work, and it was unlikely that anyone prompted her. However, if she had been more conscious of her occupational health and safety and researched the occupational disease of artists, she would've learnt that historical art luminaries, including Michelangelo, Goya, and Vincent Van Gogh, suffered from a common condition referred to, at the time, as 'painter's colic' or 'painter's madness.'

Later to be termed *Saturnism*, this condition was promulgated by an Italian doctor in 1713, when it struck him that every artist he knew had experienced painter's colic. He deduced that the disease was due to the artists' continuous exposure to the lead-pigmented paint they worked with.

On the contrary, Gillian Genser didn't use lead-pigmented paint; she used only natural materials. So, why would she be concerned about the painter's colic? If she knew that an occupational disease had afflicted artists in the past, it wouldn't matter whether she used natural materials or lead-pigmented paints. She would've been suspicious of her symptoms and possibly taken early measures.

The issue here is not to fault Gillian Genser; I would've made the same mistake because I also believed all natural products were pure and safe. However, we need to learn a lesson from her story.

Gillian Genser's doctors discovered, after several rounds of perplexing prognosis, that the pulverized blue mussel shells she used in sculpting Adam weren't entirely pure and safe as she had thought, but contained high levels of lead, arsenic, and methyl mercury.

How did these toxins get into the blue mussel shells? Ideally, blue mussels are natural and pure. However, as they explore their surroundings in search of food, their shells, which act as filter feeders, collect and accumulate environmental toxins.

Due to this characteristic, they're often used to determine the toxicity level of water. To do this, uncontaminated mussels are sourced from aquaculture farms and placed in the water whose toxicity is to be determined. After two or three months, the mussels are collected and examined for contamination in order to assess the toxicity level of the water.

Gillian Genser could have avoided her crisis if she had investigated the chemistry of the natural materials she had assumed were so safe. She would've found out from her research that shellfish can accumulate a high concentration of marine biotoxins, thereby rendering them unsafe to be eaten and even hazardous if their pulverised shells are inhaled.

This information would've prompted her to do further research on the blue mussels, and she probably would've discovered that her work materials weren't as safe as she had thought—however natural they were.

Supplementary Note

Science is soft-spoken and perhaps more reserved than it should be. Widespread beliefs are loud and perhaps more pervasive than they should be. The effect is that people are apt to assimilate whatever comes from widespread beliefs without verifying them with science. The end result can be catastrophic.

When I was a boy, my understanding of HIV was limited to widespread belief until I studied science. I then realised that information on HIV was one thing in the public domain and another in the science journals. And each one served a purpose: the widespread belief was hyped, ostensibly to stop the spread of the virus but ultimately to promote and profit from the condom business. Conversely, the information in the science journals was factual and intended to curb the spread of the virus and find a cure.

The main difference between widespread beliefs and science is that widespread beliefs are unproven, while science is proven and can be trusted.

In essence, beliefs, however widespread they are, are unfounded and can be misleading. In contrast, science is founded on principles, rationality, and common sense. Hence, the more heedless people are to science, the more gullible and irrational they will be.

Case in Point 1: Scheele's Green

In 1775, Carl Wilhelm Scheele, a Swedish chemist, invented the ravishing shade of green that became known as Scheele's green. And although he knew his invention contained a bit of poisonous arsenic, he withheld that information from the public and went ahead to market the product. Word spread, and the product became a public sensation.

The colouring was cheap and easy to produce, so it quickly replaced older green pigments and was used to manufacture various products, including children's toys and home furnishings.

Unfortunately, the poisonous arsenic constituent in the wallpaper flaked off and pulverised over time, making it easy to be inhaled. Consequently, many infants and young children got lung disease and died from breathing in the pulverised flakes. You might wonder if Scheele's green was widely believed to be safe. Yes. Was it verified with science? No.

Case in Point 2: Covid-Organics

In April 2020, Madagascar's President, Andry Rajoelina, launched the Covid-Organics tonic and touted it as an efficacious remedy for coronavirus. President Rajoelina stated in his announcement, 'I'm convinced that history will prove us, but today, there are already two cases that have been cured with the Covid-Organics, but we'll actually see what happens next.'

A wave of hysteria swept across Africa following the launch of Covid-Organics in Madagascar. For once, Africa had come out on top in the race to find a cure for a ravaging pandemic, while world powers were baffled. However, following Andry Rajoelina's claim, the World Health Organization (WHO) issued a statement, advising people against untested remedies for COVID-19:

> Africans deserved to use medicines tested to the same standards as people in the rest of the world. Even if therapies are derived from traditional practice and natural products, establishing their efficacy and safety through rigorous clinical trials is critical.

The US Centre for Disease Control (CDC) also weighed in: 'There is no scientific evidence that any of these alternative remedies can prevent or cure the illness caused by COVID-19. Some of them may not be safe to consume.'

The WHO and CDC's press releases elicited mixed feelings towards the Covid-organics, but to dispel doubt and brush aside the scientific concerns, President Rajoelina swigged the tonic in a few gulps during the launch event and said it was safe to be given to children. Though devoid of scientific proof, President Rajoelina's assurance elicited widespread interest in the tonic, and emissaries from several African countries flocked to Madagascar to fetch some and bring them back to their home countries.

But fast forward to July 2020, two Madagascan lawmakers succumbed to the deadly virus, whereas over 20 others fell sick with COVID-19. By late July 2020, Madagascan hospitals were overwhelmed with a spike in COVID-19 cases and additional deaths. President Andry Rajoelina then re-imposed a second lockdown.

Case in Point 3: Blessed Water

In Sri Lanka, a popular shaman called Eliyantha White touted a potion he claimed to have conceived in a dream. According to him, the potion could cure COVID-19, and that, he could end COVID-19 in Sri Lanka and India by pouring the potion, which he called blessed water, into rivers.

Eliyantha White had already risen to prominence after treating several politicians and cricket stars for their maladies and injuries. For instance, he's known to have treated Sri Lanka's Prime Minister Mahindra Rajapaksa, whereas in 2010, cricket legend Sachin Tendulkar publicly thanked him for healing his knee injury.

Hence, going public with his potion was given resonance by the media. Word spread, and despite having not passed scientific approval, Sri Lanka's Health Minister, Pavithra Wanniarachchi, endorsed and promoted the potion. After two months, Pavithra Wanniarachchi caught COVID-19 and was admitted to the Intensive Care Unit. Later in September 2021, Eliyantha White also caught COVID-19 and was sent to the hospital, where he succumbed.

Lesson: Widespread beliefs are often unverified, yet they could be propagated as facts by people who should know better. This is common in societies that are inclined toward beliefs more than knowledge and where even a highly educated person and the unschooled think alike.

But however misleading a false knowledge might be—for instance, the claim that the sun rises in the east and sets in the west—other false knowledge, such as the claim that consumable natural products have no side effects can be dangerous. Because, even, excessive water consumption can eventually kill.

Therefore, before you assimilate any information, verify that it's factual and sensible. Otherwise, you risk internalising false knowledge and falling victim to it like Gillian Genser and Bruce Lee. The latter's sudden death, 50 years ago, is said to have been caused by brain swelling.

You must have heard the claim that adults should drink at least eight glasses of water every day. This notion is widely believed, but where did it emerge from? In 1945, the Food and Nutrition Board in the United States published a recommendation:

> A suitable allowance of water for adults is 2.5 litres daily in most instances. An ordinary standard for diverse persons is one millilitre for each calorie of food. Most of this quantity is contained in prepared foods.

Unfortunately, people misread the publication by paying attention to the first sentence and ignoring the last two. This spawned the myth that adults should drink at least eight glasses of water per day, as though a fact, thereby rendering it common knowledge, albeit a false one.
Bruce Lee, like many people, must have believed and internalised this false knowledge, thereby stimulating his liking and craving for water. No wonder he said:

- **Be like water, making its way through the cracks**. Do not be assertive, but adjust to the object, and you shall find a way around or through it.
- **Empty your mind, be formless, shapeless, like water.** If you put water into a cup, it becomes the cup; you put water into a bottle and it becomes the bottle. You put it in a teapot, it becomes the teapot. Now, water can flow or it can crash. **Be water, my friend**.

As a result, he drank more water than his body needed. At first, brain swelling was found to be the cause of his death, but in 2022, researchers found that his habit of drinking too much water was the underlying cause.

When there's an excessive intake of water over a long period, the excess water will lower the level of sodium in the blood and prevent the body from excreting water efficiently and fast enough. This condition is called hyponatraemia, or water intoxication, and can be fatal.

Also, people who drink at least eight glasses of water per day haven't considered that water isn't the only source of hydration. They also haven't thought about the fact that the type of food we usually eat (i.e., solid, liquid, or semi-solid), the weather, and a person's level of physical activity determine how much water is already in the body and the quantity of water to drink in order to add up.

So what's the point? Drink water to slake your thirst. Drink more water if you aren't drinking enough of it. But don't force yourself to drink water because you've set a goal of consuming at least eight glasses per day. Finally, there's no scientific proof that increasing water consumption has multiple health benefits, and you wouldn't have to believe otherwise just because the masses believe it.

Learn Thoroughly

It is easy to watch someone dive into a pool and observe them swimming from one end to another and think you can do it as well. However, every magnificent performance requires a great deal of practice and preparation, during which all mistakes and corrections are made. The end result is the marvel you thought you could easily accomplish.

In short, there's more to what meets the eye; no matter how intensely you look at a performance, you won't see its intricacies. To perform any task professionally, you must first throw yourself into the practice terrain and be exposed to the actual work's dangers, mistakes, and intricacies. You can never learn everything by observing from a distance, and you'll never be well-grounded if you skip the practice terrain.

People who have dared to perform without enough practice and preparation get hurt or embarrassed. For instance, American rapper Coolio stage-dived at an event without understanding the intricacies of stage diving and learnt a lesson.

Having observed stage dives from a distance, he didn't know that there was more to seeing performers toss themselves offstage and get caught in the air by their ecstatic audience. So, in 2009, while he was performing at Staffordshire University, rapper Coolio threw himself off the stage, hoping he would be caught in the air, but the crowd flinched back, leaving him crushing on the ground. They then pounced on him and beat him up for no reason until the bouncers arrived and saved him. It was then noticed that the mob had stolen his shoe, watch, chain, and glasses while they were beating him.

If Coolio had done some research on the obverse and reverse of stage dives before his debacle, he would've discovered that not all stage dives end in a frenzy, as is frequently depicted on television. On several occasions, stage dives have ended in tears.

Case in point: Sid Wilson was known for his dangerous stage dives, but in 2008, he jumped off the stage at the Mayhem Festival and broke both heels. He had to use a wheelchair after that.

In August 2010, during a performance at the Pukkelpop Festival in Belgium, Charles Haddon, the 22-year-old lead singer of the Camden band *Ou Est Le Swimming Pool*, unexpectedly dove into the crowd when the band was about to walk offstage. As the crowd wasn't ready for his abrupt dive, they flinched, except for a girl who Haddon flattened.

A few hours later, Haddon climbed a 60-foot satellite mast and leapt to his death. Haddon's death was reported to be suicide because he was distressed and ashamed for having seriously injured the girl he flattened.

In May 2014, during a performance of the metalcore band *Miss May I*, a fan got on the stage and dove, but he fell heavily because the crowd didn't catch him. Although he could walk after falling, the concert was cut short after he fainted. He later died in a hospital.

Fred Durst climbed the massive Hammerstein Ballroom stage during the peak of the *Limp Bizkit* rock band. Upon reaching the top, his face flushed with fear of the height, but he leapt anyway and was safely caught by his fans. Coming to his senses after his near-death leap, he said regretfully, 'I could have hit the ground; I would have died for sure.'

Cheryl Cole, however, knew what was at stake with stage dives, so she heeded caution. In 2012, while she was performing Call My Name, the 28-year-old singer dived from her stage and was caught in the air by her dancers on the floor—just as they had rehearsed, and it was a spectacular stunt at the start of her performance.

Know Who You're Dealing With

Background checks wouldn't be necessary if all men and women were blameless. But the world has too many people who have done too many odd things. Yet, no one walks with their deeds written on their forehead, whether good or bad. So the only way to find out what someone is capable of is to look into their past.

Beware of Megalomaniacs

Imagine that you're the boss, and there's someone else who can't bear to see you in your position for too long, just because they feel they're superior to you and, for that matter, deserve the position you're holding. This kind of thinking is typical of megalomaniacs.

Unfortunately, history hasn't alerted us enough to their malevolence. This allows them to pull off surprises when they're mistakenly given authority or brought to the corridors of power, and indeed, their surprises often come by acting against the person who reposed trust in them, including those who brought them to the corridors of power.

They're covert in the beginning, pretending to act in your favour and doing it well enough to win your trust and confidence. But here's the catch: while they go to great lengths to act in your interest, they would be seeking attention in order to be noticed. The purpose of their unbridled attention-seeking is to outshine you while tacitly offering themselves as a better alternative.

And having grown impatient with you for still being at your post, they'll begin to behave acrimoniously towards you, and may arrogate power to themselves before you know it. This is a red flag, a dire one. At this juncture, they'll be backstabbing you and getting it into people's minds that you're unfit for the job.

In the end, they'll brazenly defy you. This is the tipping point. Your failure to read between the lines and your hesitation to counteract their malevolence will spell your doom.

Simpson had worked in marketing for nearly a decade until he was appointed branch manager. He, in turn, appointed his high school friend, Judas, as a marketing officer and his second-in-command.

Judas was a gifted strategist and an efficient marketer. Never in the company's history has anyone used a minimum budget to yield so much profit.

Simpson was so impressed with Judas that he attended management meetings with him and even added him to the managers' WhatsApp group. But Judas seized every opportunity to call attention to his sales wits and the success he had brought to the company.

It beats me how Simpson didn't notice Judas' patterns or find it concerning that sometimes the CEO sent him a message through Judas. Alas, the CEO's secretary posted a picture of Judas on her WhatsApp status, and another time, a picture of herself with Judas. Rumours made the rounds.

One afternoon, a team of government officials visited the branch office to see the branch manager, but when Simpson showed up, they said he wasn't the one they were looking for but another man named Judas. Simpson later queried Judas about his misrepresentation, but Judas retorted that he couldn't be held responsible for someone mistaking him for the branch manager. The following week, another visitor came in to see the branch manager, and when Simpson showed up, the visitor said he wasn't the one, but her friend called Judas.

Simpson remembered the previous week's visit, and it dawned on him that Judas was coveting his position. The two men bickered and brawled, after which Simpson wrote to the central administration for a dismissal letter to Judas.

The CEO heard of the conflict, and weighing the two men, he found Judas worthy of being kept in the company rather than Simpson. Besides, his secretary had whispered to him that Simpson was sleeping on the job while Judas did all the work. So, he fired Simpson and put Judas in his place.

As the new branch manager, Judas proved himself once again, and profit was going through the roof. One day, the CEO invited him for a meeting with the board of directors and investors. A month later, while on Facebook, the CEO noticed a picture of the board's secretary wearing a bikini at the pool with Judas, who was topless and wearing sunglasses.

Unlike Simpson, the sharp-witted CEO noticed a pattern, including his observation that just around the time of the board secretary's Facebook post, his own secretary was posting broken heart emojis on her WhatsApp status. He remembered the first time Judas called him and then asked his secretary if she knew how Judas got his personal number. She answered by saying that she gave the number to him because he was pestering her for it.

The CEO connected the dots and realised how Judas had used his secretary to malign Simpson. Now, suspecting that the board secretary was his next pawn, he knew what Judas was up to, and although Judas was an asset to the company, he fired him without giving any reason.

Understand: Everyone has a history of some sort, and as a professional, you must find out about the dark side of any prospect coming into your professional orbit. You can do this by simply asking about them from someone they've worked with or checking on them on the internet.

The information you gather from your search is supposed to inform you on how to deal with them or save you the regret of unknowingly bringing the wrong person into your professional orbit. Of course, everyone has a dark side, and some past transgressions can be glossed over. But you would be reckless to overlook a megalomaniac.

Do a Background Check

Don't be dazzled by people's reputations when you're assessing them. Before anyone gets into your professional orbit, find out about their conduct. They might be good or bad; you wouldn't know which one and its details unless you did a background check on them.

In 2019, I met a young man I wanted to do business with. So I inquired about him with his manager. 'Hmmm...well...he's a good person, but I can't vouch for him,' his manager said. Alas! 'What kind of good person can't be vouched for?' I asked myself. So, I inquired further about the young man from his colleague, but she was also reticent.

Finally, I asked the young man to bring me a list of referees. After a delay, he brought me a list of executives from two companies he said he had worked for. I checked out those companies and found that neither the companies nor the executives he had listed existed.

The young man's impropriety, therefore, spoke volumes about his manager's and colleague's reticence, and it was supposed to be a warning to me.

On New Year's Day of 2018, one of my clients called me for an urgent meeting. When we met, he told me he had signed a three-year contract with a middle-aged contractor to take charge of his construction projects. The contractor had been recommended as the most capable and reasonably priced contractor in town. But this was my client's issue: he had asked about the contractor from someone who knew him, and the person had told him that the contractor was a sadist and had seduced his clients and their spouses into threesomes.

This couldn't have been an issue if the parties involved were consenting adults. However, my client was afraid because his source told him the contractor enchanted his victims by staring them in the eye, and that his previous clients, who were a staunch anti-gay activist and a chastity advocate, were seduced into his enchantment-induced threesome.

It was the most absurd thing I've heard, except that I couldn't ask my client what he had smoked, but I could see that he was anxious. And after listening to him, I advised him against holding the contractor's gaze, never to be with him alone, and never allow him to meet with his wife or even have her phone number.

Three years later, my client called to inform me the contractor had finished the project and that he wouldn't even look him in the eye when they were talking, and he never ever called his wife, though he had her phone number. He also said that the thought that he would be sodomised and cuckolded by the contractor made him fret all the time, and he asked me if I thought his source lied to him about the contractor. I told him I couldn't be sure about that and reminded him that not everything we're told about others can be true.

One day, I went out for lunch and chanced on a successful businessman I had known on TV. We discussed politics and business, and I asked him about his secret to success. But he denied having any secret and said that if there was any at all, it would be that he knows everyone he works with.

He said, 'I know everyone's history, from the janitor to the general manager. I know the astute, the honest, the dishonest, the talkative, the licentious, the secretive, the lazy, the hardworking, the bold, the timid, the liar, the idealist, and the realist; I know them all. I even know their beliefs and their thinking patterns. And I assign leadership roles to the most selfless and intelligent people. Pay them well, and they'll treat your business as their own. That day, I left the restaurant feeling more enlightened than ever.

In any case, beware of certain character traits in your professional orbit. Megalomaniacs are too dangerous to be brought near the corridors of power. They're those who can sink a ship just because they won't be made the ship's captain.

An avaricious person is loyal to money and money alone. A confused person is unpredictable and can make you lose your mind. A liar is a breathing hazard. Mind you, 'You can't grow a quality network of supportive troops to fight the frontline battles with you if you allow liars to join the platoon.' Hence, you must keep a liar at bay, come what may.

The Confused Person

Once, I was having a coaching session with a client when a lady barged in crying, 'I can't work with him anymore. He delivers the wrong message and believes everything he's told. He once served us tea with salt instead of sugar, and he even drove to church on a Monday morning, thinking it was a Sunday.'

'Who?' my client asked. 'Him,' said the marketing officer, pointing to a smallish, middle-aged man who walked in grinning. 'He's the most confused person I've ever known,' the marketing officer remarked.

Explication

In January 2020, news about the suspension of a Ugandan imam from his clerical post made the rounds. This was after it emerged that his hijabwearing wife, whom he had known as Swabullah Nabukeera, was found to be a man.

The revelation came to light after Swabullah Nabukeera was arrested for stealing TV and clothes from her neighbour at her new matrimonial home. Upon her arrest, an officer frisked her and felt something unusual with her breasts. When her breasts were checked, they were found to be pieces of cloth in her bra. A further check on her body revealed 'her' genitalia, and lo and behold, Swabullah Nabukeera was a complete man identified as Richard Tumushabe.

He was subsequently charged with impersonation, theft, and obtaining goods by false pretence. During the investigation, the police questioned the imam about why he had married a man who pretended to be a woman, but he swore he had no clue his wife was a man. According to him, they hadn't had sex in their two-week-old marriage because, all the while, his wife had been telling him 'she' was menstruating.

Understand: The eccentricity of the Imam is typical of a confused person, and you would think they're funny until one gets into your professional orbit. It is then you'll know they're a pain in the neck.

At an abstract art exhibition in Yekaterinburg, western Russia, a security guard, on his first day at work, took a ballpoint pen and drew pairs of eyes on two of Anna Leporskaya's faceless Three Figures artwork, thereby damaging the $1 million painting. He was fired then and there!

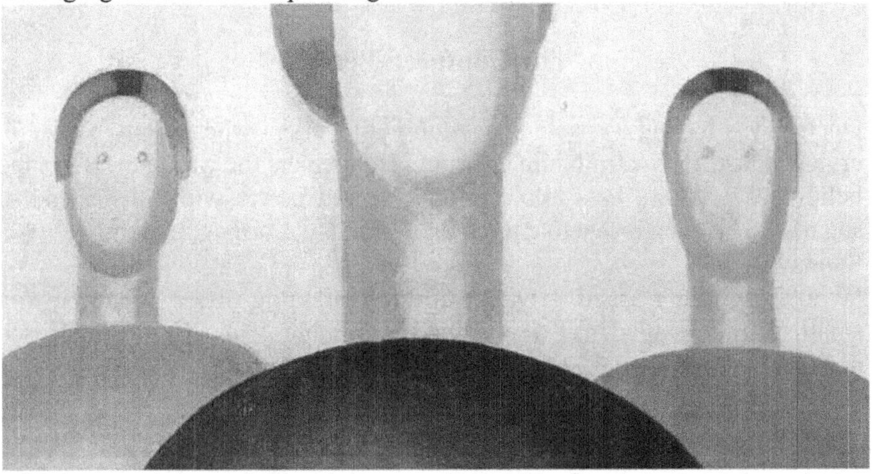

Did the security guard intend to cause harm? No. But he ruined the painting anyway just because he was bored and didn't know what to do until he had the idiotic idea to draw those eyes on the high-value painting.

If you've never dealt with a confused person but heard about their antics, you would think they're funny. But if you've ever had one in your professional orbit, you'll know they're a pain in the neck, and you'll surely need blood pressure medication to put up with them.

And though they might not mean harm, nonetheless, their actions and inactions can render you culpable and liable for compensatory damages. You may not notice a confused person early enough because of their education and qualifications, but it won't be long before they surprise you.

In December 2020, when the COVID-19 vaccine rollout was in full swing, a certain pharmacist was arrested for destroying 570 doses of COVID-19 vaccines. He did it during a night shift by removing a box containing the vials from a refrigerator. Could he have destroyed the vaccines unintentionally? No. As a pharmacist, he knew the vaccine could survive only up to 12 hours outside the refrigerator's temperature. Hence, he knew he was spoiling the vaccines.

Did he intend to cause harm? No. He genuinely believed he was doing the right thing. And despite his education and the fact that COVID-19 was the leading cause of death, he believed the pandemic was a hoax. He had also internalised the belief that the earth is flat (against the fact that the earth is spherical) and that the sky is a 'shield put up by the government to prevent people from seeing God.'

The Avaricious Person

Name anything worth flaunting, and there wouldn't be any that an avaricious person doesn't desire. Mention any vice people perpetrate, and there isn't one that an avaricious person cannot do to get money. The longer you deal with them, the higher the likelihood they'll sting you.

Holding a position is their greatest enabler; their potential victims are anyone they do business with, and their clients are their most convenient victims. That's how Dr. Farid Fata was able to pull off the most scandalous healthcare fraud in the history of the United States.

He was well-known and influential because he owned Michigan Haematology-Oncology (MHO), which was one of the largest cancer practices in Michigan.

In 2013, he was arrested on charges of prescribing chemotherapy to his 500-plus victims, who were either perfectly healthy or whose conditions didn't require chemotherapy. He also submitted $34 million in fraudulent charges to insurers over a period of six years.

One of Fata's victims, a disabled auto worker, reportedly suffered teeth loss and an uncontrollable body twitch after Dr. Farid Fata misdiagnosed him with rare blood cancer and subjected him to monthly chemotherapy and three weeks of radiotherapy.

Later, when the victim visited a different oncologist, he was told he never had cancer.

During the trial of Dr. Farid Fata, his victim, then 62 years old, told NBC News, 'I have so much hatred toward Fata. His name causes an instant headache. He gets my stomach turning. It is hard to explain… the things I want to do to that guy, I couldn't say in public. I hope he gets life imprisonment.'

Dr. Farid Fata was sentenced to 45 years in federal prison. Of course, everyone has a dark side, and some past transgressions can be glossed over, but this one is too dire to overlook, even if he comes back repentant.

Explication

We live in an era where you can present the public with a curated image of yourself to influence how you want to be perceived. Thanks to publicists and social media. And it's okay if you're sincere. Otherwise, it wouldn't take long for people to see through your fakery and tell others about their bad experiences with you.

This will cost you your reputation, as people will learn to be cautious when dealing with you, whereas others will avoid dealing with you entirely. Another way people can build their reputation and boost their influence is to earn titles. Titles have a way of eliciting admiration and respect for the bearer. And they deserve it because they earned it. But again, you should still ask about the character of anyone coming into your professional orbit. Because they are still humans, whether they have the titles Honourable, Doctor, Professor, Colonel, or Mister.

Dr. Farid Fata's misconduct, for instance, attests that prestige doesn't tell a person's integrity, and the only way you can be sure about someone's character is to do a background check on them.

The Guy Who Comes Around

It's been three weeks since Eric first saw Dr. Abotsi on campus. He graduated two months ago but still visited the campus to study for his professional exams. In a lecture room on the first floor, where he often sat to study, he saw Dr. Abotsi having a confab with the janitors, and he greeted him when their eyes met. They ran into each other for the second time at the university's library and exchanged greetings.

Since then, Dr. Abotsi passed by once in a while on the first floor to have a pep talk with Eric, during which they discussed academics and scholarships. Eric assumed Dr. Abotsi was a university lecturer without asking him; after all, he had told Eric his name was Dr. Abotsi. And realising that he knew a great deal about international scholarships, Eric began to enjoy his company.

One Friday afternoon, while Eric was studying, Dr. Abotsi came along and greeted him. He then told Eric that he had promised to pay part of a student's tuition fee but had forgotten the deadline was 2:00 pm and he had a staff meeting to attend in the next 20 minutes. So, he implored Eric to lend him GH¢ 4000.00 for the student's fee before the 2:00 pm deadline, and that he would pay it back the next Monday.

Eric didn't have the money in his wallet, so he went across the street to the ATM and returned to give it to Dr. Abotsi. When Monday came, Dr. Abotsi didn't show up on the campus. Eric was too engrossed in his studies to find out why, but Tuesday, Wednesday, and Thursday passed, and there wasn't a sign of him; his phone was off, and there wasn't any trace of him on the internet.

Eric inquired about Dr. Abotsi from the janitors. 'Who's Dr Abotsi?' They asked Eric. When Eric described him, they told him they didn't know his name and hadn't seen him since last Friday. Eric then asked the janitors to direct him to Dr. Abotsi's office. 'Which office?' The janitors asked Eric. 'Is he not a lecturer at this university?' Eric inquired. 'He isn't,' the janitors responded. 'He is not a member of the university's staff. He's been coming around to chat with us, but we don't know him or where he comes from.' When Eric heard this, he wept.

Explication

Any sting you experienced in college as a student couldn't be as costly to your studies as it'll be to your career if you experience it as a professional. This is the aspect Eric should be thankful for. At least, his experience with Abotsi exposed his gullibility, thereby nudging him into self-awareness and making him wiser and more thoughtful when dealing with strangers.

It cost him GH¢4000.00 to learn a lesson, and had it not been for this college experience, he probably would've gone on being gullible in his career, which would've cost him his reputation and an opportunity.

In my early years as a career coach, a client visited me and talked about wanting to quit his high-paying job. He held a master's degree and was the project manager at his workplace.

One morning, a well-dressed gentleman visited his office with a friendly demeanour and told him he wanted to buy some merchandise from the company. According to my client, before he could direct the gentleman to the sales office, he took 10 hundred-dollar notes from his wallet and gave them to him as a tip. He immediately handed him a two-million-dollar cheque for the merchandise and said he wanted to see samples.

My client then left him in his office to go get the samples from the sales office, but when he returned, the gentleman was gone, his project documents were gone, the cheque was a dud, and the hundred-dollar bills were counterfeit.

The matter was referred to the CID, and although they didn't indict my client, he became an object of scorn at his workplace and was ridiculed at every opportunity. He could tell from everyone's face that they didn't want him anymore. Hence his desire to resign!

In Europe, Carlos Hector Flomenbaum, known as such to the staff of a bank in Antwerp's diamond district, Belgium, looked between 55 and 60 years old, had grey hair, spoke American-accented English, and bore an Argentine passport.

He had identified himself as a successful businessman, and for at least a year, he frequented the bank with chocolate gifts. With his jovial nature, the bank employees liked him, and he often had a confab with them on non-banking issues. He eventually won the bank's executives' trust and was given VIP access to the vault.

At the bank, certain customers were given passcards to access their diamonds during non-banking hours. Carlos Hector Flomenbaum became one of those trusted passcard holders, and between March 2 and 5, 2007, he walked into the vault and out the front door with 120,000 carats of diamond, 41 blue stones, and two rare green stones valued at $28 million.

No one saw him again, and it turned out that he was an imposter with a stolen passport.

Understand: Through our college and career experiences, we cross paths with diverse individuals. Some become our friends, and the rest become our acquaintances. As social beings, we express our niceness to our acquaintances by greeting them, responding to their greetings, and occasionally having chitchat with them. But in the midst of these, we keep them out of our personal orbit and at an emotional distance. When they try to be intrusive, we show our displeasure to discourage them from further intrusion. However, sometimes people scale our impersonal barriers and become friends with us before we know it. And it wouldn't be hard for them to scale our personal barriers if they could figure out our interests. For instance, most men are fond of dirty talk and will remain so for a lifetime. That was what Abotsi used to scale Eric's impersonal barrier.

He began visiting the campus to scam an unsuspecting victim, and Eric, unfortunately, became his target. Initially, Eric regarded Abotsi as a stranger and wouldn't look at him for a second after responding to his greeting. But one afternoon, while both men stood apart facing the main entrance of the campus, a lady in a racy dress with the biggest derrière passed. Both men noticed her derrière, turned to look at each other, and smiled. Voila! Abotsi knew Eric would be a fan of dirty talk, so he brought up the conversation, to which Eric responded well.

On that day, they exchanged phone numbers and became 'friends'. In their next conversation, Eric opened up to Abotsi about his savings for a new laptop and a consultation with a scholarship expert when he completes his professional exam.

That was how Abotsi knew of Eric's savings and capitalised on it to scam him. First, he alluded that he was a lecturer at the university, lied about being a scholarship expert after knowing that Eric had an aspiration for post-graduate studies, and then promised him he would work out a scholarship for him immediately after his professional exam.

At a certain point in their acquaintanceship, Eric met with Abotsi every day. This gave Eric a false sense of friendship with Abotsi, though he didn't know him. Moreover, Abotsi had promised Eric he would secure a scholarship for him, and thinking Abotsi was a lecturer with a PhD, Eric didn't doubt Abotsi's credibility. Therefore, when Abotsi asked Eric for the GH¢4000.00, Eric had no reason to be unkind to him, considering the greater benefit he would soon enjoy from him without paying for consultation. So, Eric lent Abotsi the money before he knew he had been swindled.

Finally, when someone is being overly kind to you or too sacrificial for your gain, don't get too carried away or relish the favour. Instead, be concerned about their motive and what they may ask for in return.

Be Cautious in Unfriendly Territories

In February 2018, a client I was coaching for a job hunt visited me with his cousin. This cousin had a degree but hadn't gotten a job since he completed university three years ago. He was frustrated and had resolved to join his friend in South Africa to work.

According to him, his friend in South Africa had already secured a job for him, and the job was guaranteed if he could get to South Africa in three weeks. I asked him if he had his CV with him, and he pulled one from a brown envelope and handed it to me. After I had perused it page by page, I told him that no serious employer would call him for an interview with the kind of CV he had written. He admitted he had never received a call for a job interview.

I offered to coach him, as I was coaching his cousin, so that he could still look for a job in Ghana. He replied, 'My mind is made up. I have a ready job in South Africa, and I'll leave next week.' I asked him which province in South Africa he was heading to. 'Gauteng,' he replied. The name sounded familiar, and I did a quick internet search.

According to the search result, the Gauteng Province is cited for a high incidence of xenophobic attacks on foreign African nationals. So I asked him if he knew about xenophobia in South Africa and how deadly it could be? He answered, 'Yes.' I also asked him if he was aware that the recent xenophobic attacks in South Africa were not the last, and that they would occur again. He responded, 'It won't happen in Jesus' name.' I then cautioned him to always save money for contingencies and that he should leave the province promptly when xenophobic tension began to brew.

That was the first and last time I saw or heard of him. In 2019, the following year, xenophobic riots broke out in Johannesburg, in the Gauteng Province, leading to several casualties, including the murder of at least seven people.

Even if there aren't many educational and job opportunities in your country, you can always avoid places where people have been atrocious toward a group you belong to in the past, whether it's because of your sexuality, ethnicity, tribe, nationality, religion, or race.

In September 2018, news about the arrest and 10-year conviction of Kylie Moore-Gilbert in Iran on espionage charges made the rounds. Moore-Gilbert is a British-Australian academic in Islamic studies at the Asia Institute of the University of Melbourne. She had travelled to Iran on an invitation to an academic conference but was arrested by the Iranian Revolutionary Guard Corps on her return at the Tehran airport.

No public evidence of her guilt was shown, and the Australian government condemned her conviction.

Moore-Gilbert denied any wrongdoing, explaining that she had rejected an offer from Iran to be a spy in exchange for her release. However, according to a 2020 report, she was arrested because the Iranians discovered she was in a relationship with an Israeli, which fuelled an unfounded suspicion that she was a spy.

Understand: When bad blood exists between your country and another country, avoid that country if you can, lest they target you for their political interests. And if they do, your home country may not be able to intervene as swiftly as you would expect. For Kylie Moore-Gilbert, it took the Australian government 804 days to negotiate her release in exchange for the release of three Iranians serving long prison sentences in Thailand. Could this have been the actual purpose of Kylie Moore-Gilbert's arrest?

Human rights organisations described Iran's actions as 'hostage diplomacy'. Moreover, the relationship between Iran and the West has been trepidatious.

One of the biggest mistakes you can make as a citizen of a feuding country in this situation is to regard yourself as apolitical in the feud. Even if you genuinely disagree with your government's policies against the other country, it still doesn't change the fact that you're a citizen of an adversary country, and if you're on the soil of that country, they may target you.

In 2017, a British-Australian blogger called Jolie King, and her Australian boyfriend, Mark Firkin, left Perth to embark on a globetrotting adventure across Asia to the UK. They blogged and posted drone footage and pictures of their adventure on their Instagram timeline and YouTube channel, where they had more than 20,000 fans. They wrote online, 'Our biggest motivation... is to hopefully inspire anyone wanting to travel, and also try to break the stigma around travelling to countries that get a bad wrap in the media.'

King and Firkin began their journey by driving north to Darwin, where they shipped their car to Timor-Leste. From there, they drove through Indonesia, shipped their car to Malaysia, and drove through Southeast Asia, India, and Pakistan. They posted on YouTube once a week until, suddenly, their fans no longer had updates from them as their posts on Instagram and YouTube ceased.

This became a cause of concern among their online followers until news emerged about their arrest and incarceration in Tehran's notorious Evin Prison on charges related to drone flying without a permit. Their conviction, albeit not based on a trumped-up charge, evoked public sentiment. But ignorance of the law is no excuse in any land.

While you may be able to get away with a pardon or warning in your home country, in another country, foreign policies and national security concerns may cause authorities to exact the full rigours of the law on a foreigner, particularly one from an adversary country.

Jolie King and Mark Firkin, however, were later released following sensitive negotiations by the Australian government on their behalf.

So whenever you're on the soil of a foreign country, be mindful that you're no longer in your homeland, and you must behave accordingly, especially if your home country is an adversary to the foreign country you're in.

Vacate When Tension is Brewing

On December 7, 1941, the Japanese Imperial Navy Air Service launched a preemptive, unprovoked, and surprising attack on Pearl Harbour. The attack was launched from six aircraft carriers by 353 Imperial Japanese aircraft, comprising torpedo bombers, fighters, and level and dive bombers, in two waves of attacks that crippled the US Pacific Fleet.

Four US Navy battleships sank out of a total of eight that were damaged. Three cruisers, three destroyers, an anti-aircraft training ship, and a minelayer were sunk or damaged. A total of 188 US aircraft were also destroyed, and a death toll of 2,403 Americans was recorded, aside from the 1,178 wounded.

The next day, the US declared war on Japan and formally joined WWII, leading to Japan's eventual defeat and surrender. Seventy-eight days after the Pearl Harbour bombing, American-Japanese living in the US would bear the brunt of the infamy.

President Roosevelt issued Executive Order No. 9066, authorising the Secretary of War to forcibly remove more than 110,000 people of Japanese ancestry in the United States from their homes in California, Washington, and Oregon and send them to a detention camp in a desolate location, depriving them of the basic freedom guaranteed by the US constitution. Families were forced to live in poorly built, overcrowded barracks with no running water and almost no privacy as everyone had to use public bathrooms. The camp was fenced with barbed wire and guarded by heavily armed soldiers.

The Executive Order was backed by Congress without a single vote against it, and the Supreme Court ruled that it was legal.

The Pearl Harbour bombing, although unprovoked and unexpected, was the tipping point of years of tension between Japan and the US. And it wasn't a period for Americans living in Japan and Japanese living in America to feel comfortable, even if their purpose in the other country was well-intentioned.

They could've relocated to neutral territories while the tension was brewing in order to avoid the unknown. And then return when there is calm. This is because, in times of war, anger and vengeance for an enemy's infamy will be vented on their available citizens, as happened to the innocent Japanese residents living in the US.

Even if the government doesn't sanction such vindictiveness, the citizens who have lost loved ones in combat can be unpredictable. However, after 50 years, the US government apologised and compensated the Japanese for their internment.

It's, therefore, important to be mindful of the diplomatic relationship between your country and the country where your sense of purpose is taking you. Even in the absence of war but during a period of prevailing bad blood between your country and an adversary country, avoid the latter if necessary.

Finally, wherever your sense of purpose takes you, research how the people there have dealt with people like you in the past. If they've been cordial and welcoming to your people in the past, they'll likely remain the same in the present. If they've recurrently been atrocious to your people in the past, you should expect traces of their past behaviour in the present.

In 2005, 56 West African immigrants, including 44 Ghanaians, Nigerians, Togolese, and Ivoirians, who attempted to illegally enter The Gambia were slain by the Gambian Junglers squad at the behest of the Gambian President, Yahya Jammeh. Also, the sporadic xenophobic attacks in South Africa by black South Africans against other African nationals should be a caution to any foreign African national whose sense of purpose is leading them to South Africa.

Sharpen Your Axe

On May 14, 2018, the Nigerian Inspector General of Police (IGP), Ibrahim Idris, commissioned a Technical Intelligence Unit, dubbed COBWEB Solutions Technical Intelligence Platform at the Kano State Command. Soon after the event, a video showing IGP Ibrahim Idris reading the speech below to an English-speaking audience went viral:

> ...The Commissioner of Police, I mean the A.G in charge of POLAC, police academy, who is here with us this afternoon, the Commissioner of Police in the state of Kano State Command, Rabu'i, the Commissioner of Police in charge of the monitoring unit, Abu Sani, senior police officers of the command, ladies and gentlemen.
>
> I am delighted to make this remark at the official, official commissioning of the COBWEB transmission, I mean, intelligence platform of the federal, I mean of the Kano state command as it remarks yet another milestone in the effort of this administration to commission the Nigerian Police Force to make an important effective and impulsive responsive in the art of policing in Nigeria.

> On appointment, that is regional police on 22nd June 2016, I promise to take the Nigerian Police Force to a higher level where it will be more accountable, effective and transmission, I mean, transmission to available with a effective, I mean *erh*... with …sorry… with a …I mean errh reprehensive on corruption to have effective forth faith, I mean errh.. *free* faith in the commission, I mean transmission…I mean effort at the transmission commission to transmission mean, I mean transmission. To have effect on *errm*…apprehend, I mean apprehensive at the transmission of the royal prevention and detection and transmission and transmission for the effective of the transmission of the Nigerian Police Force and the men in the command.
> The effective, the effective, transmission transmission and I mean apprehensive transmission transmission, I mean cultivative, I mean cultivative transmission. Transmission and transmission, I mean apprehensive transmission and other transition [he paused and continued] of effective transmission tran, I mean errm Sorry…..Sorry please.
> [An aid came to his side speaking indistinctly while he continued reading]
> ….I present of all kidnapping transmission transmission other effective transmission transmission other transmission. I can state without fear of contradiction that trans… I have commission what? Over transmission of, over transmission of, over all kidnapping, armed robbery and other heinous crime. I mean *erh* commission transmission, I mean errm recommendation transmission *erm* ok ordered submission.

The speech went viral and caused confusion among the public, who were unsure of whatever omissions and commissions that the Inspector General of Police wanted to transmit. However, the actual speech was later made available on the internet:

> I am delighted to make this remark at the official commissioning of the COBWEB Solutions Intelligence Platform of the Kano State Command, as it marks yet another milestone in the efforts of this Administration to reposition the Nigeria Police to make it more effective and responsive in the art of Policing Nigeria.
> On my appointment as the Inspector General of Police on the 2nd June, 2016, I promised to take the Nigeria Police Force to a higher level where it will be more accountable, effective, responsive and reliable with a Zero tolerance of corruption. I have kept faith with the promise despite efforts

at various quarters to distract me. I am so happy today that the Nigeria Police have truly been repositioned and we have recorded major achievements and breakthroughs in the areas of crime prevention, detection, prosecution and welfare of the officers and men.

The fight against insurgency, kidnapping, Armed robbery, Cattle rustling, Farmers/Herders clashes and other heinous crimes are being systematically won. I can state without fear of contradiction that over 70% of all kidnapping, armed robbery and other heinous crime cases recorded since my assumption of office have been resolved. It is also of importance to note that several thousands of arms and ammunition have been recovered, thereby making it increasingly difficult to access illegal arms and criminal activities.

These achievements wouldn't have been possible without the introduction of the technical intelligence platform in Abuja, manned by the Special Intelligence and Tactical Response Teams coordinated by the IGP – Monitoring Unit for strategic and modern crime-mapping in the country, I decided to establish two or more Technical Intelligence Platforms in Lagos and Imo States in 2017 to provide technical Intelligence assistance/support to Police Commands in the South West and South East respectively.

What we are witnessing today is the Commissioning of the 4th technical platform in Kano for the Northwest Zone to give technical aid to Police Commands in the Zone. This technical platform will certainly increase Police efficiency, effectiveness and their capacity to detect crime in the area. I therefore call on the Police Commands to utilise the opportunity provided by these four technical intelligence platforms in Abuja, Lagos, Owerri and now in Kano to boost your policing capability in these areas.

I will not relent in my efforts to ensure that the challenges of crime we are facing in this country, be it kidnapping, killings, armed robbery, militancy, terrorism, and other heinous crimes will be soon resolved with the use of technical intelligence platforms in line with international best practices. Consequently, I will endeavour to link all State Police Commands with Technical Intelligence Cobweb Platforms as soon as funds are made available.

Finally, I want to assure Nigerians that the Police is doing everything possible to protect life and property in Nigeria. I am not unaware of the concerns of Nigerians about the challenges of crime and criminality across the country. I appeal to you to be patient with the police and government as the president and the Commander-in-Chief of the Armed Forces of the Federal Republic of Nigeria is doing everything humanly possible to end these challenges. Thank you.

Explication

Abraham Lincoln said, 'Give me six hours to chop down a tree, and I will spend the first four sharpening the axe.' (IGP) Ibrahim Idris's *transmission transmission* speech debacle leads to one conclusion: he didn't prepare for the speech. The result was his hilarious reading, which never ceases to confuse and entertain.

Sir Winston Churchill is widely regarded as the greatest politician and orator in modern history. To attain that prominence, he always planned, prepared, and practised his speeches. He began by drafting the speech and reading it to himself. Then he would imbibe sentences and progress to paragraphs. At this point, he regurgitated what he had imbibed while pacing his room until he could recite the entire speech by heart. During his practice, he adjusted his tone and the pitch and loudness of his voice to iron out the stammers in his speech.

At old age, Churchill still wrote his speeches, usually dictating them to a secretary and editing them himself. He would then ask for the final copy to be presented as a poem showing spaced lines and breaks in the text so that he could pinpoint where to pause, hesitate, and accentuate. He was a relentless reviser of his speeches, just as he often edited his books. The final version would be retyped on notepaper, yet he would still strike through some texts and make insertions at the last minute.

And after all the preparation, he would take the stage and captivate his audience with an enthralling speech that would reverberate in their minds long after the event.

Learn from this: Don't perform in public what you haven't prepared for in private.

Quit and Shrink

Knowledge has to be improved, challenged, and increased constantly, or it vanishes – Peter Drucker.

A sword will remain sharp as long as its user sharpens it. On the other hand, its continuous use without sharpening will make it blunt. Similarly, bodybuilders will have to continue training to keep their muscles; if they quit training, their muscles will atrophy.

So, in truth, whatever gain we make through practice would be eventually lost if we quit practising. In ancient Greece, the Spartans rose to dominance as a formidable warrior society and the most feared military force in Greece. They didn't explore art, science, or innovation. Their main focus was valour and war, for which they trained and lived.

After defeating Athens in the Peloponnesian War, the Spartans attempted to expand into an empire. Initially, they occupied a small geographic space and knew one another. So, they were all under the watchful eyes of their neighbours, which was how they conserved the Spartan way of life. But when they expanded into an empire, they dispersed themselves through the Greek city-states, beyond the watchful eyes of their fellow Spartans.

Gradually, they relaxed their social values and mingled with an alien culture. This eventually eroded their warrior way of life and sense of valour. Hence, they became less badass than they used to be, and in the Battle of Leuctra, they lost and fell from prominence, never to rise again.

Be Dynamic and Adaptable

It is not the strongest of species that survives, nor the most intelligent. It is the one that is most adaptable to change. – Charles Darwin.

The rise and fall of Nokia is a testament to complacency. Complacency has consequences as it instils a false sense of constancy against the intrinsic nature of market dynamism.

The market is the people, and people get bored with monotony. However, Nokia remained steadfast and continued to produce diverse phone designs with the same monotonous user experience. Then, in 2007, Steve Jobs walked on stage and rolled out the iPhone, touting its diverse user experience and novel interface.

The interface had no buttons. As such, a user only had to touch a screen, and he would get the feel of a whole computer in his hand. It was novel and had a wow factor!

Initially, Nokia dismissed the touchscreen as a gimmick, saying it used too much battery. But then, from a 49.4% market share in 2007, they plummeted woefully until, in 2010, they decided to ditch their Symbian Operating System and join the smartphone wagon. But they went in too late because other smartphone brands had already taken the market.

By 2013, Nokia's market share had eroded to 3%, and in 2014, they sold their mobile phone business to Microsoft for $7.2 billion—against a $300 billion market value during their peak.

Facebook, on the other hand, isn't taking a chance with complacency. Since its launch in 2003, Facebook has been the social media website with the most dynamic evolutionary pattern. Thus, by introducing new features from time to time and strategically acquiring WhatsApp and Instagram, Facebook makes itself relevant to subscribers for its diverse user experience and dynamic features, thereby making it difficult for rival social networks to catch up with it, let alone outpace it.

Learn this lesson: For every milestone you reach, always strive to better yourself at what you do. Because people get bored with monotony, and after some time, they would want to try something new. In any event, be the person to provide them with that 'something new'. And whatever the situation might be, don't stay the same way for too long: do a makeover, do a rebrand, and add a new feature.

Don't be adamant when the wind of change is blowing. This is how you can keep up with dynamism and remain relevant in the system.

Don't Multitask

Multitasking is like constantly pulling up a plant. This kind of constant shifting of your attention means that new ideas and concepts have no chance to take root and flourish. – Barbara Oakley.

When you begin one task, stick to it with faith and grit until you succeed or your experience shows that it's not worthwhile, then you can move to the next task. Never scatter your energy by engaging in many things at a time. Because, if you do, your brain will trick you into thinking you're being productive when you aren't.

Meanwhile, you would be prolonging the time it takes to complete a task. Factoring in the human body's susceptibility to fatigue, multitasking diminishes the concentration you need to accomplish a goal, which, in effect, can lead to burnouts, mistakes, accidents, and costs you could've avoided.

CHAPTER FIVE

Your purpose and Society

The greatest ability in business is to get along with others and influence their actions. – John Hancock.

Cultivate Social Graces

A sense of purpose is the motivation that drives us to accomplish our life goals. It instils in us the impetus to push ourselves through the difficulties on the path to success and guides us to avoid distractions that may keep us from reaching our goals.

Accomplishing your sense of purpose puts an end to your old life and marks the beginning of a successful life. How you lead yourself in this new life is what will accord you dignity or put your hard-earned name into disrepute.

The latter, in other words, refers to a fall from grace and can shatter your reputation into unmendable pieces. The consequence can be dire; this is evident in the lives of public figures who, after a long and prestigious career, were caught pants down in sex scandals, corruption scandals, unethical business conduct, power abuse, et cetera.

In developed countries, a fair trial and conviction of the rightly accused person are likely, whereas in corruption-laden countries, a narrow escape after an initial brush with the law is the norm for the rightly accused person who is politically connected or has the means to pay their way out. In any case, they're disgraced.

Christopher Columbus had become a dignitary in the Court of the Spanish Crown. He had persisted in his lobbying for sponsorship to embark on the Enterprise of the Indies, which he succeeded in, upon which he was bestowed with the rank of Admiral of the Ocean Sea, and appointed as Viceroy and Governor of all the lands he claimed for Spain.

He was also allowed to keep 10% of all the money made from the new land forever. He could also buy an eighth of any business that used the new land and get an eighth of the profits.

In 1500, however, accusations of tyranny and incompetence against Columbus reached the Spanish Crown. The narratives of his misconduct in the West Indies were nerve-racking, panicky, and scandalous, thereby prompting Queen Isabella I and King Ferdinand II to sanction Columbus' ouster as governor of the West Indies.

He was then arrested, sent back in chains to Spain, and incarcerated. His replacement was Francisco de Bobadilla, who was commissioned by the Spanish Crown to inquire about the accusations of brutalities against Columbus. When Francisco de Bobadilla arrived in Hispaniola, he was immediately met with complaints about Columbus' three brothers, thereby lending credence to the allegations being levelled against them in Spain.

So, Francisco de Bobadilla told the Spanish Crown that Columbus had used torture and mutilation to rule Hispaniola and that he was not liked by the colonists.

In 2006, a 48-page report was found in the Spanish city of Simancas detailing the testimonies of 23 people, including friends and foes of Columbus, on the tyranny suffered by colonial subjects at the hands of Columbus and his brothers during his seven-year rule in Hispaniola.

The report reveals that Columbus once punished a man who was found guilty of stealing corn by having his ears and nose cut off and selling him into slavery. The report also shows that Columbus congratulated his brother, Bartholomew, on 'defending the family' by making a woman parade naked through the streets and cutting out her tongue for insinuating that Columbus was of lowly birth.

To stop unrest and rebellion among the natives, Columbus ordered a harsh crackdown in which many natives were killed and their dismembered bodies were paraded through the streets as a warning to others who might try to rebel.

According to Consuelo Varela, a Spanish historian who had perused the report, it states that even those who loved Columbus had to admit the atrocities that had taken place.

For this abuse of power, the Spanish Crown ousted Columbus as governor and had him, along with his brothers, sent back to Spain and incarcerated. They languished for six weeks before King Ferdinand II ordered their release.

Not long after their release, the Spanish Crown summoned them for a fair hearing, and upon considering their pleas, the Spanish Crown restored

Columbus and his siblings to their freedom and wealth. They also funded his fourth voyage, but he was never again appointed governor.

Explication

A show of excellence and extraordinariness wins us the hearts of ordinary men, nobles, kings, queens, and even corporations, thereby making us influential. For instance, in a film series on Soviet television, Russian actor Vasily Livanov played the role of Sherlock Holmes with such perfection that the British Monarch was enthralled by his acting and conferred upon him the honorary membership of the Order of the British Empire.

Similarly, Songne Yacouba was gifted a carton of an herbal mixture for treating malaria and piles. The gift was given to him for emerging as the man of the match between his team, Kumasi Asante Kotoko Football Club, and Accra Hearts of Oak.

This is why you should strive to be excellent at what you do; you might not know who's watching you.

And be mindful of your behaviour when you become an influential person. Some people become heartless and abusive when power and status get into their heads. This led to Columbus's fall.

When you lead with an iron fist, in the beginning, you'll instil fear in your subjects. If you continue to lead in this manner, their fear of you will harden them and embolden them to rebel against you. I've seen this fate befall several business owners and managers who had repressed their staff and subordinates for far too long until each subordinate was determined to undermine the business in any way they could.

The owner of a school I knew managed his employees with a fist of iron and mistreated them for any little mistake they made, until one busy Monday morning, he found himself all alone with the students without a teacher or any other staff. Upon realising that they had all abandoned him, his heart started racing, and he was rushed to the hospital, where he was resuscitated, but he never recovered from the shock and died a few days later, after being discharged.

In August 1498, Columbus returned to Hispaniola from an expedition and found that many of the Spanish colonists were in rebellion against his rule. A number of them returned to Spain and badmouthed him in the Spanish Court, accusing him and his brothers of tyranny and gross mismanagement.

The Spanish Crown forced Columbus to make peace with the rebellious colonists on humiliating terms. Columbus was eventually kicked out of his job as governor and taken to Spain in chains, where he was locked up.

Had his expeditions not been beneficial to the Spanish Crown, and had he not cleverly enticed the King and Queen with the fortunes of a fourth voyage, his misdeeds, including the enslavement and brutal subjugation of the indigenes, would've had him sent to the gallows and quashed his sense of purpose.

On sexual misconduct, the internet has made it possible for victims to quickly identify with themselves and campaign against their past abusers. Social media is a great tool for this, and it has brought down a number of powerful men who were otherwise well-known and respected.

Among them in recent years are Harvey Weinstein, Bill Cosby, and R. Kelly, who ended up disgraced and incarcerated after decades of fantastic careers, fabulous successes, and global prominence.

Men should keep this in mind. Those who don't know should be told, and those who have forgotten should be reminded that sexual misconduct can kill a man's career in the long run, while constant abuse of power and repression breeds hatred and will eventually lead to a rebellion.

Understand the Social Milieu

Mamoudou Gassama, like most people from third-world countries, was hopeful for a better life Europe. To achieve his purpose, he first travelled from Burkina Faso through Niger and finally to Libya, where he was arrested and beaten. Undeterred by the beating, he still made his way through the Mediterranean and obtained papers to stay legally in Italy.

In 2017, he travelled via the Mediterranean migrant route to join his elder brother in France, where he worked in construction and lived in a hostel in the eastern suburb of Montreal, a place known as 'Little Bamako.' Mamoudou Gassama's stay in France, however, was illegal without having been granted asylum.

On May 26, 2018, the 22-year-old Mamoudou Gassama noticed a child dangling from a fourth-floor balcony of a building, and amid onlookers and honking cars at the nerve-racking sight, he ran across the street and sprang into a climbing action to save the child.

A viral video of the incident showed Gassama pulling himself up from balcony to balcony, like Spiderman. On reaching the fourth floor, he placed one leg over the balcony, reached out with his right arm, and lifted the child to safety.

Firefighters arrived shortly afterwards, but fortunately, Mamoudou Gassama had already saved the situation. Paris Mayor, Anne Hidalgo, praised Mamoudou Gassama on Twitter for his 'act of bravery' and personally thanked him on the phone.

Gassama told reporters that he had acted without thinking: 'I saw all these people shouting, and the cars sounding their horns. I climbed up like that, and thank God, I saved the child.' He added, 'I felt anxious when I saved the child...(when) we went into the living room, I began to shake, I could hardly keep standing, so I sat down.'

President Emmanuel Macron tweeted that in recognition of Gassama's 'heroic act,' his status in France would be made official with a residency card 'as quickly as possible.' The following week, Gassama sat next to him at the Élysée Palace.

He was awarded the Honour Medal for Courage and Devotion, offered a job in the fire service, and was granted French citizenship at the behest of President Macron. In addition, on June 24, 2018, he received the BET Humanitarian Award in Los Angeles.

If all these benefits went to a man who saved a child's life in France, you may guess what would've become of a man who saved the life of a US president, and your guess would be wrong.

On September 22, 1975, a 33-year-old former Marine called Oliver Sipple was among a crowd of onlookers in San Francisco to cheer and catch a glimpse of President Gerald Ford.

By sheer luck for President Gerard Ford, Oliver Sipple found himself standing next to Sara Jane Moore, a 45-year-old mother of four who wanted to assassinate the US president. Moore suddenly pulled her revolver and shot at the president, but she narrowly missed his head. And just before she could aim for another shot, Sipple moved swiftly to grab her arm before she pulled the trigger and accidentally shot a taxi driver, who survived.

Sipple was praised for his bravery, but soon after risking his life to save the president, he was outed by Harvey Milk, a prominent gay-rights activist.

Harvey Milk and Oliver Sipple had been close friends and associates. Milk was running for office as San Francisco city supervisor, and Oliver Sipple was on his campaign. So, when Oliver Sipple made the headlines for his heroism, Milk decided to ride on Sipple's fame to boost the fledgling gay-rights movement, without Sipple's consent.

While Oliver Sipple's heroism was trending, Harvey Milk reportedly said, 'It's too good an opportunity. For once, we can show that gays do heroic things, not just all that caca about molesting children and hanging out in the bathrooms.'

The press immediately switched from Sipple's heroism to his gayness, and the headline turned to, 'How a gay hero had saved the President's life.'

Sipple, who was raised in Detroit but had lived in San Francisco, was known in the San Francisco gay community, where he was an activist for gay rights. Back in Detroit, however, he was closeted.

Nonetheless, the new news headlines did Sipple a great disservice. First, he was a soldier who had served his country in Vietnam; during that time, he was wounded by shrapnel, and his hospital was shelled while he was on admission. Second, for risking his life to save the life of the US president.

Sipple's family became the subject of blazing gossip in the ensuing days. His mother was scandalised to hear about his sexuality; she disowned him and said she never wanted to speak to him again. His father and brothers were harassed and taunted at work.

Sipple became estranged from his family as a result. For President Ford, the best he could do for a man who had saved his life was to send him a polite thank you note rather than invite him to the White House or award him a medal of honor:

> I want you to know how much I appreciated your selfless actions last Monday. The events were a shock to us all, but you acted quickly and without fear for your own safety. By doing so, you helped to avert danger to me and others in the crowd. You have my heartfelt appreciation.

President Ford denied that his blatant shunning of Sipple, who had risked his life to save his, had anything to do with his sexuality. On the other hand, Sipple was unperturbed by the president's tepid attitude and treasured his appreciation note anyway.

His brother, George, stood by him despite his family's rejection. Apparently, George was more appreciative of Oliver Sipple for saving the president's life. But in the long run, Oliver Sipple came to regret saving the president's life as his own life went awry with depression and alcohol abuse.

Oliver Sipple felt he owed no one an explanation as to how he led his life, and that his sexuality was no man's business. Yet, for the anguish he felt the press/media had caused him, he sued seven different papers and 50 executives of magazines, newspapers, and news agencies for $15 million in damages, adding that his outing by Milk had caused him 'great mental anguish, embarrassment, and humiliation.'

The legal battle dragged on until the California Supreme Court dismissed the case, ruling that Sipple's sexual orientation was already known to hundreds of people prior to the news story. So, the media wasn't responsible for his issues.

When his mother died, his father reportedly barred him from attending her funeral. He was depressed for the next 14 years of his life, possibly due to schizophrenia.

He died in his apartment with a bottle of whisky in his hand. To no one's shock, President Gerald Ford didn't attend his funeral; instead, he sent a letter of condolence.

Explication

We live in societies that have distinct norms and those that are considered deviant. So far, the legal wrangling surrounding LGBTQ+ has settled in most developed economies, where people who identify as LGBTQ+ are no longer mistreated by the law.

But this situation isn't the same everywhere. A religious demography despises LGBTQ+ people. In this case, the last thing you want to do is out your sexuality among people who are religiously homophobic.

While writing this book, I coached a fresh graduate for a mid-level career in procurement. She passed the job interview and started work as a procurement officer. A month later, when the 2021 anti-LGBTQ bill frenzy was bubbling in Ghana's parliament, her boss brought her and the other recruits a human resource form on which she was to indicate, among other things, her sexual orientation.

She called me about the form, telling me for the first time that she was a lesbian, and she asked me if it was a good idea to indicate her sexuality. I advised her against it and told her to indicate that she was straight. I also reminded her of the fact that she was in a religious demographic where the majority of people are homophobic. But she insisted that she must be herself and went ahead and indicated on the form that she was lesbian.

Some days after she submitted the human resource form, she began experiencing prejudice at her workplace and was eventually handed a dismissal letter that only said her service was no longer needed. When she asked her colleagues what she had done wrong, they told her their boss thinks she harbours an evil spirit because whenever he calls them to his office for prayer, she doesn't close her eyes.

To avert these mishaps, you better be closeted, and if you're outed against your consent, as was Oliver Sipple's case, never admit it; deny it and leave the matter to public scepticism. You should rather be focused on your career and stay clear of LGBTQ+ discourse, lest you go canting like an Ohio lawmaker did. In 2017, the male lawmaker, who had been vocal about his Christian faith and anti-LGBTQ+ views, resigned after he was caught pants down making out with a man in his office.

Be Mindful of the Cultural Climate and Religious Factors

Wherever you find yourself, you must tread cautiously with the traditions and culture of the people. In truth, there are several turn-offs about traditions and culture, yet in public, you must be civil about what you detest and avoid acting in a manner that insults the culture of the people. Because you may go overboard and be met with fierce antagonism by cultural fanatics.

The same goes for religion. In a religiously tolerant society, you can only share your dissenting views politely and respectfully. But let me add that you must resist the temptation of pouring scorn on other people's fetishes, especially in jurisdictions governed by religious laws.

In August 2020, a 22-year-old musician from Kano State, in northern Nigeria, called Yahaya Sharif-Aminu, composed a song that was said to be derogatory towards Prophet Muhammed. The song went viral on WhatsApp and fuelled anger among the locals, who regarded the song as blasphemy.

This stoked a fierce protest, during which Yahaya Sharif-Aminu's family home was burnt amidst calls for authorities to take action against him. He was later arrested, found guilty of blasphemy, and sentenced to death by hanging.

While some locals lamented his fate, the leader of the protest who called for Yahaya Sharif-Aminu's arrest told the BBC that the judgment would serve as a warning to others contemplating toeing Yahaya's path. He added, 'When I heard about the judgment, I was so happy because it showed our protest wasn't in vain. This judgment would serve as a deterrent to others who feel they could insult our religion or prophet and go scot-free.'

If I had the privilege to be heard on this issue, I would've pleaded for mercy on Yahaya Sharif-Aminu's behalf. The next thing I would've done was to caution everyone else not to repeat what he did.

Some years ago, I coached a client on job hunting, during which he told me he was an atheist. I immediately cautioned him against professing atheism at his forthcoming job interview and told him that if a question on his religion came up, he should profess Christianity or Islam.

The reason is that many Christians in this demographic regard atheists and heathens as weird and unconventional due to years of incessant demonisation by the Christians' predecessors against African traditional believers, atheists, and heathens. This can be a reason for a Christian to withhold an opportunity from the latter. It's absurd; it shouldn't happen, and no one will admit to this bigotry, yet it happens.

A client of mine, who was brought up in a conservative Christian family, grew up believing that only members of his denomination were just. This belief became the basis of his recruitment policy, and he wouldn't employ heathens in his company. However, he continued to incur losses due to the dishonesty of his managers and the incompetence of his general manager.

In a meeting with his godfather and a fellow believer (in which I was present), he lamented how hard it is to get honest people to work with. In response, his godfather praised his deputy for being smart and said that his deputy was the brain behind his success.

My client then asked him which Christian denomination his deputy belonged to. His godfather replied, 'He has never stepped foot in a church or mosque, yet he's the most honest, selfless, and smartest person I've ever worked with.'

Of course, there are also religious adherents who are honest, selfless, and smart, but this boils down to their upbringing and individualities, not necessarily the fact that they're religious or irreligious.

Be Mindful of the Political Climate

Understanding the political climate of your resident country is crucial for your sense of purpose. In a typical democracy, citizens call out their leaders for wrongdoing. In Ghana, for instance, free speech and free press are pronounced, and we speak truth to power without fear of intimidation. But without incentive, I suggest you leave certain matters to the press, political adversaries, and freedom fighters to voice out. Why? Because speaking out against the authorities can make them vindictive. And if you're a soft target, they can show you where power lies.

Some years ago, a nurse friend caught some executives in the upper echelons of the health service in an act of corruption and decided to expose them on Facebook live. Fortunately, she called to tell me about her intention, and I asked her one question, 'Do you intend to work happily after exposing your superiors?' She responded, 'Yes'. Then I advised her to contact a certain journalist, pass on the information to him, and stay out of the matter. She later thanked me for the advice.

What could've happened if my nurse friend had acted on her initial thought? First, the exposé would trend and the culprits would be called out, but if they have strong ties with the ruling political party, they will get off scot-free. Second, my nurse friend would've been victimised at work.

In an authoritarian regime, however, criticizing the authorities is frowned upon, and the consequences of dissidence can be too harsh, if not extreme. In November 2020, Chinese regulators pulled a break on Ant Group by suspending its listing at the eleventh hour when the Ant Group was about to go public and raise as much as $37 billion. This would've been the biggest stock sale in modern history, and Ant Group would've been the biggest Fintech company in the world.

Jack Ma, the richest man in China at the time and the boss of Ant Group and Alibaba, was the target of the suspension, and it cost him dearly. What did he do?

On October 24, 2020, a week before the suspension of Ant Group from the Shanghai Stock Exchange, Jack Ma berated the Chinese financial regulatory system at a press conference. He called the system outmoded and said that the financial regulators seem like a kind of club for the elderly who want to play it too safe, something that isn't good for 'youth' economies like China.

He further called out the financial regulators for being extremely cautious and said that there's no innovation in this world without risk. And he said that Chinese banks were like pawnshops that would only lend money to people who had something to put up as collateral.

In response to Jack Ma's criticism, the financial regulators introduced a new regulation that rendered the Ant Group unqualified for making an IPO, thereby preventing Jack Ma from raising the $37 billion. Following the suspension, the Chinese government launched an antitrust investigation into Alibaba.

At this juncture, Jack Ma had to play it safe by keeping silent and out of public view to prevent further provocation.

Whenever I hold a career coaching session with fresh graduates, I caution them against doing national politics in the office. First, I examine their online footprints and delete anything that would be offensive to someone on the other side of the political divide.

Be mindful that people are fanatical about national politics, and since the proliferation of social media, recruiters check the online footprints of job applicants the same way that employers check on their employees. And when they find something politically distasteful, they disfavour the applicant.

To play it safe, you either have to leave your political views at the door before you enter the office or play along with the dominant force of your work hierarchy. If the latter is true, they'll regard you as a like-minded comrade and treat you accordingly. This can somehow pay you dividends.

As for office politics, you better know what you're getting from it before you get involved; otherwise, don't participate

CHAPTER SIX

Talent Acquisition

One of the mistakes hiring managers make in the 21st century is assuming that academic qualification is the only attestation of a candidate's capability and career readiness. But this notion is flawed because it doesn't pay heed to a candidate's aptitude, initiative, and skill set, thereby precluding the possibility of hiring a genius.

Notice that most of the luminaries and creative geniuses we've discussed had no degree, and those with degrees were usually ordinary college students. Yet, they were the most brilliant living things to which we owe gratitude for modern civilisation, economic fortune, scientific breakthroughs, and the spread of knowledge.

They include Albert Einstein, Winston Churchill, and John Gurdon. The rest were Michael Faraday, Thomas Edison, Nikola Tesla, and the Wright Brothers, to name a few.

Paradoxically, though the most outstanding college students show great promise in the classroom and still have the potential to reach the pinnacle of their career, they hardly get into the orbit of luminaries and creative geniuses whose common denominators are self-learning, a burning desire to pursue their vocation, and the zeal for wealth creation and extraordinary achievement. Also, not every extraordinary college student and 'well-qualified' job candidate will perform extraordinarily on the job.

In fact, some people are highly learned and have garnered a lot of certificates, but they come up short on aptitude, initiative, and skill set, and without having fire in their bellies, they simply can't deliver on the job. I've known people like that, and there are many of them. I've also known people with talent, skill set, and initiative, but due to their very limited education, they're not as competent as they should be.

The good news is that whether in the closet, classroom, or on the job, anyone with the desire to learn can do so and make up for their shortcomings. On the next page, you'll be inspired by some extraordinary achievers who proved that their brainpower carried more weight than a dozen paper qualifications.

Benjamin Franklin

In 1718, when Benjamin Franklin was 12 years old, his father apprenticed him to his elder brother, James Franklin, who was a pressman in Boston. This marked the beginning of Benjamin Franklin's career development.

Over the next five years, he acclimatised well to the press business and became versed therein. He also observed that effective writing was an uncommon skill, and that he could easily court attention with a well-turned piece. This made him consider becoming a career writer.

At first, he tried writing poetry, but he soon realised that he couldn't write effective lines, so he gave up. His next try was prose writing, and before he could find any book to learn from, he chanced on a volume of *The Spectator* in which were published Joseph Addison and Sir Richard Steele's famous periodical essays, which had appeared in England in 1711–1712. Benjamin Franklin became enthralled by their writing style and studied their essays to improve his writing.

From then on, he would spend hours reading and rereading *The Spectator* papers and copying excerpts to regurgitate. He would also attempt to rewrite those excerpts over and again until he could write them seamlessly from his memory. At this point, he was able to cull poetry from feature articles and turn it into prose.

He kept to this self-learning endeavour until he felt in his gut that he had developed his writing forte and was ready to show readers what a good writer he had become.

In 1721, James Franklin founded a weekly newspaper—*The New England Courant*—and invited contributors to submit content. Young Benjamin Franklin, then 16 years old, had a duty to proofread and typeset the manuscripts submitted by the contributors before they were published.

On several occasions, Benjamin sought James's consent to write for the *New-England Courant*, but James repeatedly denied him the opportunity. So, Benjamin hatched a plan: he created a persona of a middle-aged widow named Silence Dogood, and once every two weeks, he would drop a letter with an essay, up to a total of 14, at the door of his brother's printing shop.

The first of his series of 14 essays is on the next page, and they were all originally published in *The New England Courant*, to which they were subscribed, Silence Dogood:

Silence Dogood, No.1
Printed in the New-England Courant, April 2, 1722.
To the Author of the *New-England Courant.*

Sir,

It may not be improper in the first place to inform your Readers, that I intend once a Fortnight to present them, by the Help of this Paper, with a short Epistle, which I presume will add somewhat to their Entertainment.

And since it is observed, that the Generality of People, now a days, are unwilling either to commend or dispraise what they read, until they are in some measure informed who or what the Author of it is, whether he be *poor* or *rich*, *old* or *young*, a *Schollar* or a *Leather Apron Man*, &c. and give their Opinion of the Performance, according to the Knowledge which they have of the Author's Circumstances, it may not be amiss to begin with a short Account of my past Life and present Condition, that the Reader may not be at a Loss to Judge whether or not my Lucubrations are worth his reading.

At the time of my Birth, my Parents were on Ship-board in their Way from London to N. England. My Entrance into this troublesome World was attended with the Death of my Father, a Misfortune, which tho' I was not capable of knowing, I shall never be able to forget; for as he, poor Man, stood upon the Deck rejoicing at my Birth, a merciless Wave entered the Ship, and in one Moment carry'd him beyond Reprieve. Thus, was the *first Day* which I saw, the *last* that was seen by my Father; and thus was my disconsolate Mother at once made a *Parent* and a *Widow*.

When we arrived at Boston (which was not long after) I was put to Nurse in a Country Place, at a small Distance from the Town, where I went to School, past my Infancy and Childhood in Vanity and Idleness, until I was bound out Apprentice, that I might no longer be a Charge to my Indigent Mother, who was put to hard Shifts for a Living.

My Master was a Country Minister, a pious good-natur'd young Man, and a Batchelor: he labour'd with all his Might to instil vertuous and godly Principles into my tender Soul, well knowing that it was the most suitable Time to make deep and lasting Impressions on the Mind, while it was yet untainted with Vice, free and unbiass'd. He endeavour'd that I might be instructed in all that Knowledge and Learning which is necessary for our Sex, and deny'd me no Accomplishment that could possibly be attained in a Country Place; such as all Sorts of Needle-Work, Writing, Arithemetick, &c. and observing that I took a more than ordinary Delight in reading ingenious Books, he gave me the free Use of his Library, which tho' it was but small, yet was well chose, to inform the Understanding rightly, and enable the Mind to frame great and noble Ideas.

Before I had liv'd quite two Years with this Reverend Gentleman, my indulgent Mother departed this Life, leaving me as it were by myself, having no Relation on Earth within my Knowledge.

I will not abuse your Patience with a tedious Recital of all the frivolous Accidents of my Life, that happened from this Time until I arrived to Years of Discretion, only inform you that I liv'd a cheerful Country Life, spending my leisure Time either in some innocent Diversion with the neighbouring Females, or in some shady Retirement, with the best of Company, Books. Thus I past away the Time with a Mixture of Profit and Pleasure, having no affliction but what was imaginary, and created in my own Fancy; as nothing is more common with us Women, than to be grieving for nothing, when we have nothing else to grieve for.
As I would not engross too much of your Paper at once, I will defer the Remainder of my Story until my next Letter; in the meantime desiring your Readers to exercise their Patience, and bear with my Humours now and then, because I shall trouble them but seldom. I am not insensible of the Impossibility of pleasing all, but I would not willingly displease any; and for those who will take Offence were none is intended, they are beneath the Notice of Your Humble Servant,

Silence Dogood.

The essay above became the talk of the town, as did the rest that followed, and soon, Silence Dogood became a household name. The essays made jokes about certain aspects of daily life during the colonial era in America, and readers were amused. Male readers, in particular, were enthralled by Silence Dogood's articles, and they began sending her flirtatious remarks. Nobody suspected it was 16-year-old Benjamin Franklin.

In the end, James found out that Silence Dogood was non-existent and that it was his 16-year-old little brother, Benjamin, who was pretending to be her. James became angry with Benjamin, and they brawled. Benjamin felt bitter toward James for his overreaction, so he quit the job and left for Philadelphia.

In Philadelphia, Benjamin Franklin became a successful newspaper editor and pressman at the age of 23. From 1729 on, he published the *Pennsylvania Gazette*, which was generally acknowledged as the best of the colonial newspapers. He also made immense gains from publishing *Poor Richard's Almanack*, which he authored under the pen name Richard Saunders and circulated annually from 1732 to 1757.

Benjamin Franklin made a lot of money and gave out loans at interest during those years. He also invested in rental properties in Philadelphia and many coastal towns. By the late 1740s, he had become one of the wealthiest and most influential colonists in the northern part of North America.

In 1737, when he was 31 years old, he was appointed postmaster of Philadelphia. The position didn't pay much; however, he had the opportunity to mail his newspapers to readers at no cost, thereby making the *Pennsylvania Gazette* the most widely circulated publication in the colonies.

The postmaster job also enabled him to build an extensive network, which he leveraged for publicity on his achievements. He eventually became an intellectual celebrity and was the most admired American.

On August 10, 1753, he was promoted to deputy postmaster general, then to postmaster general in 1775. According to Carla J. Mulford, a professor of English at Penn State University and author of an upcoming book, *Benjamin Franklin's Electrical Diplomacy*, 'When he was appointed postmaster general for the American confederation in 1775, it clearly showed the extent to which he was trusted by American leaders to have Americans' best interests at heart.'

Benjamin Franklin's civic achievements include founding the Library Company, Philadelphia's first fire department, and the University of Pennsylvania, where he became its first president. As an accomplished diplomat, he became widely popular in France and was influential in forging the diplomatic relationship between France and America, referred to as Franco-American relations. This development was a monumental milestone for the American Revolution, during which America received shipments of vital munitions from France.

Mulford explains, 'Franklin had good foresight. He was a good system analyst. He was agreeable to work with when others were agreeable. And he was an excellent troubleshooter, who was able to figure out problems and finding solutions when plans went awry.'

What was Benjamin Franklin's Educational Attainment?

You may wonder which university Benjamin Franklin studied at or what degree he had. Could it be English, literature, linguistics, communication, journalism, or administration? Guess what? Benjamin Franklin didn't go past primary school, and it wasn't even likely he completed it as his formal education ended at the age of 10.

From then on, he worked briefly with his father before being apprenticed to his elder brother in the printing business. His accomplishments, thus, are solely credited to his inclination for self-learning.

His secret was his passion for reading; as a matter of fact, Benjamin Franklin was a voracious reader and sharp-witted.

In 1772, he wrote a letter to Joseph Priestley, the English chemist who invented carbonated water and discovered oxygen, carbon monoxide, nitric oxide, nitrous oxide, ammonia, sulphur dioxide, nitrogen peroxide, and the carbon cycle. In the letter, Benjamin Franklin explained the pros and cons list for the first time. Because of this, he is considered to be its creator.

> ...My way is to divide half a Sheet of Paper by a Line into two Columns, writing over the one Pro, and over the other Con. Then during three or four Days of Consideration, I put down under the different Heads short Hints of the different Motives that at different Times occur to me for or against the Measure. When I have thus got them all together in one View, I endeavour to estimate their respective Weights; and where I find two, one on each side, that seem equal, I strike them both out: If I find a Reason pro equal to some two Reason con, I strike out the three. If I judge some two Reasons con equal to some three Reasons pro, I strike out the five; and thus, proceeding I find at length where the Balance lies; and if after a Day or two of further consideration nothing new that is of Importance occurs on either side, I come to a Determination accordingly.

Benjamin Franklin was also a genius, known for inventing the lightning rod, the glass harmonica, the Franklin stove, bifocal glasses, and the flexible urinary catheter. He was indeed a polymath.

Elon Musk

Elon Musk obtained his bachelor's degree in economics and physics from University of Pennsylvania, then he enrolled at Stanford University to pursue a PhD in applied physics and material science. But he dropped out after two days and co-founded Zip2, a company that developed maps, directions, and yellow pages for online newspapers.

Compaq acquired Zip2 in February 1999 for $307 million. A 7% cut, amounting to $22 million, went to Elon Musk. He was 27 years old and went on to co-found x.com, an online financial service and email payment company, with $10 million from the $22 million cut he received from the sale of Zip2.

A year later, x.com merged with Confinity, which had an online money transfer service called PayPal. The merger then focused on the online money transfer specialty and was renamed PayPal in 2001. In October 2002, the online auction company, eBay, acquired PayPal for $1.5 billion, out of which Musk received $165 million. He was 31 years old.

Elon Musk had always been interested in space travel and wanted to get more people interested in it. He thought that for life to continue, humans needed to live on more than one planet. In 2001, he came up with the idea for the Mars Oasis project.

The project's aim was to land a miniature experimental greenhouse containing seeds on the planet Mars. It was expected that the seeds would germinate and grow into food crops on Martian soil, confirming the possibility of human survival on Mars.

But Elon Musk realised that actualising this idea would be prohibitive with the prevailing space transportation system. He needed a cheaper system to reduce the cost of spacefaring in order to enable humans to colonise Mars, so he sought out refurbished intercontinental ballistic missiles (ICBMs) to transport the greenhouse payloads into space.

In October 2001, Elon Musk travelled with Jim Cantrell (an aerospace consultant) and Adeo Ressi (his best friend from college and an investor) to procure cheap rockets from Russia, but Musk's naivety in rocket science was noticed and he was ridiculed by one of the Russian chief designers. Yet they still didn't get the cheap ICBMs they were looking for and returned to the US empty-handed.

The group returned to Russia in February 2002 with Mike Griffin, who, at the time, was working with Orbital Sciences (a maker of satellites and spacecraft) to procure three ICBMs. In their meeting with the Russian firm, they were offered one ICBM for $8 million, but Musk considered it too expensive and backpedalled. On their flight back to the US, a light-bulb moment dawned on him: 'What if I build the affordable rockets I need?'

Elon Musk, however, knew nothing about building rockets, nor did he have an academic qualification in rocket science. But if you look back at his lifepath, you'll notice a pattern shared by most creative geniuses.

At an early age, he had shown aptitude, skill, and initiative. He had also been a voracious reader and had an inclination for applied knowledge. For instance, he taught himself computer programming at the age of 10, and when he was 12 years old, he created a BASIC-based video game called Blastar, and sold the code to a magazine company for $500.00.

If Elon Musk had to build his own rockets to further his Martian ambitions, where would he begin? As a creative genius, he believed he was better off learning on his own. So he began studying from textbooks and consulting with the rocket scientists around him, and soon, he was deeply immersed in rocket science.

The depth of his immersion was such that he wouldn't part with his textbooks, including the books he borrowed from Jim Cantrell. They were *Rocket Propulsion Elements*, *Aerothermodynamics of Gas Turbine and Rocket Propulsion*, *Fundamentals of Astrodynamics* and *International Reference Guide to Space Launch Systems.* He became so versed in his studies that, at some point, he could quote excerpts of the books verbatim and was communicating with rocket experts in rocket science jargons.

It took Elon Musk two years to teach himself rocket science. With $100 million of his personal fortune, he founded SpaceX in 2002 as CEO and Chief Engineer. He also joined Tesla Motors as chairman and became the CEO and product architect in 2008.

As of 2022, he had been the longest-tenured CEO of an automotive manufacturer and the richest man on earth. However, what truly sets Elon Musk apart is his unquenchable thirst for knowledge and his incredible achievement of teaching himself how to build rockets. Musk's story serves as a powerful reminder that with enough determination and dedication, we can learn anything on our own, even surpassing what is typically taught in the most advanced college lecture rooms.

How Did Elon Musk Perform in College?

People are curious about Elon Musk's college GPA: how well he performed at UPenn, given his career accomplishments, reach of influence, wealth, and all the other reasons he is a household name. Before we get to that, let's get into how people he worked with have assessed him over the years. According to Jim Cantrell:

> Once he [Elon Musk] has a goal, his next step is to learn as much about the topic at hand as possible from as many sources as possible. He is by far the single smartest person that I have ever worked with.

> Period. I can't estimate his IQ but he is very very intelligent. And not the typical egghead kind of smart. He has a **real applied mind**.

In an article titled 'How Did Elon Musk Learn Enough About Rockets To Run SpaceX?' published on Inc4.com, an employee wrote:

> He was the quickest learner I've ever come across. You had this guy who knew everything from a business point of view, but who was also clearly capable of knowing everything from a technical point of view, and the place he was creating was a blank sheet of paper.

And according to Elon Musk himself: 'I know my rocket inside out and backward. I can tell you the heat-treating temper of the skin material, where it changes, why we chose that material, the welding technique…'

Having studied the lifepaths of hundreds of creative geniuses and extraordinary achievers, I found that they have a preference for applied learning, which explains why they learn better as self-learners, mentees, or apprentices.

College learning, on the other hand, may be too academic and thus too boring for them, especially if what they're learning has little relevance to their vocations and aspirations. This is why they might not perform too well in college because it's hard for them to commit study time to subjects they find irrelevant. This is also why they may drop out or score GPAs that are way below their high IQ. That notwithstanding, they can score excellent grades in subjects they find interesting.

Elon Musk might not be different. Below is an excerpt from an anonymous response on the Quora thread (107) What was Elon Musk's GPA at UPenn? - Quora

> When I taught Elon, he was just another student in the class. Not in my wildest dreams did I see him go on to build his tech empire.'
> Wait, you taught Elon? What was he like as a student?
> 'Fairly unremarkable. I didn't even remember teaching him until long after he graduated.'

Not long after I began writing this book, I met Christie, the mother of a pupil I taught some years ago. His name is Ryan. Christie lamented that Ryan's health problems put him in the hospital too often and made him miss too many classes, which led him to graduate with a pass.

I told Christie not to worry about that because there wasn't anything anyone could do about Ryan's GPA, and I assured her that if Ryan cultivated a sense of purpose, he would be accomplished and successful the same way he would've been if he had graduated with a first class and had a sense of purpose.

Two years later, I was waiting for a friend at a bank's parking lot when a gentleman drove past me in a newly registered posh SUV. He parked his car next to mine, came directly to where I was standing, and greeted me.

His suit, his shoes, and his sunglasses were on point. When he took off his glasses, I recognised him. It was Ryan, and I was happy to see him, more so after seeing on his business card that he was the project manager of a logistics company.

He told me, 'Thank you, Sir.' I asked him, 'What for?' He responded, 'My mum gave me your message on cultivating a sense of purpose; I digested it, and it has brought me this far.'

Degree Inflation

Amos had worked for more than 20 years as a technical officer (junior rank) in a research institution. He knew the ins and outs of every task performed by his department and had a firm grasp on every task performed at any desk in the department.

He was the go-to person in case there was any technical challenge, and he would fix it. He had also mentored several research scientists when they were technical officers, but he had no postgraduate qualification. That's the reason he was still a technical officer, though he had worked for more than 20 years.

In 2021, a vacancy for the head of department position was advertised, and Amos's colleagues urged him to apply. However, his application was disqualified, and one of his former mentees, who had a PhD, was given the appointment.

Amos was vexed and wanted to resign until a mutual friend with whom he worked told him to see me. When Amos and I met for the first time, knowing I was privy to his issue, he gave me his CV. I perused it, and I was impressed. We discussed books, politics, and education. He was one of the most erudite guys I've met, and I offered him a job as operations manager on behalf of a friend.

The pay and perks were much higher than a professor's salary at his workplace. Despite this offer, he kept whining about being denied the HOD position. He told me, 'Francis, I swear, I know the job better than anyone in the department, and I can play the role of HOD better than this boy they've appointed. I even mentored him, and he still doesn't understand the procedures.'

Obviously, Amos had missed an important point about his field of work. I told him, 'Amos, I've known you before your friend asked you to see me. I first heard about you from some student friends who came to work with you as interns. They told me you're phenomenal. But unfortunately for you, in your field of work, you won't get anywhere without a postgraduate qualification, and you already know this, so why did you apply for the position?' Amos didn't say a word. I continued, 'I know you're capable; that's why I'm offering you this job. However, if you want to continue working in research and rise to the top, then you must get a doctorate. Now tell me, are you interested in the job I'm offering you?'

At this point, Amos seemed to be reflecting on what I was saying; he accepted the offer and began working the following month.

After some months, a friend of mine named Collins, who has a PhD and works at the same institution where Amos worked, told me Amos couldn't have been an effective researcher or HOD without a PhD.

I chuckled at Collin's simple-mindedness on judging aptitude and potential, and I asked him if he knew of Tu Youyou. He answered, 'No.' 'How about Michael Faraday?' 'I know him,' he responded. 'Tell me about him.' 'He was a genius,' he replied. 'What was his highest academic qualification?' 'He had a PhD.' 'That's incorrect,' I refuted.

Michael Faraday wasn't a PhD holder. As a matter of fact, he never had a master's degree, a bachelor's degree, a diploma, or a senior high school or junior high school certificate. He never really had a formal education, as he was taught to read, write, and cipher at Sunday school.

The rest of his education was obtained through self-learning, and his career development was through an apprenticeship under an acclaimed chemist at the Royal Institution of Great Britain. He was called Humphry Davy.

Sir Humphry Davy's scientific endeavours include using electricity to isolate potassium, sodium, calcium, strontium, barium, magnesium, and boron. In other words, it was Humphry Davy who discovered the elements mentioned above. He's also renowned for inventing the miner's safety lamp, which he named after himself, the 'Davy' lamp. His most acclaimed achievement, however, was his discovery of Michael Faraday, the most influential scientist of the nineteenth century, whose picture Albert Einstein kept on his study wall.

According to Britannica:

> Faraday, who became one of the greatest scientists of the 19th century, began his career as a chemist. He wrote a manual of practical chemistry that reveals his mastery of the technical aspects of his art, discovered a number of new organic compounds, among them benzene, and was the first to liquefy a 'permanent' gas (i.e., one that was believed to be incapable of liquefaction). His major contribution, however, was in the field of electricity and magnetism. He was the first to produce an electric current from a magnetic field, invented the first electric motor and dynamo, demonstrated the relationship between electricity and chemical bonding, discovered the effect of magnetism on light, and discovered and named diamagnetism, the peculiar behaviour of certain substances in strong magnetic fields. He provided the experimental, and a good deal of the theoretical, foundation upon which James Clerk Maxwell erected classical electromagnetic field theory.

In 1832, Oxford University awarded him an honorary Doctor of Civil Law degree, and he received other accolades and medals in recognition of his works.

After I briefed Collins on Michael Faraday's accomplishments, I asked him if he still thinks Amos couldn't have been an effective researcher without a PhD. He smiled and said, 'Don't blame me; it's not my fault for misjudging; it's the system that made me think the way I thought, and I bet that if Michael Faraday finds himself with us today, the system will prohibit him from effectuating his aptitude, and his potential will amount to nothing. I guess it's the same system that has prohibited Amos from climbing; it's a flawed system that doesn't recognise aptitude but only credentials. Yet, considering Michael Faraday's limited education, I bet that there isn't any academic in my institution, whether a doctor or a professor, whose work can match up with his contribution.'

I was glad Collins had had a change of mind about his view of credentialism as an absolute measure of competence. Of course, I admit, some people can't be effective researchers without a PhD, and Collins couldn't be entirely wrong about that. However, there are still some PhD holders who aren't effective researchers, whereas some other people were born with fire in their bellies. With them, whether they have a degree or not, a PhD or not, once they get to the field, they'll excel and outshine everyone. Michael Faraday was one of them.

Next, Collins and I spoke about Amos' suitability for the head of department position:

Just as credentialism doesn't always equate to competence, being the most technically capable person doesn't guarantee effective leadership. Charles Steinmetz, for instance, was a genius and a standout in the field of electricity. However, as HOD at General Electric Company, he was a failure and had to be fired. But because he was an important technical person, they gave him a new title as a consulting engineer and gave the Head of Department job to someone else.

Similarly, being the most learned person in the room doesn't necessarily make you an effective leader. Contrary to this reality, in the public sector, one becomes automatically qualified to lead if he has the highest educational attainment.

This is one of the reasons for the widespread incompetence in the public sector, where some organisations thrive only because they're statutorily not-for-profit, state-funded, and monopolies, and not because they've had a succession of managing directors with meritorious academic qualifications.

In principle, effective leadership doesn't come with academic qualifications. It's either inherent or learnt; if you don't have it, you must learn it. There are five things to look out for in order to tell if someone would be an effective leader: First, a leader must be intelligent; this attribute must not be overlooked or downplayed. Regardless of the enormous affluence or influence a person wields, making them a leader if they're clueless and unintelligent is akin to shooting yourself in the foot, and there'll be the devil to pay. Second, consider their previous initiatives and problem-solving proclivity. Third, a leader must be bold; a timid person must not lead. Fourth, they command respect by leading by example, appreciating their subordinates, and rewarding the deserving ones; and fifth, an effective leader is feared by the group, not because they bully, but because they're intolerant of nonsense, instil discipline, and punish the bad guys accordingly.

'Now tell me,' I asked Collins. 'Do you think Amos couldn't have been an effective head of department without a PhD?' Collins smiled once more and admitted that he had made a mistake.

Fortunately, Amos had both aptitude and initiative, and I saw leadership qualities in him too. However, his strife about being denied the head of department position was pointless because he already knew that academic credentials came before competence in his field of work. This brings to mind the Chinese meritocracy system and Project 523.

Chinese Meritocracy

In the Chinese meritocracy system, ability and virtue are the first and last criteria for a public office appointment. According to Zhang Weiwei, Director of the China Institute at Fudan University, China's rise to global prominence isn't necessarily attributable to an economic model.

> By the meritocracy system, competent leaders are selected based on performance and broad support, through a vigorous process of screening, opinion surveys, internal evaluation, and various types of elections. This is much in line with the Confucian tradition of meritocracy. After all, China is the first country to invent the civil service examination system. Today, China practices meritocracy across the whole political stratum. Criteria based on poverty eradication, job creation, local economic growth, social development and environmental protection are all key criteria for selecting and promoting officials. From the Chinese point of view, the nature of the state, including its legitimacy, has to be defined by its substance, that is good governance, competent leadership and success in meeting people's needs. So despite its many deficiencies, the Chinese polity has delivered the world's fastest-growing economy and has vastly improved living standards for most Chinese. While Western governance allows for the exit of bad leaders through regular elections, but in China's Confucian tradition of meritocracy, a state should always strive for the best of the best options by choosing leaders of the highest calibre. This is by no means easy, but the effort to this end should be ceaseless and continuous. China's political and institutional arrangements and innovations so far have produced a system that has in many ways combined the best option of selecting well-tested competent leaders. – Zhang Weiwei.

You may be wondering which one is appropriate for the economy. Meritocracy or credentialism?

While cronyism, nepotism, and credentialism are conspicuous in feeble and flawed economies, they're also not appropriate for business and enterprise. The Chinese meritocracy system, on the other hand, has worked well as an economic model, thereby placing China's economy second only to that of the United States.

What does this mean for your sense of purpose or as a leader of an institution? Meritocracy as a talent acquisition model is more effective than credentialism, nepotism, and cronyism. Period!

Project 523

In 1969, during the 14th year of the Vietnam War, the Vietnamese soldiers were ravaged by malaria in equal measure as their enemies' firepower. China was an ally of Vietnam, and alarmed by the malaria death toll, they funded an antimalarial medication development project. The project was codenamed Project 523, and a Chinese scientist named Tu Youyou was appointed to lead the project.

Tu Youyou began her research by reviewing a myriad of traditional literature and perusing ancient texts that were written thousands of years ago. She also travelled to remote regions and foraged for herbs that might be efficacious. After several months, she identified about 600 plants and 2,000 possible remedies.

She methodically narrowed the prospective herbs down to 380 and tested each one after another on laboratory mice. This was the most demanding aspect of the project. Tu Youyou said, 'It was a very laborious and tedious job, particularly when you faced one failure after another.'

Tu Youyou and her team ran hundreds of tests that continuously yielded nothing until they tested an extract from the sweet wormwood plant, known in Chinese as *qinghao*. This extract showed promise, and Tu Youyou was excited about the result. But to her disappointment, she began observing inconsistencies in the extract's efficacy, and though it had taken her two years to get to that phase, she stopped the process and started all over.

To begin anew, Tu Youyou reviewed every test she had run and reread every piece of literature in search of a clue she might've missed. Then she chanced on a single sentence in the book, *Handbook of Prescription for Emergencies*, written over 1500 years ago.

The sentence had to do with heat, explaining that high temperatures denature the active ingredient in sweet wormwood plants during the extraction process. This insight led Tu Youyou to redesign the extraction process, using solvents with low boiling points until she got an extract that was consistently efficacious.

Now, it was time for human trials, but there wasn't a facility in China they could use, and due to the secretive nature of the project, going outside China for a trial was out of the question. They reached a dead end, and Tu Youyou volunteered herself for the human test because she couldn't see any other way out.

Her plan to be the first person to try her own medicine was one of the bravest things a scientist in the field of medicine could do. Together with two other members of Project 523, they infected themselves with malaria and took the first doses of their new drug. The trial was successful, as the three volunteers recovered quickly and safely.

Despite the project's success and her self-sacrifice, the Chinese government had strict rules that barred Tu Youyou from publishing her research findings. But she continued her research and learnt of the drug's structure, which she identified as artemisinin, upon which she developed a second antimalarial medication.

After this point, Tu Youyou had to wait until 1978 to publish her work, and the World Health Organization had to wait until 2000 to approve artemisinin as a medicine to treat malaria.

So far, artemisinin has been administered to malaria patients over 1 billion times and has saved millions of lives. For her accomplishments, Tu Youyou received the 2011 Lasker–DeBakey Clinical Medical Research Award as the first Chinese, and in 2015, she won the Nobel Prize in Physiology or Medicine as the first Chinese female.

Tu Youyou's accomplishment is all the more remarkable because she has no PhD or master's degree. She also had no international research experience and was not even a member of any Chinese national institution. This earned her the moniker 'The Professor of the Three Noes.'

Tu Youyou would never have been chosen to lead Project 523 in a credentialing system because she lacked postgraduate academic credentials. But there she was in a meritocracy system, where aptitude comes before academic credentials, and she achieved a feat that not every postgraduate degree holder with the highest credentials and research experience could achieve.

The Hiring

Some time ago, a human resource friend of mine named Abdul was tasked with recruiting top-tier candidates to fill various administrative roles. He called for graduates with first-class degrees to apply for the administrator positions and those with other classes to apply as administrator deputies. In essence, Abdul was about to designate positions based on GPAs, and when he received the job applications, he shortlisted only candidates from elite universities.

However, his boss didn't find his method impressive. He took the opportunity to share some valuable advice, saying, 'Son, not every high achiever in college will excel in their job, and conversely, those with average grades can still be extraordinary in their careers. In fact, some of the most outstanding professors, lawyers, teachers, engineers and doctors I've known were only average students. Moreover, some of the world's most accomplished professionals were individuals who dropped out or never attended elite universities. Lastly, a candidate's competence and suitability for a job cannot be solely determined by their GPAs, no matter how high or low they may be. Exceptional abilities cannot be captured by certificates. Take a moment to absorb this.'

Explication

Abdul's outlook on talent acquisition was lame and commonly shared by many hiring managers. His boss, however, wasn't the only person to disagree with his method of recruiting top-tier talents. According to the CEO of McDan Shipping Company, Dr. Daniel McKorley, he doesn't put much premium on certificates before he employs. He averred that he had witnessed several circumstances where those with the best certificates had failed to deliver. He said, 'Running interviews, you can see eloquent and smart people, but when you put them to work, it is very appalling.' He, however, maintained that certificates should be the basis, though he wouldn't put much premium on them.

'Now, restart the recruitment process,' Abdul was instructed. 'Your method will bring us the best students from school, but the best candidates for the job may fall through the cracks.'

Mortified by his boss's reproof, Abdul called and asked for my thoughts on his boss's viewpoint. I told him his boss was absolutely right.

It is indeed true that many highly talented individuals might not have equal opportunities or resources compared to others, which can hinder them from showcasing their skills and abilities. Nevertheless, it is of utmost importance to acknowledge that talent and extraordinary capability can emerge from any corner, making it crucial to establish a diverse and inclusive hiring process that enables individuals of all walks of life to demonstrate their worth. Companies that invest in considering candidates from diverse backgrounds may uncover hidden gems capable of adding tremendous value to their organisation.

With this insight, I referred Abdul to Elon Musk's talent acquisition strategy and Warren Buffet's quote. Putting the strategy and quote together will give you the corporate version of the Chinese meritocracy system.

Elon Musk, a visionary genius who holds the esteemed position of being the wealthiest individual globally (as of the time of writing this chapter) while also leading the iconic companies Tesla and SpaceX, has keenly observed that degrees, in all their various forms and sizes, do not provide a comprehensive representation of a candidate's true competence, proficiency, and character.

So, when hiring, though he would notice a candidate's academic qualifications, he looks beyond them. To Musk, evidence of exceptional ability and a track record of exceptional achievement are far more important than a degree from a prestigious university. He averred that if a person has a track record of exceptional achievement, then it's likely that it'll continue.

When he was asked whether he considered the name of the college a job applicant attended when evaluating a potential Tesla employee, he responded, 'There is no need even to have a college degree at all or even high school diploma to work at Tesla. If somebody graduated from a great university, that may be an indication that they'll be capable of great things, but it's not necessarily the case. If you look at say, people like Bill Gates or Larry Ellison, Steve Jobs, these guys didn't graduate from college, but if you had a chance to hire them, of course, that would be a good idea.'

Could Elon Musk be wrong about his talent acquisition strategy? No. I bet he had observed that ingenuity emanates from the brain, not from degrees. And being the boss of Tesla and an avid reader, I have no doubt that he had read how Nikola Tesla was hired by Thomas Edison.

Thomas Edison never went to college but was a self-taught genius who, until 2013, was the most prolific inventor in history, with 1093 US patents.

In June 1884, Nikola Tesla arrived in New York City with only four cents in his pocket and a letter of recommendation to Thomas Edison from his former employer, Charles Batchelor. The letter of recommendation read: 'My Dear Edison: I know two great men, and you are one of them. The other is this young man!'

As succinct as Charles Batchelor's recommendation of Nikola Tesla was, it informed Thomas Edison about everything Nikola Tesla was and would be: a genius and prolific inventor. The most notable of Nikola Tesla's inventions, to which we owe him gratitude, is the alternating current (AC) electric system: the most widely used electrical system today. Yet, Tesla was a dropout.

Elon Musk further explained that when he interviews prospective employees, he asks them to give him a summary of their career and describe to him how they solved some of the most difficult challenges they encountered. He would further inquire about the details of the problem they described, and by doing so, he could tell if they were being truthful about their participation. If they hadn't been responsible for solving those problems, they wouldn't be able to answer.

Elon Musk has used this strategy to recruit some of the best talents in the world (not the best graduates) to work with. However, this strategy was already known and had been applied for centuries against credentialism. Sir Humphry Davy, for instance, recruited Michael Faraday after Michael Faraday presented him with evidence of exceptional ability.

Michael Faraday had a limited education. He learnt reading, writing, and ciphering at Sunday school. When he turned 14, he became a bookbinder and bookseller apprentice for seven years. It was during his apprenticeship that he thoroughly educated himself by reading extensively. One of his most cherished books was *The Improvement of the Mind*, authored by James Watts, and he assimilated the principles and suggestions therein.

Michael Faraday had already developed an interest in science, especially electricity. However, he was mostly influenced by the book *Conversations on Chemistry*, which stimulated his interest in chemistry.

In 1812, towards the end of his seven-year apprenticeship, Michael Faraday attended several lectures by Sir Humphry Davy. At each lecture, Faraday took notes, which eventually ballooned into a 300-page book and sent it to Sir Humphry Davy. Sir Humphry Davy was impressed, and his reply to Michael Faraday was immediate and kind.

In 1813, one of the Royal Institution's assistants was fired, and Humphry Davy was asked to find a replacement. Michael Faraday came to mind, and he offered him the job as a chemical assistant at the Royal Institution.

Hence, starting off as an apprentice of Humphry Davy without pursuing further studies or anything of the sort but self-learning, Michael Faraday excelled above any chemist of his time, including his mentor, Sir Humphry Davy, and became the most accomplished scientist the world had ever known.

Google has recently taken a turn from the norm of hiring talent from specific top schools. As of 2013, up to 14% of some of their programme teams were filled with employees who had never been to college.

Google shifted from the norm based on an analysis of its employees. Being led at the time by their Executive Chairman, Eric Schmidt (PhD, University of California, Berkeley), they found no relationship between job performance and GPA or college affiliation. The former Senior Vice President of People Operations at Google, Laszlo Bock, even said that GPAs are worthless criteria for assessing a job candidate.

My last referral to Abdul was Warren Buffet's quote: 'In looking for people to hire, look for three qualities: integrity, intelligence, and energy. And if they don't have the first, the other two will kill you.'

Look into Mischievous Behaviour

Top-notch corporations are pools of top-tier talents and should be the first point of consideration if you want to recruit the crème de la crème, but I can bet that the finest talent may not be there yet. It could be a lowlife on the street or a ghetto hustler who never gets the chance to prove their worth, and even if they do, they may not be properly recognised.

Given the accounts of the fascinating people I've discussed thus far, none of them could quickly learn a medical procedure and perform it on the spot, but Ferdinand Demara did it.

Demara was born in the town of Lawrence, Massachusetts, in 1921, and was said to enjoy pranking his townspeople more than anything else. He eventually lost interest in school and dropped out at the age of 16. Even so, he was mischievous but smart, and he was said to have had a photographic memory. After dropping out, he ran away from home to Rhode Island, where he became a Trappist monk.

Two years later, he was told he couldn't be a Trappist monk, probably because he did something mischievous! So, they sent him to a Brothers of Charity home near Montreal, Canada, instead. Later, he was sent to the Brothers of Charity boys' home in West Newbury, Massachusetts, to teach a fourth-grade class. But he quit and left after getting into an argument with his boss.

The following year, he stole the identity of his army friend, called Anthony Ignolia, and joined the army, but he soon went AWOL. This marked the beginning of his imposter escapades. Next, he joined the United States Navy and trained as a hospital corpsman, but because he didn't attain the position he desired, he faked his death and re-emerged with the identity and credentials of Robert Linton French (PhD) and had a job as a religion-oriented psychologist.

But Demara didn't stay on one job for too long and had to leave. Yet, still as Dr. French, he applied for various jobs at the Catholic College and landed a psychology teaching role at Gannon College. He was later appointed dean of the School of Philosophy, during which he taught general psychology, industrial psychology, and abnormal psychology. He even wrote and published a booklet titled *How to Raise Your Child*, which was well received. However, he was forced to resign too soon after being caught forging cheques.

He was finally caught by the FBI, but not for fraud or impersonation. Instead, he had left the Navy. He was found guilty of desertion and handed an 18-month sentence at the Naval Disciplinary Barracks, San Pedro,

California. He stole another identity after being released from prison and used it to study law and join a Roman Catholic brotherhood.

While with the brotherhood, he met and became acquainted with a young Canadian surgeon named Joseph C. Cyr. Joseph C. Cyr had recently moved to the United States and sought help from Demara to complete his immigration process. With all of his legal documents in hand, Demara jumped at the chance to impersonate Dr. Cyr. He moved to Canada promptly and joined the Korean War as a surgeon.

At first, he was stationed at the base. During his time there, he lied to the other surgeons, saying that he was writing a handbook for lumberjacks on how they could perform life-saving operations on one another. And while he pretended to be writing instructions on how to perform certain procedures, he got the other surgeons to also write step-by-step instructions on how to perform other procedures. He was adamant that they write in plain English because he wanted to learn quickly from the manual.

The war intensified, and Demara was called to duty on the Pacific front, aboard the *HMCS Cayuga*, a Royal Canadian Navy destroyer. At the time, there was a naval captain on board who had a terrible toothache and wanted the tooth taken out. Demara had no idea how to extract a tooth, so he looked in the handbook he had 'co-authored' with the other surgeons back at base and successfully extracted the captain's tooth.

As the war raged on, 16 Korean combat casualties were brought to the *HMCS Cayuga* for treatment. They needed immediate surgery, or else they would all die. All eyes were on Ferdinand Demara, the ship's sole 'surgeon,' and after ordering that the wounded soldiers be taken to the operating room and prepared for surgery, he vanished for a few moments.

Apparently, he sneaked into his office with a textbook on general surgery and speed-read the procedures he needed to perform on the soldiers, which included a major chest surgery. After a short while, he re-emerged and operated on the soldiers. They all survived.

Demara's most profound procedure was removing a bullet from a wounded soldier. It was a big deal at the time, and his success at it made headlines in the Canadian newspapers. One of the newspapers landed in the hands of the real Dr. Joseph C. Cyr's mother, and she noticed that an imposter was impersonating her son. Word spread and reached the *HMCS Cayuga.*

Captain James Plomer, however, didn't press charges against Demara because he felt embarrassed for allowing a quack into the navy unnoticed. So, he dismissed him quietly.

Ferdinand Waldo Demara, however, continued impersonating, and his escapades were legendary, including his impersonation of Brother John Payne of the Christian Brothers of Instruction.

Acting as though he were Brother John Payne, he wanted the teachings of the religious brotherhood to be better known and more widespread. To further his cause, he founded LaMennais College in Alfred, Maine, and proceeded on his own to have the college chartered by the state. LaMennais College is now Walsh University.

You could say that Captain James Plomer should've let Ferdinand Demara, who never went to medical school but was a skilled self-taught 'trauma surgeon,' keep doing his job on the *HMCS Cayuga*, but that would've been an abetment. Still, I would've suggested that he be sent to medical school for training, regardless of the admission requirements, and retained as a surgeon.

In hindsight, looking into a mischievous act is another way to find a great person or a person with a lot of potential, especially if there is a way to stop them from being mischievous. That is exactly what FBI agent Carl Hanratty did to change Frank William Abagnale Jr. from his old ways.

In the film, *Catch Me If You Can*, Frank William Abagnale Jr. impersonates a Pan Am pilot and forges airline paycheques worth millions of dollars. The FBI took up the matter, and agent Carl Hanratty was assigned to track down Frank. Agent Carl kept track of Frank's other impersonation schemes, like when he pretended to be Dr. Frank Conners and practised medicine as if he were him.

Frank was eventually caught by Agent Carl, and while he was in prison, Carl would sometimes visit him. On one of these visits, he showed Frank a fraudulent cheque from a case he was investigating. Frank immediately figured out that the bank teller was involved in the fraud. Carl was impressed, and he convinced the FBI to allow Frank to serve the rest of his sentence in the FBI Financial Crimes Unit. Frank agreed to the deal, and his performance on the job was sterling.

In real life, Frank Abagnale Jr. did not finish high school, but after doing his time, he used his knowledge and experience in fraud and impersonation to assist businesses and government agencies in preventing and detecting fraudulent activity. He works as a secure document consultant and has written four books on how to avoid fraud and identity theft.

Whose Idea was it?

Abbey's enterprise was failing due to his son's mismanagement. So, he fired him and took over as CEO, but it was nearly too late as the enterprise was on the brink of collapse.

He called me as his last recourse. I listened to him and advised him to solicit ideas from every manager and staff of the company. I also asked him to announce a reward for whoever brought the most practical idea. He responded, 'I've held several meetings with my managers, and we've exhausted every option.' I immediately drew his attention to what I had just told him, 'Every manager and staff' 'Oh, my bad,' said Abbey. 'The staff certainly aren't as smart as their managers, but I'll see.' And he left cheerless, perhaps due to the simplicity of my advice. Before he left, I told him to come back for a wrap-up when he got the most practical idea.

The next day, Abbey held a forum with his managers and staff and promised 2% equity to the person whose idea would save the company. They did the math on the 2%, and it was substantial. This engendered all kinds of ideas from the management and staff.

Finally, Abbey received a proposal with the title *Project Save Ship*, which gave him a glimmer of hope. It was from Smith, an understated staff driver who hadn't been to college. Abbey invited Smith to meet with him and his investors for a presentation, and Smith impressed them. Afterwards, he left the boardroom and went back to his driving duties with a written contract on the 2% equity, which was applicable only if the idea worked.

Abbey then commissioned the *Project Save Ship* team with every dime he had. The team was to execute Smith's proposal in a bid to salvage the enterprise.

In the first quarter of its execution, *Project Save Ship* showed promise. By mid-year, the enterprise was yielding a steady stream of revenue, but the project tanked before long and the enterprise collapsed, owing to the fact that the team's leader was bereft of ideas and direction. Abbey lost his investment and blamed his son for collapsing his enterprise.

The Wrap-Up

I chanced on Abbey again at a friend's wedding reception, and I asked him why he didn't return. He admitted his regret for not coming back for the wrap-up and narrated everything that led to the collapse of his enterprise.
I had much to tell him on that day, including the advice I would've given him if he had returned, and I'll share it with you.

During the reign of Ramesses II, the Pharaoh of Egypt (1279–1213 BCE), he had a dream in which he was standing by the Nile, and out of it came seven cows that were sleek and fat and grazed among the reeds. Seven other ugly and gaunt cows followed in succession from the Nile, stood beside the sleek and fat cows, and ate them up.

Pharaoh woke up from the dream, fell asleep again, and had a second dream. In this dream, he saw seven heads of healthy and good grains growing on a single stalk, and seven other thin and scorched heads of grain sprouted and swallowed up the seven healthy full heads.

At daybreak, Pharaoh woke up and was confounded by the dream. He summoned all the magicians and wise men of Egypt and put his dream before them for interpretation, but none of them understood it. Pharaoh's chief cupbearer was present, and looking upon the confused magicians and wise men, he remembered someone he knew from his days in Potiphar's prison; his name was Joseph, son of the Jewish patriarch, Jacob. When he was in prison, the chief cupbearer had a perplexing dream that no one could interpret but Joseph.

> Then the chief cupbearer told his dream to Joseph, and he said to him, 'In my dream, now behold, there was a vine before me, and on the vine were branches. And as it budded, its blossoms came up, and its clusters of grapes grew ripe. And the cup of Pharaoh was in my hand, and I took the grapes and squeezed them into the cup of Pharaoh. Then I placed the cup into the hand of Pharaoh. Then Joseph said to him, 'This is its interpretation: The three branches, they are three days. In three days, Pharoah will lift up your head and will restore you to your office. And you shall put the cup of Pharaoh into his hand as was formerly the custom when you were his cupbearer.' (Genesis 40:9–13, Lexham English Bible).

The chief cupbearer excitedly recounted his meeting with Joseph to Pharoah. Intrigued, Pharoah sent for Joseph, who listened intently as Pharoah described his dream. With rapt attention, joseph interpreted the dream:

> The dream meant that there would be seven years of abundance followed by seven years of famine, and the reason why the dream was twofold is that it's certain to come to pass and imminent.

To offset the famine, Joseph proposed to Pharaoh that he appoint a discerning and wise Overseer of Egypt and put him in charge of commissioners who would take a fifth of all harvests in Egypt during the seven years of abundance. These harvests were to be stored in silos as the country's buffer stock for the seven-year lean season.

Egypt, by then, was the most civilised nation on earth. In its north, on the coast of the Mediterranean Sea, was the city of Alexandria, known as the intellectual centre of the world, where Archimedes studied to become the most reputed mathematician of antiquity. So for a country so replete with intellectuals, Ramesses II would have no trouble finding an expert for the role Joseph had proposed, but it didn't matter to him that Joseph hadn't been schooled in Alexandria. First, the problem was interpreted by Joseph; he also proposed the most laudable solution, and if there was anyone more suitable to execute the solution, it would be no other person but Joseph himself. Ramesses II, therefore, appointed Joseph as Vizier of Egypt, answerable only to the Pharaoh, and he delivered on his mandate.

Abbey, at this point, was scratching his head, 'I made a mistake,' he yielded. 'How?' I asked him. 'My son lacks discernment and wisdom, despite the expensive schools I sent him. I shouldn't have made him the CEO. I should've made him begin from the bottom and work his way to the top.' 'What else have you learnt?' I asked him. He responded remorsefully, 'I should have put Smith in charge of *Project Save Ship*. It was his idea. I erred big time. I thought Kamal (the marketing manager) could have handled the project better; he holds two master's degrees and he's smart, but *Project Save Ship* was Smith's idea, and only he would've conceived the most sense of direction in executing it.'

Is Postgraduate Degree a Must?

Education doesn't just take place in stuffy classrooms and university buildings; it can happen everywhere, every day to every person. – Richard Branson.

Is a postgraduate degree a must? Three categories of graduates have asked me this question. And the answer I've given them has always been 'yes' or 'maybe', but never 'no.' These graduates either wanted to be entrepreneurs, academics/researchers, or corporate workers. The former were considering MBAs, and the latter didn't point to any particular field. I'll address the former first.

The Entrepreneurs

Unlike the MBA class, where you need a high level of cognitive function and IQ to be a standout student and excel in your exams, in entrepreneurship, you need grit, a high Adversity Quotient, and street wisdom to succeed.

That's why a one- or two-year MBA programme can't compare to what an entrepreneur learns through years of blood, sweat, and tears. It's for this reason that Mark Cuban, who took MBA classes at Indiana University and also has hands-on experience as a business founder, said that the MBA is the most overrated college degree and that one can still get the same value of knowledge from other online portals for less cost, adding that experience is more valuable.

But take note: Mark Cuban is an accomplished entrepreneur, a billionaire as proof of his entrepreneurial success, and a luminary. No one would ask him to show his degree to prove a point. Moreover, his statement comes against the backdrop of his entrepreneurial experience, which, as I've already stated, an MBA can't compare with.

So, how valuable is entrepreneurial experience? The facts speak for themselves. As of 2022, Elon Musk was the richest man in the US and the world, Aliko Dangote was the richest person in Africa, Mukesh Ambani was the richest man in Asia, Carlos Slim was the richest man in Latin America, Bernard Arnault was the richest man in Europe, and Gina Rinehart was the richest person in Australia. All of the above-mentioned individuals are business tycoons, and none of them has an MBA or any other master's degree.

How did they learn to keep their momentum? The knowledge they gained from starting their enterprises, the mistakes they made, the failures they encountered, the resilience with which they kept moving, the perseverance that kept them from giving up, and their years of blood, sweat, and tears were what kept their momentum.

These experiences make entrepreneurs well-grounded and inspire them to act more decisively than they would possibly do with merely an MBA. On top of that, they read books. Whenever Elon Musk was asked how he learnt to build rockets, he answered, 'I read books and talked to people. I mean, that's how one learns anything. There're lots of great books out there and a lot of smart people.'

As such, reading more books than those with formal education will make you more knowledgeable than them. Even so, it's still worth getting an MBA, and it's not unusual for a billionaire to hold one. Michael Bloomberg, for instance, is among the list of billionaires who believe they wouldn't be where they are today without the knowledge and networks they built during their years in university. He ranks as the 13th richest person in the world, with a net worth of $76.8 billion as of the time I was writing this paragraph. He holds an MBA and a degree in electrical engineering.

The Academic/Researcher/Corporate Worker

A PhD is crucial and non-negotiable if you're an aspiring academic or researcher. And the earlier you pursue it, the better. Similarly, if you're an employee, whether in the private or public sector, a postgraduate degree might be the only means to qualify for an executive position and augment your earning potential.

There's no question about that: in the United States, for instance, education plays a significant role in determining a person's net worth. The typical graduate of a four-year college has a net worth four times that of someone who began college but did not complete it, and five times that of someone with only a high school diploma. This is the status quo, but again, there are exceptions.

Ideally, it's better to be sure of your career aspiration before deciding on the postgraduate programme to pursue. This will save you the time and cost of studying a programme that might not be relevant to your career. Above all, postgraduate studies can give you a deeper insight into your career and improve your proficiency.

By now, I'm sure someone has concluded that first class students and people with high academic inclinations aren't ingenious. But read over from page one, and you won't find such a statement, and I couldn't have said that because there are people whose aptitudes alone didn't make them geniuses until after they had pursued postgraduate education.

One of such geniuses was a chemist, an engineer, and a scientist called Marvin Pipkin. In high school, he showed an aptitude for chemistry, and he's said to have known chemistry better than all his classmates combined.

Following a stint at a prospecting firm, he had his second job at the International Mineral and Chemical Corporation, where he found himself in the midst of college-educated staff. He soon realised that he was way behind them in his knowledge of chemistry, and seeking an in-depth understanding of some chemistry theories, he enrolled at Alabama Polytechnic Institute (now Auburn University) and graduated with a degree in chemical engineering (1913).

After graduating, he worked for a year in a fertiliser laboratory and returned to API to study for his master's degree (1915). From there, he enrolled at Case Western Reserve University and graduated with a PhD in chemistry.

During his time in the US Army, Marvin Pipkin worked on gas mask innovation projects. These masks were worn by both soldiers and civilians during World War I to protect themselves against chemical weapons. He obtained 15 US patents in his lifetime, and he's mostly renowned as the inventor of the inside-frosted light bulb.

In the 1920s, General Electric tasked its newly hired engineers with developing light bulbs that were frosted on the inside. But it was a prank, and they did not expect them to attempt it. Besides, the experienced engineers thought it was impossible.

Marvin Pipkin joined General Electric in 1925 and was tasked with the same old prank. Unknown to him that the task was a fool's errand for new hires, he rolled his sleeves and went to work. But Marvin Pipkin accomplished the task in the same year, even though everyone thought it was impossible. This surprised everyone.

What made the inside-frosted bulb sensational was that when it accidentally hit the floor, it only bounced and settled; it didn't break. This feature also became the pith of the inside-frosted bulb's commercial success.

During one of my career coaching sessions with a client, we settled on academia as his most suitable career path. There was no question about that, but he also had a taste for wealth creation and feared that working in academia would stymie his impetus to amass wealth.

His reason was that he didn't know any wealthy academic. I disagreed with him, telling him that the academics he knew are probably content with their incomes or they simply aren't pursuing any wealth creation endeavour, but those who do can amass a fortune. For instance, Irwin Jacobs (PhD), one of Qualcomm's founders and its first CEO, was a professor at MIT and a billionaire; his cofounder, Andrew Viterbi (PhD), was a billionaire and a UCLA professor. Henry Samueli (PhD), one of Broadcom's founders, was also a UCLA professor and a billionaire.

In the end, we both agreed that amassing colossal fortunes, just like career development commitments, boils down to an individual's sense of purpose and cannot be hindered by scholarly endeavours.

CHAPTER SEVEN

The Creative Process

Safeguard your Brainchild: Don't Blab

One fateful night in 1953, in Ontario, Canada, a 26-year-old American engineer called Robert Kearns was celebrating his honeymoon with his wife when an errant champagne cork hit him in the left eye and injured him.

Upon recovery, Kearns began to think about the mechanics of the eye and eyelid, and he learnt that the eyelid doesn't blink at a predetermined rate but only when the eye is drying or when a foreign object lands on it. As he mused over the eye mechanics, he conceived the idea of creating an intermittent windshield wiper based on the mechanics of the human eye—which blinks every few seconds—as opposed to the regular windshield wiper, which operated nonstop. Moreover, in conditions of mist or light rain, the nonstop action of the regular windshield wiper dried the windshield and caused the rubber of the wiper's blade to stick and squeak as it swung left and right. The intermittent windshield wiper, therefore, was an innovation of the regular wiper.

For the next decade, Robert Kearns devoted himself to the invention of the intermittent windshield wiper, during which he built a workshop in his basement and made several prototypes, using the dashboards of salvaged cars.

By 1963, he had completed his invention and deemed it market-ready. His next move was to pitch it to a carmaker for a licensing deal. Ford Motors came across his mind, and one day, he retrofitted a prototype in his *Ford Galaxie* convertible and drove to the Ford factory in Dearborn, Michigan, to pitch his invention to them.

According to Kearns, though the managers he met with on that day seemed interested in his hardware, they were noncommittal. However, they invited him for another meeting, where he found himself amidst a geek of engineers who were eager to ask him questions about his intermittent windshield wiper.

As the meeting ensued, the Ford engineers showed him, though from a distance, a device they claimed to be an intermittent windshield wiper system they had developed and intended to install in their new Mercury line of cars. At this point, Kearns lost himself in the feeling of comradeship with his fellow engineers, and expecting that they would make him an offer, he divulged the innards of his invention to them.

For two years, Kearns met with the Ford engineers from time to time to discuss intermittent windshield wiper technology. Yet, contrary to his expectation, they still didn't make him an offer, and by the close of 1965, they stopped calling him.

Four years later, Ford rolled out its first electronic intermittent windshield wiper. Robert Kearns noticed it and looked askance at it, but believing that Ford was acting in good faith and optimistic that they would soon invite him for a deal, he didn't question what they were up to.

However, having expected their call for too long and still not hearing from them, he put his plan for the intermittent windshield wiper on the back burner and went to work as an engineer at the US National Bureau of Standards.

In 1976, Robert Kearns' eldest son brought home a Mercedes-Benz intermittent wiper control box. When Robert Kearns noticed it, he became suspicious and examined its innards. To his shock, he found that the innards were an exact copy of his intermittent windshield wiper system. He further obtained the patent filings of Ford, Volkswagen, Renault, General Motors, Mercedes-Benz, and others, and upon examining their filings, he noticed that they had all replicated key elements of his invention.

Having realised that he had been double-crossed, he was enraged, and in 1977, he filed lawsuits against Ford, Chrysler, General Motors, Mercedes-Benz, and several European carmakers.

The ensuing litigation was costly and daunting, and it took 10 years. Robert Kearns referred to his occupation during that period as 'litigant,' and he had to represent himself at some point because he couldn't afford to pay a lawyer. This led the judge to strike out some cases against him due to missed deadlines and the mediocre court-ordered filings he presented to the court.

Nonetheless, in 1990, Ford Motor Company agreed to settle with Kearns for $10.2 million. Also, in 1992, Kearns won $30 million against Chrysler for patent infringement.

Explication

As a matter of principle, whenever you're inventing something, avoid telling people about it. And when you finish, patent it immediately. This is crucial. Had Robert Kearns been late on his patent filing and the carmakers filed theirs ahead of him, he wouldn't have had the legal basis to claim inventorship of his invention. This would've also meant that his 10-year-long endeavour had gone down the drain, and his dividend would've been pain and grief.

In the 1970s, while working as a biological scientist in the Public Health and Reference Laboratory of Ghana Health Service, Madam Veronica Bekoe noticed that the staffers washed their hands in the same bowl of water and rinsed in another bowl. Her concern was that the practice was unhealthy, which made it conducive for an infection to spread.

She decided to solve it, at which point she conceived the idea for what would later be known as the Veronica Bucket. To invent it, she retrofitted a spigot into an aluminium utensil to make a prototype. By 1992, she had improved the prototype of the Veronica Bucket and introduced it in the Public Health and Reference Laboratory of Ghana Health Service, where it was first used.

Clinics and hospitals noticed the Veronica Bucket, and it has since been widely used for handwashing in schools, hospitals, and events. But it wasn't until 2020, when COVID-19 emerged, that its use gained prominence and became more valuable.

However, because Madam Veronica Bekoe didn't patent her invention, the manufacturers of the Veronica Bucket raked in all the profit without paying a dime in royalties to her, and by the time she decided to file for a patent, it was too late.

The next lesson you should learn from Robert Kearns's experience is to never divulge the innards of your brainchild to anyone. That was actually where he erred. When he met with the Ford engineers, he should've limited his pitching to only what the device does, its benefits, and a demonstration of how it worked. Divulging his invention's innards was unnecessary and led to the stealing of his idea.

Finally, there were two reasons why Robert Kearns should've shied away from Ford Motors and taken his pitching elsewhere. First, the managers he met with were noncommittal. Second, they claimed they had developed an intermittent windshield wiper. So, what was it about Robert Kearns' invention that they wanted to know, thereby necessitating the back-and-forth meetings they called him for?

Robert Kearns ought to have demanded a straight answer from the Ford managers about whether they would have a deal with him or not. And if not, he should've withdrawn and pitched his invention to another carmaker.

Understand: Whenever you go out to pitch something to someone, be humble but never assume the posture of being at their mercy. If they aren't forthright in their response, look out for signs that they aren't on the same page with you, then silently withdraw and look elsewhere before you end up wasting your time.

You may as well do simultaneous pitching with several prospects. This will enable you to know what others have to offer so that you can strike the best deal. Finally, don't blab, lest you reveal information to them that they shouldn't know.

Don't Waste Time

You cannot stand in hell; you can only keep moving, and that is how you should be working, like you're in hell, to keep everything moving.

There has never been a time in human history with as much jet-speed technological advancement as there is in the 21st century. Though designed for everyday convenience, these technologies, particularly the handy ones, such as our mobile phones, have a tendency to distract users from work.

A distracted mind leads to protracted work and can drag out a project that could be accomplished in a week to a month or months. To offset this tendency, you must begin to see distraction as an enemy of productivity and treat it with the contempt it deserves. So far, no one other than Maneesh Sethi has demonstrated this resolve in a very self-intimidating way and produced the best results.

The Indian-American CEO, Maneesh Sethi, reviewed his timesheet and realised that his hours spent at work didn't match his productivity. He identified his social media engagements and watching film episodes on the internet as the culprits, upon which he devised a genius solution.

In 2012, Maneesh Sethi hired a woman named Kara for $8 per hour. All Kara had to do was sit close to Maneesh while he worked on his computer, and if he switched to social media, she was obliged to slap him.

Result: Maneesh Sethi revealed that his average productivity ran around 35%–40% on most days, but since he brought Kara on board, his productivity soared. He posted, 'When Kara sat next to me, my productivity skyrocketed to 98%.'

Setting goals with timelines and consistently putting in the hours are crucial to accomplishing your goals on time. Your maxim then should be, as Elon Musk puts it, 'Don't waste your time on stuff that doesn't make things better.' That said, a habitual indulgence in idle social engagements, which protract beyond leisure, culminates in wasted time.

> Time is one thing that can never be retrieved. One may lose and regain friends. One may lose and regain money. Opportunity, once spurned, may come again. But the hours that are lost in idleness can never be brought back to be used in gainful pursuits. – Winston Churchill.

Understand: Our societies are beset with problems. Fortunately, there exist in our brains the latent solutions to these problems. These latent solutions manifest as our aptitudes and proclivities, for which we owe a duty to ourselves, society, and nature to leverage every resource at our disposal to develop them. This is the first step in proficiency development. Ultimately, the man or woman who develops herself better and faster than the rest and provides the most satisfactory solution will be recognised as a luminary

Herein, our aptitude is our urge for a particular occupation—hereby referred to as a 'vocation'—thus, our 'calling.' As a certified career coach, I offer career guidance and career development coaching to individuals, I also guide job seekers to find jobs and help professionals navigate work-related issues, including career decision-making; as a life coach, I help people map out their life goals, help them achieve them, and advise them on personal and confidential issues; as a communication/start-up consultant, I help early-stage founders find their feet in their entrepreneurial endeavour; and as an editor, I help people write personal and professional communication that is clear and free of mistakes. These are my vocations, and the more people I help in this regard, the more helpful I'll be to society. This applies to you as well—whether you're a teacher, a lawyer, a doctor, or a creative professional, to name a few.

It'll be sad and regretful that, in the end, you'll look back at your active years and reflect on something you could've done but didn't do. All the more because you wasted your time on things that didn't matter.

The most regrettable thing, however, will be something you started but went too slowly until someone else came in swiftly and stretched his hand ahead of you for the prize. This was how closely Alexander Graham Bell nearly lost his inventorship of the telephone to Elisha Gray.

Alexander Graham Bell

Born on March 3, 1847, in Edinburg, Scotland, Alexander Graham Bell didn't excel in school. However, he showed aptitude for invention and a proclivity for problem-solving at an early age. For instance, at the age of 12, he invented a device with rotating paddles and nail brushes with which farmers could quickly remove the husk from wheat grain.

After his education at Edinburg High School, he went on to study at Edinburg University, where he was trained to remove impediments in speech. But he left for London in 1867 and enrolled at the University of London to study anatomy and physiology. He later dropped out and relocated to Canada with his father in 1870. He moved to the US in 1872 and invented the telephone four years later.

On February 14, 1876, he filed his patent for the telephone, only a few hours before a lawyer also filed a caveat—a type of announcement of an invention—for the telephone on behalf of Elisha Gray, whose effort towards the invention of the telephone was known to Alexander Graham Bell.

If Alexander Graham Bell had delayed in filing his patent, it could've been granted to Elisha Gray, and he wouldn't have been known as the inventor of the telephone.

Lesson

There isn't any idea you would conceive that hasn't already been conceived by someone else. Even when you're considering a project, someone somewhere is also considering it. In the end, it doesn't matter who had the idea first; it matters who put it into action. This is particularly true for inventorship: The person who secures the patent first is recognised as the inventor. But going forward, however, whoever innovates better than the rest will get the most subscriptions and profits.

Speed and consistency are crucial for accomplishing every task. If you fall short of them, you'll likely end up as one of those great starters who finishes last or never finishes at all. It's therefore necessary to shut down every distraction that gets in your way.

Alexander Graham Bell, the inventor of the telephone, didn't tolerate the distraction of the telephone, and kept it away from his study. So, why would you, as a phone user, let your phone get in the way when you have something important to do?

I read about Paulo Coelho, author of *The Alchemist,* during the 2020 COVID-19 pandemic, and my jaw dropped when I learnt that he wrote the novel in two weeks.

While I tried to imagine him through his two-week period of writing, the words of Dale Carnegie, 'It is easier to make a million dollars than to put a phrase into the English language,' reverberated in my mind, and as a writer, I could imagine the phenomenal speed and consistency with which Paulo Coelho wrote *The Alchemist*. I could also imagine how he had strictly kept distractions away during the period of his writing. This is the part I find most enthralling about an author and a book that became a bestseller and a global sensation.

How often have you spent years on a project you could've completed in a year? How often have you procrastinated and postponed tasks because you lack focus? How often have you left your work to engage in an unproductive group chat on your phone?

You must work like hell in any endeavour you commit to. As Elon Musk said:

> Work like hell. You just have to put in 80-to-100-hour weeks every week. This improves the odds of success. If other people are putting in 40-hour workweeks and you're putting in 100-hour workweeks, then even if you're doing the same thing, you know that you will achieve in 4 months what it takes them a year to achieve.

This piece of advice is a productivity hack. If internalised, speed and consistency will become your second nature and make you super productive!

Paulo Coelho & The Alchemist

Paulo Coelho wanted to become an author since his teens, but his mother wasn't happy about his career aspiration because she saw no prospects in Brazilian authorship. She told Paulo, 'My dear, your father is an engineer. He's a logical, reasonable man with a very clear vision of the world. Do you know what it means to be a writer?'

When Paulo heard her mother say those words in one ear, the words went out as fast through the other ear, and he clung to his resolve to become an author more than ever before.

He also showed no interest in his parents' staunch religiosity; they realised that he wanted to be different and chart his own lifepath, which they found strange and weird. By the time he turned 17, his parents could no longer put up with his weirdness, so they sent him to a mental institution, where he escaped three times before his official release at the age of 20.

Paulo Coelho proceeded to study law at the behest of his parents, but he dropped out before long and lived as a hippie, travelling through South Africa, North Africa, Mexico, and Europe. When he returned to Brazil, he worked as a lyricist for musicians protesting against Brazilian military rule. This led to his eventual arrest, jailing, and torture for subversive activities.

He also switched between acting, journalism, and theatre until 1986. When he turned 39, he visited Spain and walked more than 500 miles along the road to Santiago de Compostela in northern Spain. On this path, he experienced an awakening that inspired him to write his first book, *The Pilgrimage,* which was published the same year.

In 1987, he wrote *The Alchemist* in two weeks and published it in 1988. Paulo Coelho explained that he wrote *The Alchemist* so fast because the story was already written in his soul.

At first, the book flopped, and Coelho felt crushed, but he believed in the thesis of *The Alchemist* and took the trouble of marketing the book himself. He then went knocking on doors to sell his books; other times, he visited his buyers purposely to persuade them to read the book.

He kept to this strategy until he found another publisher who took a chance with *The Alchemist*. The outcome was a phenomenal success: *The Alchemist* sold over 65 million copies worldwide, and Paulo Coelho was awarded the Guinness World Record for being the most translated living author.

After *The Alchemist*, Paulo Coelho wrote at least one novel every two years. He has sold hundreds of millions of copies of his books in 170 countries and translated them into 80 languages. In December 2016, Coelho was listed by a UK-based company, Richtopia, as number two of the 200 most influential contemporary authors. His net worth as of 2021, according to *CelebrityNetWorth*, was $500 million.

Be Health and Safety Conscious

For most of us, whenever we get a call for a job, we become excited about the pay and neglect the health and safety issues associated with the work. For instance, your job may require that you sit behind a computer for the better part of your working time. This will expose your sight to overextended screen time and make you susceptible to a sight defect.

But a screen time-induced sight defect can be averted if you wear screen glasses from the onset of your work. On the other hand, if you're actively using screen devices with your naked eyes and you haven't yet experienced any effect on your sight, you should begin to wear screen glasses as soon as possible. This is in order to offset the eventual effect of screen time on your sight.

Overextended exposure to noise can also hurt your hearing. Hiram Maxim, the inventor of the automatic machine gun, spent so much time test-firing his guns without wearing a hearing protection till he eventually lost his hearing.

While you might not be concerned about first aid, firefighting installations, and emergency exits at your workplace, putting these systems in place can make the difference between surviving a workplace accident and perishing in one.

In 1990, a 36-year-old man named Julio Gonzalez had an altercation with his former girlfriend at the Happy Land nightclub (Bronx) and was thrown out by the bouncer. Gonzalez then stomped three blocks away from the nightclub to a service station, where he found an empty one-gallon container into which he bought $1.00 worth of petrol. He returned to the nightclub, and with no one at the entrance, he poured the petrol at the bottom of the rickety staircase—which was also the club's only exit—and torched it. He immediately loped to his house and slept.

Firefighters arrived at the scene within a few minutes and recovered 87 dead bodies in what became America's worst single mass murder at the time. Only six people escaped the fire, including the target of the arson, Lydia Feliciano, Gonzalez's ex.

Explication

Happy Land nightclub was found to be unlicensed. Further investigation revealed that they lacked fire exits, alarms, and sprinklers, among other safety installations.

This means that the nightclub had long been a deathtrap. However, it would not be the world's last infrastructure to operate without a license or permit. Several other buildings have been erected elsewhere without permits, whereas some businesses continue to operate without a license. But what the owners of these unlicensed businesses and unpermitted infrastructure don't realise is that by circumventing the licensing process, they also avoid the opportunity to have authorities inspect and assess their infrastructure and businesses for their safety. This poses danger to the buildings' occupants and puts them at risk of losing their lives in case of a disaster.

In 2012, Melcom's five-storey shopping mall at Achimota in Accra collapsed and killed 14 people, while others were injured. It was found that the building was put up without a permit. In 2014, the multi-storey Grand View Hotel at Nii Boi Town in Accra collapsed, killing one person and injuring another. It turned out the building had no permit. In 2015, a three-story building under construction at Cantonment, Accra, collapsed and killed three people, injuring 18 others. That building was also put up without a permit.

In retrospect, the habit of circumventing operational licences, evading permits, and disregarding regulations is an ill-conceived blunder and a false economy. That said, property developers who comply with the licensing process, heed regulations, and obtain operating permits either don't encounter the mishaps mentioned above or can mitigate risks.

Harry and Harris visited me during the 2020 COVID-19 pandemic. Harry was an engineer at the mines, and Harris was a chemist in an industrial laboratory. Both men were health and safety conscious, and while they were exposed to a significant level of risk at work, Harry's employers provided all the safety equipment to mitigate his risk. In addition, his salary and conditions of service could afford him absolute comfort. So whenever he reflected on the risk he faced at work, he considered his income and the company's strict adherence to health and safety regulations as compensatory and mitigating.

Conversely, Harris could only get by on his income. The laboratory he worked in was substandard, which exposed him to all manner of chemicals, including those he literally breathed in whenever he was at work.

Knowing the repercussions of cumulative exposure, Harris became concerned about his health and complained to his employer about the company's nonadherence to safety regulations. But his employer told him to improvise, and when Harris mooted concerns about his health, he told him to endure and added, 'Many people are sending in their CVs for your job.'

Now, the twins had come to me for advice, and after listening to them, I asked them if they knew about Phossy jaw.

Phossy Jaw Disease

In the early 19th century, research and development in matchmaking revealed that adding yellow phosphorus to a matchstick head enhanced its ignition. This discovery made it easier to light a match, which led to more customers and more money for the match-making industry.

This innovation, however, was accompanied by a new occupational disease that lasted until around 1906, when the production of phosphorus matches was prohibited. Phossy Jaw was the name of the occupational disease!

Phossy jaw was caused by cumulative exposure to yellow phosphorus vapour: the active ingredient in matches.

The disease was a result of phosphorus deposits in the jaws and manifested as a painful toothache and swelling of the gums within five years of cumulative exposure. It then aggravated into a severe mouth abscess, disfigurement, and fatal brain damage. The lower jaw was usually affected more than the upper jaw, and the affected jawbones glowed greenish-white in the dark.

Phossy jaw was excruciatingly painful, with tissues in the jawbone getting rotten and giving off a foul-smelling discharge. Surgical treatment required the removal of the affected jawbone, making it difficult for the victims to eat and thereby exacerbating their health. Organ failure and cancer were also common with cumulative exposure to phosphorus.

By the time I ended my discourse on Phossy jaw, both Harry and Harris had developed goosebumps, and Harris asked me if he should quit his job.

Before I could urge him on his decision, I directed both Harry and Harris to list the reagents Harris worked with and share a copy of the list with me. The three of us—all with chemistry backgrounds—did independent research on each reagent and put them in the categories of harmful and harmless. And after considering the long-term effect of the reagent in the category of harmful, the three of us agreed that Harris should look for another job, which I was happy to help him do.

After all, his boss wasn't concerned about his hazardous work environment, which wasn't surprising. At Bryant & May, a 19th-century British company that made matches, they fired workers who showed symptoms of phosphorus exposure and hired new ones. The same would've happened to Harris.

You're Not Late to Repurpose or Diversify

Your work is going to fill a large part of your life, and the only way to be truly satisfied is to do what you believe is great work. And the only way to do great work is to love what you do. If you haven't found it yet, keep looking. Don't settle. As with all matters of the heart, you will know when you find it. – Steve Jobs.

Our social environment determines how early or late we can develop our potential, if at all. For example, a natural-born storyteller who was born and raised in a lowbrow social environment in a third-world country may go through life unaware that they could've developed a career in storytelling and made a fortune from story writing.

Sometimes, I reminisce about my childhood in the village, where I had a playmate who could tell fantastic stories and never run out of them. I had another playmate who was mechanical and could design something out of anything; he was born an engineer. But when we grew up, the former became a peasant in the village, and the latter became a hustler in the city. Had their parents been educated and well-off, either of them would have turned his talent into a rewarding career.

On the other hand, if fate had landed them in the UK or US, I'm sure they would've grown to rub shoulders with J.K. Rowling or Elon Musk. But in a third-world country, the odds were against them: the odds that they would be discovered and groomed, the odds that they would develop themselves on their own, and the odds that the education system would recognise their talents.

As of 2022, I hadn't met a single millennial in Ghana who had received personalized career guidance during their education. In fact, most of the graduates I talked to didn't even know their universities had such a resource. This is unfortunate and accounts for why many gifted people have no sense of purpose.

Years ago, I knew I had a knack for writing and coaching, but I didn't think they were worthwhile. Fortunately, it didn't take long until I realised that writing and coaching were my vocations. I was in level 200, studying Applied Chemistry, and upon realising my vocation, I immersed myself in deliberate practice. And despite my consistency and commitment, it took me 12 years to fully develop my writing and editorial forte. I trained in career and life coaching during the same period and practised both till I was poised to write this book. Similarly, not long after completing national service, some of my coursemates, already with degrees, followed their dreams to medical schools in Ghana and abroad and became fully-fledged medical doctors by our mid-30s.

Most people, however, couldn't figure out the worth of their vocations early enough, or perhaps they lacked the resolve to divert from the path the education system took them. The consequence is that they will hold on to boring occupations that are at odds with their aptitudes and proclivities.

This situation is called *misplaced vocation.* It's a misplaced vocation if a gifted teacher is working as a doctor, a 'doctor' is working as an engineer, an 'engineer' is working as a banker, a 'banker' is working as a nurse, a 'nurse' is working as a journalist, and everyone else is working in fields that are at variance with their calling.

The prevalence of *misplaced vocation* among a demography undermines the human resource base of that demography and accounts for the root cause of incompetence across diverse sectors of the economy. Is it any wonder why some countries find it hard to get nifty football coaches from among the millions of their compatriots to head their national teams?

One of the reasons is that the people born with the aptitude for football coaching are probably engaged in different occupations, while the coaching jobs are mostly left for people whose aptitude and intellect don't match up with the technical competence needed for effective football coaching.

But it's never too late; you can either repurpose yourself or diversify your career to embrace your calling, and your age shouldn't deter you.

Among her friends and relatives, Anna was the most compassionate person towards sick children. She was the only person in her circles who had visited and contributed to the medical bills of every sick child of a relative or friend on admission to the hospital. Also, when a sick child didn't want to take their medication, Anna was the one to call, and when she went up to the child, she knew what to tell them to make them relent. Her success rate was 100%.

At 37 years old, she was an accomplished engineer and was among the top echelons in the firm she worked for. Success beckoned! But Anna hadn't found fulfilment in her engineering career. She had excelled in every class she took in school and was among the best students in her engineering class.

But 25 years ago, she wanted to become a medical doctor, a paediatrician to be precise, and it was all she dreamt of until unfortunately, she missed out on the admission requirement to the medical school and had to study engineering instead.

There are few reasons people become doctors; for some, they love the title; for others, it's the prestige; and for some others, it's their parents' choice. Anna, however, was among the aspirants who genuinely cared about sick people and wanted to help them recover. Thus, medicine was her calling, and her engineering career was rather incidental.

Now she was poised to go back to school to study medicine, which would take her at least the next five years to complete. She would be 42 years old by then, after which she would have to follow through with a three-year residency in paediatrics.

'Your university mates have been practising medicine since they were 25 years old; you will have less than two decades to work until you're due for pension; it's not worth it'; 'You're a successful engineer earning a good living; why bother becoming a doctor?'

These and other words of discouragement were hurled at her by those with whom she first discussed her aspirations. She became confused, and at some point, she thought she should focus on her engineering career, but deep within her, she was experiencing discontentment with her engineering work as a result of her urge to practise medicine.

It took one session of career coaching with Anna for me to understand her calling and the details I've written in the previous paragraphs. In the end, we both reached a consensus that she could go to medical school and kickstart her career as a medical doctor at the age of 42. But the idea of having a 'short' time to practise until her pension in the next 18 years had gotten to her. In other words, she thought that, unlike some seasoned doctors she had admired all her life, she would have a 'short-lived' medical career.

To assuage Anna's worries, I reminded her that her pension at age 60 would not retire her from practice and that she could work for as long as she had the desire; what mattered most was for her to stay alive and kicking.

I referred her to Dr. Leila Denmark. She was the oldest practising paediatrician until she retired in 2001 at the age of 103. I also mentioned Dr. Howard Tucker, who, as of his 100th birthday in 2022, had no intention to retire anytime soon, and whom, on the conferment of the title of the World's Oldest Practising Doctor by the Guinness World Records, said, 'I regard this Guinness World Records title as a singular honour and look upon it as another achievement in a long, satisfying, and happy life.'

Anna was teary and all smiles at this juncture. I knew immediately that my advice had sunk in and that she was appreciating me as her career coach. She enrolled in medical school the following year and couldn't be happier or more fulfilled, even as a medical student.

Repurposing

Ava DuVernay didn't start making movies until she was 32. Other directors started their careers young and went to film school to learn how to use the tools of the trade.

Without knowing she would become a film director, she majored in English and African American Studies at the University of California. She wanted to be a journalist at first, but her internship at CBS News made her change her mind.

In 2008, she created a budding documentary about a hip-hop movement that flourished in Los Angeles in the 1990s. The title of the documentary was *This Is the Life*. Ava DuVernay later admitted to the *Washington Post* that even then, filmmaking wasn't part of her plan. But as her interest in working behind the camera piqued, she took private classes in film directing while keeping her day job.

After several years of working her fingers to the bone, Ava DuVernay became the first Black woman to win the directing award in the US Dramatic Competition category of the 2012 *Sundance Film Festival.*

She was also the first Black woman nominated for a *Golden Globe Award for Best Director* and the first Black female director to have her film nominated for the *Academy Award for Best Picture*. Also, in 2017, she was nominated for the *Academy Award for Best Documentary Feature* for her film *13th*.

> 'If you're on a path that's not the one that you want to be on, you can also pivot, and you can also move, and age doesn't make a difference, race or gender. It's about putting one step in front of another, about forward movement to where you wanna be.' – Ava DuVernay.

Diversifying

You can cultivate a skill set and use each one in a different occupation, or you can use them all as complementary skills in your profession. This kind of work-practice is called portfolio career', and it's conducive to augmenting your earning potential and boosting your career.

Personally, taking the portfolio career path has helped me. First, as a career/life coach and a startup consultant, I've been able to help more people than I could possibly do if I wasn't also a writer. As an editorial manager, I self-edit my books, format the pages, and design my book covers exactly how I envision them.

This saves me time, especially the time it sometimes takes for authors to wait for their editors to finish other clients' projects. It saves me money as well, considering the high cost of professional editing service. Furthermore, as a communication consultant, my delivery as a career/life coach and startup consultant extends beyond advisory to assisting my clients with strategic communication and professional writing needs.

I want to be clear that my success in my portfolio career is due to talent, but it took me years of practice and hard work to fully develop myself.

To pursue a portfolio career, you must first recognise your willingness and energy to work multiple jobs. Second, don't let anyone dissuade you with the 'Jack of all trades, master of none' adage, because the adage applies only to people with limited energy who either lack multiple skills or have multiple skills but can't put them to use in an effective way.

If, on the other hand, you have a lot of skills and know how to combine them well, you might be a good candidate for a portfolio career. This is especially true if you don't make enough money at one job or if you have many skills and want to use them all.

Above all, a portfolio career pays dividends, and I can guarantee that. As Robert Greene puts it: 'The future belongs to those who learn more skills and combine them in creative ways.'

My client, Nicholas, had a degree and work experience in building construction. He also had a flair for designing, so I urged him to learn interior decoration or draftsmanship in addition to his expertise. This was after he had worked with a multinational construction company for some years and had come to me to discuss his desire to start his own construction company.

Initially, he didn't think he could effectively combine his construction expertise with another occupation, but I encouraged him to try. I also told him that if he could reskill successfully without affecting his regular job, that would be an indication that he would be successful with a portfolio career.

The idea resonated with him, and he spent two years learning draftsmanship and interior decoration in turns, under the tutelage of two mentors, each day after he finished his regular job.

When Nicholas completed his apprenticeships, he indeed started his construction company, and in a country where the ordinary person is more familiar with draftsmen than architects, he gets a lot of clients in need of building plans and sells them his interior decoration service.

So, working now as a self-employed house builder, Nicholas also draws building plans and does interior decoration for the same clients. He is very pleased with his work and thanks me for encouraging him to use his vocations to develop a portfolio career.

The most interesting thing I've observed about people who diversify their occupations in the field of their vocations is that they're able to upskill/reskill with speed and can easily catch up with the old hands in the industry or surpass them.

Persevere, Success is in the Offing

When you really want something to happen, the whole universe will conspire so that your wish come true. – Paulo Coelho.

Success is much harder to attain than you can imagine. Because the obstacles on the path to success are daunting, and many people lack the impetus to push themselves past those obstacles, so they quit and settle for ordinariness.

This is typical of an employee who attempts entrepreneurship, but fails on his first try and retreats to his day job, never to venture into entrepreneurship again. Such an employee lacks grit and is unlikely to succeed.

To succeed, you must persevere against all the odds. And especially for those of us born without a silver spoon, we have no chance to succeed unless we persevere. That's why I take so much inspiration from J.K. Rowling, author of the *Harry Potter* book franchise.

Joanne Rowling was only 6 years old when she wrote her first book. It was a story about a rabbit called *Rabbit*, and Joanne received a favourable review of the book from her mother. Years later, at Wyedean School, Joanne Rowling's favourite subject was English, and she scored straight As and A-pluses in creative writing.

But this was in her early school years. Decades later, however, Steve Eddy, Joanne's first secondary school English teacher, said of her: 'She wasn't an exceptional student but one of a group of girls who were bright and quite good at English.' And I wasn't surprised to learn this due to the pattern I had observed about extraordinary achievers and creative geniuses.

In 1986, Joanne Rowling graduated from the University of Exeter with a degree in French and Classics and had her first job in London as a researcher and bilingual secretary for Amnesty International.

In 1990, while she was on a four-hour trip from Manchester to London, she had an inspiration for a story about a boy who attended a wizardry school. By the time she arrived at her destination, the story had taken shape in her mind, and she began writing it immediately. This was the beginning of the *Harry Potter* novel!

Joanne's mother died in December of that year after her decade-long battle with multiple sclerosis, and she described her bereavement as the most traumatic moment of her life.

Seven years after attending the University of Exeter, Joanne began to feel depressed. She had lost her mother, her marriage had failed, and she had no job but a child to care for. She saw herself as a failure and suffered clinical depression to the extent that she contemplated suicide. Meanwhile, she'd been writing the *Harry Potter* story while projecting her experiences onto the story's characters. At this period of her life, she came to terms with the reality that she was poor and signed up for welfare benefits.

By 1995, Joanne had completed her manuscript and titled it *Harry Potter and the Philosopher's Stone*. The manuscript received a favourable review from a beta-reader who agreed to be Joanna's literary agent. Subsequently, they pitched the manuscript to 12 publishers, but they all rejected it. In 1996, the manuscript was accepted by the 13th publisher after an eight-year-old child of the publishing house's chairman had read the first chapter of the manuscript and asked for the next chapter to be read.

To publish *Harry Potter and the Philosopher's Stone*, the publishers agreed with Joanne to disguise her gender. They averred that the anticipated readership of her fantasy novel was young boys who might not want to read a book authored by a woman. Joanne Rowling's name was thus modified to J.K. Rowling, and she was paid £1,500 as an advance. Her editor also advised her to get a day job since she had little chance of making money in children's books.

Later, in 1997, J.K. Rowling received an £8,000.00 grant from the Scottish Art Council to enable her to continue writing. The rest is history.

Explication

Ellen G. White said, 'The road to success is not a smooth way, over which we are born in palace cars; but it is a rugged path, filled with obstacles which can only be surmounted by patient toil.'

This is true for any endeavour. To succeed, you must persevere, only halfwits think greatness can be attained overnight.

J.K. Rowling's life was hard for many years before she wrote *Harry Potter and the Philosopher's Stone*. Her mother died, she had a miscarriage, her marriage was bad and ended in divorce, she lost her job, she had to raise her daughter alone, and she was depressed and suicidal.

When she had finished writing her 6-year-long manuscript, she still had to cope with the disappointment of having it rejected 12 times. Nothing could be more soul-wrenching. But Joanne didn't give in to despondency.

Paradoxically, those rejection letters rather inspired her, and she pinned her first rejection letter on her kitchen wall because it gave her something in common with her favourite authors, who also had early rejections but went on to succeed. So anytime she saw the rejection letter, she saw success in the offing.

In the spring of 1997, the same year Joanne received the grant from the Scottish Art Council, an auction was held in the US for the right to publish the fantasy novel and was won by a publisher for $105,000.00. *Harry Potter and the Philosopher's Stone* was a big hit, and the sequels that came after it were a smash in the UK and the US.

The film rights to the first two novels were sold for a seven-figure sum in US dollars, and the fantasy series has since won multiple awards and sold over 500 million copies, becoming the bestselling book series in history.

J.K. Rowling became the world's first billionaire author. As of 2019, she was rated as the highest-paid author globally, whereas the *Harry Potter* brand was worth an estimated $15 billion as of 2020.

The most important thing *Harry Potter* did was to get kids reading again at a time when people thought they were giving up reading in favour of computers and TV.

Rejections and Missing the Mark Do not Portend Failure

Jack Ma would've been dead if successive rejections could kill a man. If successive rejections could kill a dream, Alibaba wouldn't have happened, and if successive rejections portended failure, Jack Ma would've been the poorest man.

In 1999, while in his office in his modest apartment, he filmed a meeting of himself and his inaugural team in which he asked them, 'In the next five or ten years, what will Alibaba become?' He responded to his own question, 'Our competitors are not in China but in Silicon Valley. We should position Alibaba as an international website.'

Every step Jack Ma took toward his goals was hard and full of frustration, but he kept going until he reached his goal.

His first step was to learn to speak English, and he would ride his bicycle for 40 minutes to an international hotel where White tourists lodged. When a group of tourists caught his attention, he struck a deal with them to allow him to be their tour guide, and they were to teach him English in return.

One day, Jack Ma happened upon an Australian family who accepted his offer to be their tour guide. After they went back to Australia, they invited him to visit. In Australia, he witnessed a high life he had never seen in China and continued to improve his English, but mathematics was a problem for him.

He failed the standardised university entrance exams, scoring 1 point out of 120. And when he took a resit, he scored 19 points out of 120. His aggregate, nonetheless, didn't qualify him for university. He kept trying until he gained admission at Hangzhou Teachers College and graduated with a degree in English.

In 1995, he travelled to the US, where he experienced the internet for the first time and envisaged the prospects of the internet in years to come.

He founded his first company, China Yellow Pages, in a single-room office with a workstation and an old computer with unstable internet. Yet, he managed to persuade his contacts in China to commission him to develop a website for them, which he, in turn, subcontracted to developers in Seattle. Jack Ma would later lament that in the first three years before he found his feet in the business, he was treated as though he were a con man.

Four years after founding his first company, he founded Alibaba as a business-to-business e-commerce website. Once again, he struggled as he tried to pitch his idea to investors. But, without a business plan, he faced rejection until he persuaded the Goldman Sachs employee in charge of China to invest $5 million in Alibaba. This was his turning point!

Jack Ma would later prove that being intuitive and open-minded was more important for entrepreneurial success than book knowledge. He acknowledged that, though schools impart knowledge, it takes wisdom to succeed in business, and this wisdom only comes from experience.

Even as of 2014, he admitted to not being exceptionally good with technology, and as far as computers were concerned, all he could do was send and receive messages and browse the web.

In 2000, he became the richest man in China, with a $38.8 billion net worth. Jack Ma still acknowledges that he first had to get used to failure.

He failed his primary school exams twice and his middle school exams three times. After graduating from Hangzhou Teachers College and before he had his first job as a teacher, he applied for 30 jobs in his home city of Hangzhou, China, and was rejected by all of them. When KFC first went to China, 24 applicants applied to work there; 23 were hired, and he was rejected. He tried police recruitment with four other candidates. The four passed for recruitment, and he was rejected. He proceeded with his cousin to look for a job as a waiter at a four-star hotel in his home city; his cousin scored a lesser mark than him, yet his cousin was accepted, and he was rejected. Again, he tried to enter Harvard but was rejected on all 10 attempts. Jack Ma admitted to the pain of his successive failures and rejections, but he didn't give up and went ahead to be accomplished and fabulously rich.

How many times have you been rejected? Ones, twice, or thrice? Or 12 times as J.K. Rowling? Or many times as Jack Ma?

In 1987, when Bill Gates became a billionaire at age 31, he was asked, 'What is the secret to this success?' He replied, 'There's no secret; I worked really hard on my idea to get it as good as I could, and then knocked on door after door. I ended up showing my idea to 1200 people. Nine hundred said no. Three hundred people showed some interest. Only 85 people actually did anything. Thirty took a serious look. And 11 made me a multi-billionaire.'

When graduate job-seekers come to me for career coaching, they tell me they've sent several job application letters but still haven't gotten a job. And when I asked them how many application letters they had sent, the usual reply I got was: 'A lot.' Then, I would insist that they tell me the actual number of times, and the figures they often mentioned were 4, 5 or 6. And when I asked them if 4, 5 or 6 was what they considered a lot, they would grin over their exaggeration.

Most young wannabe entrepreneurs behave the same way. When I first met with some of them, they would express their frustration at not being able to find investors, and when I asked how many prospects they had pitched their ideas to, they usually counted less than five.

But success goes beyond the number of times we try. Ideally, you should go back to the drawing board after every attempted task and opportunity. This is in order for you to review your methods and strategies. It'll interest you to note, after you've done the review, that you weren't as thorough as you should've been. In this case, you must reflect and rework before you try again.

Go back to the Drawing Board

Every task, initiative, or opportunity would result in a positive, negative, or indeterminate outcome. But whatever the outcome might be, you must inculcate the habit of going back to the drawing board to assess your performance. This is critical for determining what worked and what didn't, as well as making changes, adjustments, or reinforcements as needed.

Above all, ask for feedback. But mind you, asking for positive feedback can elicit a misleading response. So, ask for negative feedback first, and if you have to pay experts to assess your work, do it and make the necessary corrections until there's no mistake left to correct. As Elon Musk said, 'You want to be rigorous about making the best possible thing you can, find everything that's wrong with it and fix it. Seek negative feedback.'

If you embrace this idea in the creative process, it'll prevent the recurrence of past mistakes, improve your competence, and accelerate your career success.

CHAPTER EIGHT

Beware of Superstition

Our goals can only be reached through a vehicle of plan, in which we fervently believe, and upon which we must vigorously act. There's no other route to success. – Pablo Picasso.

There are differences in our thinking patterns, perceptions, and understanding. We portray these differences in our social functioning, and they're due to our education, gender, ethnicity, geography, generational gap, and beliefs. However, our social functioning has a baseline that reflects our sanity and determines our acceptance into a group. Let's call this baseline rationality. Without our rationality, it becomes easy for us to be influenced into repulsive behaviours that might not necessarily be due to insanity but to indoctrination, stemming from the inculcation of mind projection fallacies. This is a concern in many societies, particularly those with a strong religious demographic, as beliefs and ideologies can be a powerful force in shaping people's thoughts and behaviour.

God, gods, and Natural Phenomena

During the prehistoric era, before any religion was founded, nature was already functioning, humans were already living, natural phenomena were already happening, good and evil were already present, and fortune and misfortune were already part of the affairs of men.

As creatures of curiosity, our early ancestors sought out explanations for these events. Diverse ideas emerged. The idealists believed that there were spiritual entities in the transcendence who oversaw the affairs of life, provided men with protection, and blessed them with fortune or punished them with misfortune.

This idea became the basis of spirituality, upon which our ancestors established their belief systems. Priesthood followed and devotees of the belief systems identified with one another, thereby establishing a religion.

Religion then reinforced beliefs with superstition; hence, our early ancestors attributed every natural phenomenon and anything inexplicable to spirituality. Rainfall, for instance, was believed to be brought about by the gods of rain. This notion was widely held.

There were, however, pragmatists among them—just like today—for whom myths and beliefs didn't resonate, except for proof and knowledge. They were convinced that nature, as physical as they perceived it, could be the only cause of natural phenomena. If so, they must find out how. This marked the beginning of man's quest for knowledge, and science was born.

At first, the pragmatists' theory about rainfall was that there was a pool of water high up in the sky that collected into a solid layer with perforations. Rain, they believed, fell through those perforations.

The pragmatists, in essence, made no attribution to the gods or anything spiritual concerning rainfall and any other natural phenomenon. But though their explanation for the cause of rain was inaccurate, knowledge, unlike belief, is dynamic, and subsequent observation led to the finding that rainfall comes about as a result of evaporation on the earth and condensation in the sky. This observation was eventually proven and became established in science as the **Water Cycle**.

In modern times, rainfall and any element of the weather can be predicted with precision, thanks to meteorology!

Charles Hatfield (1875–1958) could also precipitate rainfall using science. Yet he was a man, not a god. Had he lived in the ancient era, there would've been stories about him today that he was a god who came to dwell among men, and I have no doubt such stories would've spawned a religion in his name.

In any case, Charles Hatfield's genius invalidates the prehistoric superstition about rainfall and further indicates that there's no limit to human ingenuity. Moreover, if a mortal human could cause rainfall using science, and science is being used for weather forecast, then there's little to prove that either the gods or the Creator interfere with natural phenomena. And that the ability to interfere with natural phenomena is a prerogative of man, which is only possible through science, as allowed by the Creator.

This explains why rainfall, like gravity, sunshine, day and night, and any other natural phenomenon, aren't subjected to our religious beliefs. As such, we can pray all we want, but our prayers, hopes, and wishes cannot make natural phenomena happen or prevent them from happening.

Nevertheless, as superstition continues to permeate people's minds, it makes it easy for them to be deceived due to what they've been made to believe by other men about the gods and the Creator.

Lunar Eclipse of 1504

In 1504, Christopher Columbus got stranded in Jamaica and was welcomed by the indigenes of the island. They provided him and his crew with food for six months, but they abruptly stopped due to their displeasure with the merchandise Columbus and his men were offering them in trade.

Columbus had to find a way to renew the supplies from the indigenes, so he consulted a book he had on board. It was called the *Almanac*.

The Almanac was an annual publication that had information on weather forecasts, farmers' planting dates, dates of eclipses, religious festivals, et cetera. Columbus saw in the *Almanac* the date and time of an upcoming lunar eclipse. He decided to take advantage of the natives' ignorance and use this information to his advantage.

Next, he requested to have a meeting with the local chiefs and their people, and when he had their audience, he told them his God was angry with them for how they had treated him and his men and that his God would show them a sign of His wrath by making the moon dark and turning its luminance to blood.

The indigene's laughed off and pooh-poohed Columbus's submission, but that evening, when the lunar eclipse started, the natives panicked, and feeling threatened by Columbus's God, they raced to offer Columbus food and pleaded with him to intercede with his God on their behalf. Columbus then retreated to his cabin and pretended he was praying while observing and timing the eclipse. And shortly before the eclipse would be gone, after 48 minutes of its emergence, he told the frightened indigenes that his God would forgive them and would soon show them another sign.

Lo and behold, the moon began re-emerging from the earth's shadow; the eclipse went away, and Columbus told the indigenes that his God had forgiven them.

If only the indigenes weren't superstitious and understood that the lunar eclipse was a natural phenomenon, Columbus couldn't have deceived them. The event happened in 1504, and it's one of the many instances where people have used God's name and other fetishes to fool ignorant people. This gimmick persists to this day.

What impact will this topic have on your sense of purpose throughout college and your career? Read on!

Angel's Glow

In 1862, the second year of the American Civil War, during the Battle of Shiloh in southwestern Tennessee, wounded soldiers in the marshy field noticed that their wounds had a faint-blue glow. But due to the rain, they had to stay in the marsh for two days before they were sent to the field hospitals.

At the field hospitals, medics observed a mysterious phenomenon: the soldiers whose wounds had the faint-blue glow healed fast, spontaneously, and survived their wounds. This inexplicable faint-blue glow became known as Angel's Glow.

A phenomenon like this would engender diverse attributions among religious and pragmatic groups.

Among a religious populace, oracles, priests, and prophets will weigh in and attribute the phenomenon to superstition. Their devotees will believe them unquestionably, and the phenomenon will go down in history as a miracle.

On the contrary, pragmatists would observe the faint-blue glow and guess what natural phenomenon it is, then they would investigate to understand what it actually is.

In 2001, Bill Martin, a seven-year-old enthusiast of the American Civil War who knew about the Angel's Glow, visited the battlefield of Shiloh.

Before his visit, he had shown interest in his mother's research on a bioluminescent soil bacterium called *Photorhabdus luminescens* or *P. luminescens.* This bacterium gives off a pale-blue glow, and having observed the *P. luminescens* for some time, Bill Martin and his friend, Jonathan Curtis, guessed if the *P. luminescens* was present in the marshy fields at Shiloh where the soldiers fought and whether the *P. luminescens* was actually the Angel's Glow.

Bill Martin's mother, Phyllis Martin, a microbiologist, encouraged the boys to investigate their hypothesis.

In their investigation, the boys learnt that *P. luminescens* live inside nematodes. Nematodes are tiny parasitic worms that burrow into insect larvae in soil or plants. When the *P. luminescens* gets rooted in the larvae, the nematode vomits the *P. luminescens*, which, in turn, releases chemicals that kill the host larvae and other bacteria present.

This information convinced the boys that the *P. luminescens* was most likely the cause of Angel's Glow, but there was a conundrum: if they were to attribute the faint-blue glow in the soldiers' wounds to the *P. luminescens*, then they had to explain how it became possible because the *P. luminescens* cannot thrive at a normal human body's temperature. In other words, they can only thrive in a much lower temperature. So how did *P. luminescens* thrive in the soldiers' wounds?

After some analysis and brainstorming, the boys got the answer, and it was the weather. The wounded soldiers lay in the marshy field for two days while it rained. Thus, the cold weather and the marshy field lowered the soldiers' temperature.

So when the *P. luminescens* got into the soldiers' wounds, they thrived, and by their nature, they killed other germs present, including those that could've caused infection to their wounds. So, since there were no germs to cause an infection, a natural healing process took place, and the wound healed on its own.

This explains why the soldiers with the faint-blue glow in their wounds recovered fast. They were apparently saved not by an angel, as they had assumed, but by the *P. luminescens*!

In Boho, Fermanagh, Ireland, 47 years before the Battle of Shiloh, a similar thing happened.

The Ancient Fermanagh Soil Cure

At Boho in Fermanagh, Ireland, the soil at a local churchyard is used for treating infections, and it's efficacious. This tradition can be traced back to Fr. James McGirr, a priest and healer who died in 1815. Before his death, he told his people, 'After I die, the clay that covers me will cure anything that I cured when I was with you.'

Since then, people have travelled from far and wide to fetch the soil and sent it home to treat bacterial infections. To administer it, they slept with the soil in a wrap beneath their pillows and said a certain prayer, but the soil must be returned to where it was collected in four to nine days.

The cure did happen as expected, and the people who witnessed it were mystified. Hence, the locals attributed the soil's efficacy to superstition. And though sceptics deem these stories as folklore, the soil, nonetheless, remains efficacious, and its use for curing infections prevails to this day.

Scientists Weighed In

At a time when the world is heading toward an antibiotic crisis due to the emergence of antibiotic-resistant bacteria, there's a need to rev up research to develop more efficacious antibiotics. As the World Health Organisation had cautioned, if the antibiotic crisis aggravates, people may succumb to common infections that have been treatable for decades. The reason is that the current antibiotics would be rendered ineffective against antibiotic-resistant pathogens.

Gerry Quinn (PhD), a microbiologist and member of a team of international researchers working to develop new antibiotics, heard of the miraculous ancient soil at the churchyard of Boho in Fermanagh. And having heard of the mysticism and superstition surrounding the soil, Dr. Gerry Quinn posited that if the soil truly cured, then there was a science to it.

Dr. Quinn and his research team went to the churchyard in Boho, Fermanagh, on July 28, 2015, to collect a soil sample, which they then sent back to their research laboratory. Their analysis revealed that the soil was the habitat of an unfamiliar strain of Streptomyces (a bacteria). This novel strain produced various antibiotics capable of killing multidrug-resistant pathogens, including the World Health Organization's top three most dangerous pathogens to human health.

In other words, the antibiotics produced by the newly discovered strain of streptomyces in the soil at Boho Churchyard were found to kill bacterial germs, and therefore could boost the healing of bacterial infections.

The scientists also discovered that the reason the soil must be returned four to nine days from the day it was fetched had nothing to do with superstition but was due to concerns over radon (a naturally occurring radioactive gas) emission from the limestone and shale content of the soil. As a result, it was not safe for people to keep the soil near their homes for an extended period of time.

It's the aim of the scientists to develop more efficacious antibiotics from the newly discovered strain of Streptomyces in order to offset the threat of the emerging drug-resistant bacteria.

Apparently, Fr. James McGirr's parting prophecy about the churchyard soil, the prayer said during its use, and the need to return the soil to where it was collected only engendered mysticism and superstition but had nothing to do with the soil's curing property.

Health, Spirituality, and Science

In 1937, only six months after Pastor James McKeown had arrived in the Gold Coast as a resident missionary at the Apostolic Church, he had malaria. At the time, the doctrines of the Apostolic Church prohibited their devotees from seeking medical treatment because they believed that sick people would recover if they were fervently prayed and fasted for.

So, they kept the ailing pastor in a room and prayed fervently for him; however, their attempted spiritual remediations didn't prevent Pastor James McKeown's condition from worsening. After two days, the English District Commissioner took him to the Ridge Hospital in Accra, where he was given medication, following which he recovered.

Paradoxically, the leaders of the Apostolic Church were vexed because Pastor James McKeown had sought out medical treatment and thereby defied the church's doctrine. One issue led to another, and they parted ways with him. Pastor James McKeown moved on and later founded the Church of Pentecost.

The misconception about the cause of disease and healing has a long history. In ancient times, healing was the business of oracles, priests, and prophets, whereas mysticism and superstition have always been attached to disease and healing. The emergence of epidemics and pandemics reinforces superstition the most.

In Cameroon, for instance, the founder and leader of Kingship International Ministries, Pastor Franklin Ndifor, claimed to have cured people with COVID-19 by laying his hand on them and praying. Word spread, and dozens of people with COVID-19 congregated at his church to be cured by prayer. But Ndifor himself caught the virus and died on May 16, 2020.

When Ndifor's death was announced, his followers rejected the news and blocked the entrance to his home to prevent medical staff from retrieving his mortal remains. They said their pastor was on a retreat with God and would return as they prayed and sang for his resurrection. It took the use of tear gas to disperse them before Ndifor's mortal remains were retrieved for burial.

On March 22, 2020, at the New Deliverance Evangelistic Church in Virginia, US, Bishop Gerald Glenn, in flagrant disregard for warnings against the gathering of more than 10 people, told his congregants, 'I firmly believe that God is larger than this dreaded virus.' He further said that 'people are healed' in his church, adding: 'I'm a preacher, I talk to God.' Nearly three weeks after the event, which was his last in-person church service, the 66-year-old Bishop died of COVID-19.

In Nigeria, Prophet T.B. Joshua of The Synagogue Church of All Nations made an audacious prophetic declaration that COVID-19 would go away on March 27, 2020. Delivering a sermon at his church on March 15, 2020, Prophet T.B Joshua said:

> This month, on 27th, it will be over. By the end of this month, whether we like it or not, no matter the medicine they might have produced to cure whatever, it will go the way it came.

He added, 'If it is not a medicine that brought this to the world, medicine cannot take it out. It will go the way it came.' When the prophetic date elapsed and more COVID-19 incidents and deaths were recorded in Nigeria, Prophet T.B. Joshua prescribed two lemons and hot water as a home remedy for COVID-19. He wrote on his Facebook page:

> Last meeting, I shared with you one of my habits. I am going to share with you one of my habits. I am going to share with you today, one more. My viewers, you deserve what I deserve—this is a revelation. In the morning, take a cup of hot water and two lemons. Cut the lemon into small slices and put it in the cup. After three to five minutes, begin to sip it as a drink. Refill it three times! I will advise you to move, walk around your compound or premises as you are sipping. After three to five minutes, sip it as a drink. When you are moving and sipping, it helps digestion.

The head of Aborigine Ogboni Worldwide, a fraternal institution indigenous to the Yoruba, Oba Olakisan Adetoyese, urged the Nigerian government to try traditional and spiritual means to combat the pandemic.

He also warned the government about the scientific method of tackling COVID-19, saying: 'The disease is not an ordinary one, and it demands a spiritual solution to send it packing. Several terrible epidemics in the past had always been tackled through spiritual means even when there was no medical or scientific know-how.' He added: 'I offered to embark on spiritual activities to curb the disease in the country, and I will meet with some selected governors in the South West on ways to avert the spread of the disease.' He also said: 'Also, I am ready to appease the gods through rituals in some selected cities within the South West region as a means of solving the epidemic.'

He called on traditional rulers and other religious leaders, especially Muslims and Christians, to embark on spiritual exertions to curb COVID-19.

Nigeria's COVID-19 tally at that time, in March 2020, was 30. Barely seven months later, as of October 20, 2020, Nigeria's case count was 61,558 confirmed cases, comprising 1,125 deaths, 56,697 recoveries, and 3736 active cases.

As usual, in every attempted spiritual remediation, it turns out that the solutions always come from science. In New Zealand, when they had recorded just over 100 cases as of mid-March 2020, they imposed nearly seven weeks of the strictest lockdown, which was responded to by the citizens with a level of compliance that was the highest in the world. By June

8, 2020, they were the first country to declare a COVID-19-free status, and they subsequently eased all the social restrictions they imposed to contain the spread of the virus.

They recorded a total of 1,500 cases with 22 deaths. Their success over the pandemic was wholly due to uncompromising science, driven by leadership, and had nothing to do with superstition, spirituality, or religion.

Black Death

In the mid-1300s, Europe was hit by the deadliest pandemic in the history of mankind. It was called the Black Death, and in an era where the germ theory was unknown, Europeans worried that the pandemic was sent by God as punishment for their sins. In the article: 'How Humanity's Response to Epidemic Diseases Has Stayed the Same Throughout History, Genevieve Carlton stated the facts:

> Although many flocked to church for protection, faith didn't protect Europeans from the plague. In the 14th century, the plague swept through religious communities, wiping out entire monasteries and convents. The pope himself withdrew from society instead of stepping up as a religious leader.

Smallpox

Berkeley, England, was hit by a smallpox epidemic in the 18th century, and it was the leading cause of death. Survivors were often left disfigured, and it was the worst thing to happen to a human.

As usual, people tested their faith in religion and were disillusioned. The available scientific remedy at the time was called variolation.

In variolation, a healthy person was inoculated with a matter taken from a patient with a mild condition of smallpox. The practice was based on the theory that the inoculated person would also develop a mild condition but would recover and be immune to future infections.

Unfortunately, when variolation was tried, the condition of the inoculated people wasn't always as mild as they had anticipated; their conditions often got worse, and they died, or at the very least, they infected other people.

But Edward Jenner made a profound observation during the period. He noticed that people who contracted cowpox recovered without treatment and they didn't contract smallpox, whether they were intentionally or accidentally exposed. He concluded that cowpox didn't only provide immunity against smallpox but could be transmitted from one person to another to provide protection against smallpox.

In May 1796, Edward Jenner took a matter from fresh cowpox lesions on the hand of a dairymaid and inoculated an eight-year-old boy called James Phipps, who had never had smallpox. Phipps became ill with cowpox for nine days and recovered on the 10th day.

On July 1, Jenner inoculated Phipps again, but with smallpox matter. Phipps, on the other hand, was completely immune to smallpox, and Jenner concluded his experiment as the discovery of a cure for smallpox (without ever joining the spirituality bandwagon).

For this scientific breakthrough, parliament voted him a sum of £10,000 in 1802 and another sum of £20,000 in 1806. He received worldwide recognition for his ingenuity and was recognised for discovering vaccination.

Life Purpose, Superstition, and Rationality

Since time immemorial, people have visited oracles, priests, and prophets in search of solutions to their problems and explanations for inexplicable causes and circumstances. Other people frequent places of divination to seek mojos for protection or to carry out some mischief.

Tales about these divinations abound, having been told and retold through the ages and attracting subscribers from near and far. But it's interesting to note that, unlike the fantastic stories from the past about the power of divination and the effectiveness of spiritual efforts, these things don't work in real life the way they do in stories.

So far, whereas historians, anthropologists, and archaeologists have probed and proven innumerable happenings that span as far back as the prehistoric era, no narrative about the practicality of superstition has been proven, not even by the devotees who promulgate those superstitious narratives. And, while certain phenomena, such as Angel's Glow, appeared to be real and widespread, when investigated, they were discovered to be a bioluminescent soil bacterium and had nothing to do with angels.

In 1955, during a revival service in Miami, Florida, Evangelist Jack Coe claimed to have divinely healed a three-year-old boy with polio and told the boy's parents to do away with his leg braces. However, they later found that the boy wasn't cured as Evangelist Jack Coe had made it seem, and attempting to walk without the braces caused him excruciating pain.

As a result of the sham, Evangelist Jack Coe was arrested on February 6, 1956, and was charged with practising medicine without a license. But the judge dismissed the case because Florida's law exempted divine healing. A few weeks later, Evangelist Jack Coe fell sick; his muscles were paralysed, and he underwent a tracheotomy to help his breathing. He was subsequently diagnosed with polio and died on December 16, 1956.

Throughout his ministry, Evangelist Jack Coe argued against doctors and taught his followers that they needed faith for healing, not medical treatment. So people were surprised that when he fell sick, he went to the hospital for treatment.

Supernaturality?

Unlike the numerous unverifiable stories that project supernatural powers, the following stories are about real-life events that tested the supernaturality of spirituality and superstition.

Bank Robbery in Tehran

In Iran, a man paid $500.00 to an oracle for a mojo that was supposed to make him invisible and enable him to rob a bank. He put on the mojo, and thinking that he had become invisible, he strutted into a bank in Tehran and began snatching money from the customers' hands and pulling wallets from their back pockets, but the infuriated customers smacked him down and handed him over to the police. When he was put before the court, he cried foul, telling the judge that he had been ripped off by an oracle.

The Xhosa Prophecy

Nongquawuse was born in 1841 and raised as an orphan by her uncle, who later became her special aid when she was a prophetess. In 1856, Nongquawuse said that the spirits of her ancestors came to her and told her that the British would leave their land if the Xhosa people destroyed their food, crops, cattle, and other sources of income.

Word spread, and except for a few Xhosas, the rest of them went on a cattle-killing frenzy and destroyed their crops. According to the prophecy, the expulsion of the British would happen on February 18, 1857. When the date passed, the British remained, and the Xhosas blamed the few people who did not participate in the cattle killing craze, but they soon became disillusioned and turned their rage on Nongquawuse.

The lack of food on their land caused a severe famine, reducing the Xhosa population from 105,000 to 27,000 people. Nongquawuse was subsequently arrested by the ethnic chief and handed over to a British army officer called Major Gawler, at whose residence Nongquawuse lived until she was released.

Psychic Sylvia Brown

Psychic Sylvia Brown gained prominence following a televised psychic reading. In a 2004 episode of *The Montel Williams Show*, she told Louwanna Miller that her missing daughter was dead. Miller felt sad and broke into tears on the show, but her daughter, Berry, was later found alive and kicking.

Sylvia Brown had previously informed the parents of missing Shawn Hornbeck that their son had died and that his remains could be found near two jagged boulders. Nearly four years later, Shawn Hornbeck was found alive.

While superstitious believers have so much faith in the supposed supernatural, Lt. Dave Parker of the Anchorage, Alaska Police Department said, 'We've never had a psychic lead that turns out to be correct.' His assertion corroborates the statement of former FBI agent and ABC News consultant, Brad Garret, who said that alleged tips from psychics rarely help solve a case. He also said, 'As far as finding a victim, finding remains, finding evidence, or in any way helping to solve the case, it's never been my experience.'

Understand: There isn't any domain of human consciousness that is as slippery as the path of spirituality, where belief comes before knowledge, doctrine before reasoning, faith before logic, and superstition before science. It's also the path where learning about the gods/God could be the beginning of perpetual brainwashing, manipulation, and exploitation, wherein the victims of the exploitation willingly cooperate, adore, and defend the teachings and names of their brainwashers. In one of Pastor Mensa Otabil's most circulated sermon clips, he said:

> As a matter of fact, when I started [pastoring] as a young man, I was talking to an older [pastor]; you know people who are ahead always want to advise young people, so this older [pastor], I hear he, supposedly, have been [pastoring] for a long time, and he called me and says, 'Young man, I like you, you know, I like the way you teach,' and he says, 'One thing about people; they like to be deceived,' and he says, 'You have to deceive them. Because if you

> don't deceive them, they'll go to somebody else to deceive them, so deceive them yourself.' That's what the older [pastor] told me. Because he had learned the trade and had realised that human beings generally don't think, and especially when they get born again, their spirits start working their brains, and it freezes. There's no intelligence afterwards. So some of you here run after a prophet somewhere and give all your money to him, and the next day he comes, you will do the same. Somebody is deceiving you, but you're willingly participating. Because the foolish man does not consider consequences, he doesn't sit back to analyse and say: 'I took that step last year; what are the results this year?'

Belief and Rationality Juxtaposed

Throughout history, kings, rulers, noblemen, merchants, and commoners have been enchanted by the exaggerations and hype of the supernaturality of superstition, thereby subscribing unquestionably to spirituality. So instead of being guided by knowledge, logic, strategy, and science, they draw on superstitions and fantastic bygone stories for critical life decisions. In any event, it turns out that the pragmatist who goes into a contest with critical thinking and strategy is poised to outwit and outperform his contender, who comes with his superstitious beliefs as his best foot.

Battle of Pelusium

In 525 BC, during the *Battle of Pelusium* between Persia and Egypt, the Persians learnt that the Egyptians, who had a formidable army and rarely lost a battle, worshipped cats and other animals. So, they developed their strategy around the Egyptians' superstition.

Cambyses II of Persia, who was a realist and an experienced field commander who knew about Egyptian religion, put a lot of cats and other Egyptian totems in front of his front line.

When the Egyptians saw the cats ahead of the Persians, they withheld their offensive for the fear of hurting the animals and incurring the wrath of their gods. This put them at a great disadvantage, while the Persians unleashed their assaults against them, resulting in the first Persian conquest of Egypt.

Aunty Vicky's Business Woes

While I was doing my national service, I also took on a part-time teaching job for a contractor. After work, I would visit his office to teach his children before heading home. The office was located next to a grocery store belonging to his landlady, a Ga woman in her sixties called Aunty Vicky.

She had been running the store for over forty years and her bread selection was her main source of income. The other items in the store were just supplementary sources of revenue.

Despite the presence of several grocery kiosks in the area, Aunty Vicky had essentially enjoyed a monopoly over the bread market for aeons. And if you were in her area, you had no choice but to buy her bread, whether you liked her or not.

Soon after I began teaching in the neighbourhood, a new grocery store opened on the same street, around three hundred metres away from Aunty Vicky's store. The owner, a Voltarian man in his forties known as Efo, became Aunty Vicky's main competitor. Efo's store was quite large, with a plethora of vividly coloured stock displayed on shelves, from snacks to toiletries. Old school music played in the background, which soon became a noticeable signature of the store.

Initially, Aunty Vicky felt uneasy about Efo's presence, but after a month, she got used to it and her fears allayed when she didn't notice any significant decline in her revenue. Meanwhile, Efo was also enjoying a fair share of the market, which was surprising, given that Aunty Vicky was an established figure in the neighbourhood while Efo was a newcomer.

However, this could be attributed to the two salesgirls Efo had brought with him from the start and the other items he had in stock that no other seller was offering.

Efo's salesgirls, one fair and slender, and the other dark and plump, were pretty and spunky. Additionally, he had hired three male store hands whose job was to assist customers by carrying their heavy purchases to their cars or to the nearby bus stop.

Efo didn't involve himself much with customers but sat back and observed the comings and goings of the store. He had also installed a CCTV system, allowing him to monitor the happenings in his store even when he wasn't present. He could access the footage on his phone and he once caught a shoplifter on camera. Efo shared the footage online, and it soon went viral. The shoplifter was eventually caught and arrested. On another occasion, one of Efo's store hands was caught on camera selling an item to a customer and pocketing the money. Efo again shared the footage online, and it quickly gained attention. The store hand was compelled to return the money and was dismissed.

A few months later, Aunty Vicky began to notice a decline in her bread sales as her customers started buying bread from Efo's store instead. Despite continuing to purchase other provisions from Aunty Vicky, they specifically visited Efo's store for bread. When returning from Efo's store to buy additional provisions from Aunty Vicky, or while passing by her store on their way home from Efo's store, Aunty Vicky observed her customers trying to hide the bread they had bought from Efo by stiffly holding it by their sides to avoid being noticed.

As time went on, Aunty Vicky noticed a general decline in the sales of her other items. Her customers were now buying all of their provisions at Efo's store, rather than having to hide their bread before returning to her store to purchase the rest of their items. She realised that Efo's store was becoming the preferred shopping destination for her customers, and she was losing out on business.

Aunty Vicky couldn't comprehend why her loyal customers were abandoning her, despite never being rude to anyone and selling bread that was the same size, taste and price as Efo's. She understood that Efo's attractive salesgirls were drawing in male customers, but she couldn't understand why her friends and family members were opting to buy from Efo instead. Aunty Vicky suspected that Efo, being a Voltarian, had put a hex on her and her business.

She became increasingly convinced that Efo was using spiritual means to harm her business and steal her customers. Therefore, Aunty Vicky began spreading rumours to anyone who would listen, claiming that Efo had planted juju near her store to bring bad luck. Her superstitious fears were well fuelled by her listeners, who warned her about the supposed juju practices of Voltarians. Some advised her to take action, so she decided to seek the advice of her pastor.

Aunty Vicky attended a traditional church, and when she shared her suspicions about Efo's spiritual interference with her pastor, he confirmed them. He advised her that her irregular attendance at church had left her vulnerable to the devil's influence on her business. He prayed for her and invoked the name of Jesus to neutralise any possible juju that might have been planted to drive her customers away.

Afterwards, Aunty Vicky began attending church regularly, but despite her efforts, her business continued to struggle. Eventually, she stopped calling her bread supplier since no one was buying it and instead focussed on selling a limited selection of toiletries and snacks.

Aunty Vicky's cousin, who was her age, advised her that the pastors from traditional churches were not passionate enough about spiritual matters and suggested that she seek help from a more spiritually inclined church. He directed her to a gown church located by the sea, known for its strong spiritual practices.

A prophetess at the gown church affirmed Aunty Vicky's suspicion and prayed for her while making her roll on the bare ground and having her bathe in seawater. She then gave her a crucifix to hang at the top of the wall opposite her store's entrance, where it would be visible to everyone. The prophetess assured her that the crucifix had the power to neutralise any juju that might have been planted around her store.

Aunty Vicky followed the prophetess' instructions and hung the crucifix in her store, but even after two months, there was no improvement. Her friend suggested that the solution to her problem might not lie with any church and recommended an effective oracle in the Western region who could help. They agreed to visit the oracle on Friday.

After learning about Aunty Vicky's problem on Wednesday, I approached her to listen to her concerns. She explained that her troubles began on the day Efo opened his store and that she harboured a deep-seated distrust of Voltarians due to their reputation for practising juju.

I respectfully challenged Aunty Vicky's beliefs and assumptions by pointing out that superstition and stereotyping can be self-inflicting and damaging, and that there could be a rational explanation for what was happening to her store. I also suggested that a rational approach could be helpful in understanding and solving her problem. I explained to her that people of all ethnic groups can practice juju and that it was unfair to single out Voltarians. Furthermore, I pointed out to her that the area around her store was paved, and if someone had dug out the blocks to plant juju, it would've been noticeable. I knew there was no evidence of such an occurrence, and that the problem wasn't spiritual as she believed.

After making well-intentioned efforts to help, I found that Aunty Vicky was not receptive to my suggestions. She dismissed my rational approach and rebuked me harshly, insisting that the issue was spiritual and beyond my understanding as a child–I was 24 years at the time. I felt embarrassed and unsure of how to respond as she asserted her beliefs, leaving me feeling like the only one who disagreed with her superstitions. It became evident that she was seeking confirmation of her own beliefs rather than considering alternative perspectives.

On Friday, as planned, Aunty Vicky and her friend travelled to the Western region to visit the oracle. She left the store in the care of her unemployed niece for the whole week that she spent in the Western region until she returned with the oracle. The next day, the oracle performed a ritual at the store and sprinkled a liquid in calabash, which was meant to dispel any evil spirit hindering Aunty Vicky's business. After the ritual, the oracle instructed Aunty Vicky to close the store for a month and come every midnight to sprinkle the liquid in calabash at the entrance of the store. He assured her that the store would rebound after the 30-day break.

Aunty Vicky diligently followed the oracle's instructions and performed the midnight ritual as directed. After the 30 days had passed, she eagerly called her suppliers to restock her store, hopeful that her woes were over. It was a Monday, and as midday passed, not a single buyer had come in. Then, around 2:00 p.m., a woman in a white gown walked into the store. Aunty Vicky recognised her as the prophetess she had visited at the seaside; the one who had given her the crucifix.

They had a long conversation, and as the woman was about to leave, she bought a slice of bread from Aunty Vicky.

As the woman was leaving the store, she came across a child and inquired if the little girl was feeling hungry. The child appeared confused, and before she could respond, the woman handed her the bread and continued on her way.

The little girl, who happened to be Aunty Vicky's granddaughter, ran up to her and told her about the woman who had just given her bread. Aunty Vicky looked and saw that it was the same slice she had sold to the woman. Her face grimaced with confusion as she watched the prophetess going. About 300 metres down the road, the woman turned towards Efo's store, then came back into view with a black polythene bag, presumably containing bread.

Aunty Vicky's heart sank as she realised that the spiritual woman had also rejected her bread and bought one from Efo's store. She couldn't help but feel crestfallen and foolish for relying so heavily on spirituality to solve her business woes. She regretted wasting all that money she had spent at the shrine in the Western region and the gown church. To add insult to injury, she still had bruises on her elbows and knees from being made to roll aggressively on the bare ground while a group of men and women followed her, clapping and chanting 'holy ghost fire.'

After realising that her superstitious approach wasn't helping, Aunty Vicky turned to me for advice, telling me I was the only person with a different perspective. She told me again how everything started and how much money she had wasted in her futile attempt to revive her business, including the fact that when she returned from the Western region, her niece didn't hand her any sales cash. She claimed to have heard some paranormal noise in the store at midnight while she was in her room, and when she opened the store at daybreak, all the sales cash had disappeared from the box where she kept it. Aunty Vicky believed her and attributed the 'spiritual theft' to Efo's doings.

As she told me this, I remembered the week when her niece ran the store. She had bought an expensive designer bag and a pair of shoes as gifts for the contractor's secretary. She had even written a love letter to her, promising her that she would shower her with more gifts if she agreed to be her girlfriend. This memory sparked a realisation in my mind.

The Rational Approach

I am not aware of any verified instances where superstition has triumphed and successfully solved a problem. While uncorroborated stories, hearsay, and tales abound, they do not provide credible evidence for the effectiveness of superstition.

Despite Aunty Vicky's initial resistance to my suggestions, I hoped that eventually, she would realise the limitations of her irrational beliefs. And as her issue now fell under my responsibility, I was eager to help her find a solution based on rational and evidence-based approaches.

So after conducting a survey of 20 of Aunty Vicky's former customers, I discovered that they all switched to Efo's store for the same reason: Aunty Vicky was known for chewing on a sponge all day and constantly having her hand in her mouth rubbing the sponge over her teeth. However, the real problem was that, Aunty Vicky's loaves were uncovered, and when customers came to buy a loaf or slice, she would pick it up with the same hand that had been holding the sponge in her mouth.

This disgusted her customers, but they had tolerated it in the past because they had nowhere else to buy bread. However, when Efo opened his store, customers were impressed by the fact that his bread was packaged in transparent polythene. Even when a customer wanted to buy a slice, the salesgirls would pick the bread with their hands inside the outside of a fresh black polythene bag so that their bare hands wouldn't touch the bread. They would then hand the bread to the customer in the same black polythene bag. This hygienic practice was the main reason Aunty Vicky's customers switched to Efo's store.

While trying my best to help resolve Aunty Vicky's issue, I befriended Efo and discovered that he was a practical and rational individual who believed in evidence-based strategies, not superstition or juju. He was an avid reader of books on sales and marketing, which were the source of the innovative ideas he implemented in his store, such as installing a CCTV system and playing old school music to evoke nostalgia among his customers. Even the idea of employing attractive salesgirls and store hands was assimilated from the books he read.

After relaying my observation of Efo to Aunty Vicky, she realised that her lifelong ignorance was due to her misplaced belief in superstition and her failure to seek out evidence-based solutions. She also came to realise that Efo's success over her was due to his knowledge of business and marketing strategies. In contrast, Aunty Vicky had never read a book or article on these topics and had relied solely on faith and spiritual directives from religious TV channels. Like most religious adherents I know of, she failed to recognise the difference between what she saw on TV and real-life situations.

To help Aunty Vicky recover her business, I suggested some measures, such as hiring a pretty and spunky salesgirl, and installing a CCTV system in her store among other things. Although it took some time, Aunty Vicky's store eventually regained its former popularity, and her sales returned to their pre-Efo levels. Even when she had to travel and leave her niece in charge of the store, she never experienced any **mysterious financial losses** again.

In the end, Aunty Vicky's willingness to change and my practical suggestions helped her turn her struggling business around.

Superstition Will Take Your Focus Away From Your Goals

Beginning as a social orientation, most of us born and bred in Africa were imbued with superstition before we learnt to walk and talk. And we grew to accept as true any idea about spirituality that was instilled in us, even if it was illogical.

The same is true for our religious beliefs, and whether you call it church or shrine, or you reference God, juju, or ancestral spirits, the dynamics of superstition are the same.

I must admit that I was brainwashed and entrenched in superstition in the past, but unlike the masses who remain like that for a lifetime, I snapped out of it before long. For some other people I know, their disillusionment shook them to the core, and they had to be referred to psychiatrists for help.

According to the Head of Psychology at the University of Ghana, Professor Joseph Safo, prophetic theology is one of the major causes of suicide in Ghana:

> Within the remit of African prophetic theology, there's something we call triumphalism. Triumphalism means that when you go to a lot of churches, especially, the prophetic ministries, they give you a

> picture that God's intervention is so real that no matter the existential crisis confronting a person, when they preach the word and they give you prophecy, God will intervene. Now what happens is that they become frustrated when they don't get results...It is this theology of escaping suffering that creates a problem for them.

These people gave too much time, energy, and money to their religious leaders in the expectation of meeting their life aspirations and resolving their dire issues, only to be disillusioned in the end. They include students who, instead of seeking help from academic counsellors, rather sought help from prophets; businessmen who, instead of seeking help from consultants, rather sought out mojo from oracles; job seekers who, instead of seeking help from career coaches, rather sought help from 'prophets' and diviners; and sick people who, instead of visiting the hospital, rather got carried away by unverified healing miracles on TV and fell victim to charlatans.

The list goes on and on, including athletes seeking trophies. These athletes, for instance, train very hard for a match, yet they may lose. But when they win, they attribute their victories to the oracles they consulted. But it begs the question: 'Why would they train if a supernatural power would grant them victory anyway?'

Ghanaian boxers, Braimah Kamoko, a.k.a. Bukom Banku, and Ayittey Powers later renounced their belief in juju, saying that juju doesn't work in the ring, but only hard training and preparation do. Ayittey Powers came to this realisation after an oracle he had consulted before a bout assured him of a resounding victory, yet he was beaten to a pulp and woefully lost the bout.

I once visited a sick friend called Moses. His condition was getting worse because he wasn't taking his medication. I asked him why, and he told me that in the past, he always sent his medication to his pastor to pray over it in order to be efficacious. I asked him why he hadn't sent his medicine to him, and he told me his pastor had travelled and would be back in a week. I then asked him, 'If your pastor doesn't return, how would you survive?' He didn't answer.

Moses had already hurled curses at his sister and called his mother a witch for trying to talk him out of his dogma. But he didn't dare me on that, and out of respect for me, though with reluctance, he took his medication as the doctor directed him, and without any spiritual exertion, he started getting well.

When he recovered, he apologised to his mother and sister and expunged superstition from his mindset, never to look back at it again. He had since embraced a realistic worldview and admitted that he now realises his past troubles were due to his ignorance and not witchcraft, as he had been led to believe.

Next, I'll share a real-life story of a collegian who fell for religious indoctrination, and two other real-life stories, involving a graduate job seeker and a businessman who sought out spiritual backing and paid dearly.

The Collegian

On August 5, 2015, Ghanaians woke up to the shock of the breaking news that a citizen had left the country to join the Islamic State. Nazir Nortei Alema was a 25-year-old Geography and Rural Development graduate from Kwame Nkrumah University of Science and Technology. He had sent a message to his family that he was on his way for an official assignment at Prestea, then to Takoradi. But after a while, he sent his brother a different message:

> Pray for me, I will never forget you in my prayer, and it's my hope and prayer that we will meet again, if not in this world, then in Jannah (paradise). I love you all. May Allah grant us understanding and guide us all to the straight path. Assalamu alaikum! I told you a lie to please my Allah. The deception was to go do some research work in faraway Prestea while the main idea was to move far away from you all to the Islamic State (IS). I know it might sound kind of crazy to you, but your son really had to take this bold step to get out of the corrupt system of Ghana which has democracy first on its list.

It was later revealed, to the shock of the entire Ghanaian populace and particularly disappointing to Ghanaian Muslims, that Alema had fallen for the indoctrination of a certain Badharn Diallo, a Guinean Muslim, who had come to Ghana to recruit henchmen for the Islamic State. In March of the following year, Nazir Nortei Alema was killed in a battle in the Syrian city of Homs.

The Graduate Job-Seeker

Two days before her graduation, Jane had a call from her prophet. He warned her not to eat any food her stepmother would bring to her graduation ceremony and told her to fast and pray until 2:00 pm on that day. This was to avert the unfortunate things that might befall her in the years to come. Jane revered the foretelling!

The graduation ceremony ended at midday, but Jane forgot about her prophet's warning and ate her stepmother's meal while she was revelling with her friends. She remembered the warning after she had swallowed the last morsel and was panic-stricken about the unknown consequence.

Three years after her graduation, Jane had no job. Her prophet told her there was a spiritual conspiracy behind her joblessness, which was triggered when she ate her stepmother's meal, and unless she came to church every day for special prayers, she would never land a job.

He also told Jane to sell the taxi her deceased mother bequeathed to her and bring the money to the church as an offering to God. He told Jane to trust God and believe that by obeying the prophetic directive (selling her taxi and giving the money to God), she would land a juicy job. The taxi was Jane's only source of income, but she sold it and gave the money as an offering to her church.

Two years passed and Jane was still unemployed; then one afternoon, she received a phone call. The caller introduced herself as the HR manager of a company Jane had sent a job application to, and she asked Jane to revise and resend her cover letter and CV. Jane complied and spent a lot of time wondering who the caller was because her voice was familiar.

The next day, the human resources manager called again and asked Jane to revise and resend her cover letter and CV. This time, Jane was thoughtful; the caller's voice was more familiar, and she began wondering what was amiss. But she complied anyway, and not long after she resent the email, she received a call for a job interview; Jane broke down in tears.

In the boardroom, while she awaited the interview panel, a secretary came to serve her a folder containing what was supposed to be her cover letter and CV, and she told her she could refer to them during the interview. At a glance, Jane noticed that the cover letter and CV bore her name, but the content was different from all three that she had sent.

This made her confused, and her confusion rendered her jittery and inarticulate during the interview, but the interview was short, and Jane was surprised by the news of her success over the other candidates. To Jane, this was a miracle: who was the caller with the familiar voice? Why did she call twice? Who had rewritten her cover letter and CV better than the ones she sent? Why was the interview so brief? How did she emerge as the best candidate, knowing that she was inarticulate during the interview?

She concluded that someone was behind her success, but who might it be? She spent a sleepless night thinking about these questions, and at daybreak, she informed her prophet about it. Her prophet's reply was that Jane's tears over her joblessness and the sacrifice she made to God with her taxi had reached heaven, and so God sent an angel to rewrite her cover letter and CV to enable her to get a job. Jane cried out 'halleluiah' and promised to give away her first salary to the church.

On Monday, when Jane reported to work, the secretary served her some documents to peruse, which she recognised immediately. They were the first cover letter and CV, and the other two she sent upon the caller's instruction. She noticed that the documents had been defaced with red ink strikethroughs and insertions due to typos, grammatical errors, and poor sentence structures.

She wondered if there was an English professor working with the company and why they would treat her job application documents as though it was an English 101 assignment. She was so engrossed that she didn't notice the HR manager passing to take her seat. 'Jane', she heard her name and raised her head. It was Hetty, her school mother in senior high school.

Jane lit up with excitement, seeing Hetty for the first time in 11 years, and everything made sense to her there and then: she wasn't getting a job because no recruiter would shortlist a candidate who wrote so poorly as she did, and it had nothing to do with her stepmother.

She thanked Hetty for rewriting her cover letter and CV and resolved to take a writing class to improve her writing.

I first met Jane at the University of Ghana Business School, where we had both gone to inquire about a master's programme. When she narrated her experience to me, I asked her how she coped with life after she sold her taxi and gave the money to her prophet. She replied, 'It was terrible for me. The taxi was my only source of livelihood, and after I sold it, I constantly had to rely on family and friends for my upkeep. There were days I went without food.'

I asked her how she fell for the deception. She responded, 'It started in my childhood. We were not allowed to question what they taught us about God, faith, and spirituality; we were only to believe and never to doubt what we were told in God's name. We were also made to believe that everything they told us came from God, and I grew to believe that anyone who did not share my belief was an enemy of God and an evil person. They also instilled fear in us and made us feel as though we were being haunted by evil spirits. So, I lived my whole life in fear and would do anything the prophet would ask me to do, without thinking. Little did I know, I've been brainwashed all my life.'

The Businessman Who Sought Spiritual Backing

It isn't known when the late Edward Quartey-Papafio began consulting the oracles, Gamelo Larwei, 36, and Famous Adorkunu, 37, at the Power 1 shrine, located on the outskirts of Adeiso in the Eastern Region. But it was established that Quartey-Papafio paid them Gh¢10,650.00 for a mojo he believed he could use to conjure Gh¢400,000.00 to fund his business. The two oracles, a.k.a Power and Scorpion, about whom locals had lived in awe because of their supposed mysticism, came from Togo and were domiciled in Ghana. They usually ran commercials and talk shows on a private TV station to lure prospective clients who wanted to acquire wealth overnight. It was also reported that both men, as oracles, had duped some unsuspecting victims to the tune of various sums.

On January 15, 2020, Quartey-Papafio visited the Power 1 shrine to get the mojo he had paid the oracles for, and he was never heard of again. A subsequent investigation led a team of police officers to the shrine. When the oracles were interrogated, they confessed they had shot and killed 64-year-old Edward Quartey-Papafio and syphoned his blood. They then led the police to his grave and exhumed his mortal remains.

A second and third decomposing corpses were exhumed from different graves in the shrine. A decomposed body with skeletal remains and another corpse were also exhumed within the same perimeter of the shrine. Finally, the police retrieved human skulls and other skeletal remains hidden under two fetishes in the shrine. Both Power and Scorpion were arrested and put before the court for murder.

Quartey-Papafio was not the only person who met a tragic end while seeking spiritual support in the pursuit of a goal. Many are the credulous people who fall for urban tales that aggrandise the might of oracles, magic, and mysticism. Yet, 'evidence' of their effectiveness has always been urban tales, uncorroborated bygone stories, hearsay, and unconfirmed radio and TV broadcasts.

Embrace a Realistic Worldview

If you belong to a superstitious group, you should learn about these things as soon as possible—preferably before embarking on the journey of your life's purpose. Because sooner or later, a relative, a friend, or a colleague will entreat you to seek spiritual backing.

And it makes no difference whether they're referring you to a church, shrine, or other religious entity; you could end up being manipulated, exploited, or entangled.

Take note: if you disagree with their superstitious inducement, they will try to intimidate you by predicting doom for your lifepath. On the lighter side, some people will even tell you things like 'you're carnally minded' and may refer you to scriptures that even insult your disposition toward common sense. But say nothing, don't argue with them, and don't let their words get to you. This is why: you can't change the mind of someone who isn't willing to have their mind changed. Typical of most religious adherents, their beliefs are not based on logic or reason, but identity and group affiliation. As such, they perceive any teaching or idea that challenges what they've been made to believe as an attack on their identity. Accordingly, they become even more rigid and defensive, and won't agree with you regardless of the facts and figures you present to them. Besides, most of them have been dogmatically conditioned and systematically brainwashed from the cradle and are likely to remain so until the grave.

In places I lived through my childhood, the masses believed in superstition or belonged to fellowships that identified as spiritual. These people were quick to accuse anyone of witchcraft if the person refused to reason with them on their spiritual terms. Yet they desired better lives and believed they would achieve them through their spiritual efforts. If they were right, why haven't the most religious countries in the world minted the most billionaires and buoyant economies? Also, in all my travels, I found the most ignorance and abject poverty among the most superstitious demographics, but this, might not be the case in other regions and countries though. Meantime, take a look at the developed countries, and see how they've advanced with science over the years.

Rationality is thinking, logic, reasoning, pragmatism, knowledge-seeking, strategy, intellectualism, endeavour, ingenuity, science, and technology. It's the basis of common sense and the starting point of human advancement. In contrast, superstition is an overly credulous belief in and reverence for the supernatural, which is frequently propagated through religion.

According to the Merriam-Webster dictionary, superstition is a belief or practice resulting from ignorance, fear of the unknown, trust in magic or chance, or a false conception of causation. The catchwords here are ignorance, fear, and false.

In some parts of Africa, the most common depiction of superstition is a concept called **God-will-do.** In Ghana, it's translated in Akan as *Nyame Bɛyɛ,* and it's prevalent among the vastly religious population. The problem with *Nyame Bɛyɛ* is that this concept undermines the human problem-solving impetus because when people expect their needs to be provided by someone or a higher power, they relax and withhold the effort that is needed to get things done.

But the reality is that, regardless of whatever your religion has taught you about God or your god's providence, nothing in this life is achieved without brains and effort. And it doesn't matter if someone believes in God or any other deity or has no belief at all; anyone who puts their brain and effort to work will get results and can be successful.

So, guess how a country fares when its leaders and more than half of its citizens are superstitious and excessively religious? In such countries, you'll find more religious entities than corporations, the education system is substandard, the health sector is below par, the rule of law is weak, and the social order churns out too much corruption and poverty.

What is more? Also, in such countries, the masses don't recognise that ignorance is the bane of society. Instead, they attribute every problem to spirituality, blame witches and evil spirits for their troubles, and turn to religion and superstition to solve their problems, which never get solved.

> As soon as something terrible happens, instead of us investigating-finding out what might have been the cause and therefore trying to find a solution, we go for the cheap way, spiritual, and that mitigates any attempt to do serious investigations to try to find out the actual cause of an event. – Most Reverend (Dr) Emmanuel Asante.

In the light of this God-will-do concept, in 2020, at the height of the COVID-19 panic, President Akuffo Addo invited some prominent Ghanaian clerics to the *Jubilee House* and beseeched them to pray to the God of Israel for divine intervention.

President John Magufuli's response to the pandemic in Tanzania was even more dramatic and offbeat. On April 5, 2020, at a church in Tanzania, he told the congregation that COVID-19 was satanic and did not reside in the body of Jesus (the church). He then called for three days of national prayer to defeat COVID-19 and told the citizens that they could flock to the churches.

In addition, he forbade health workers from mentioning COVID-19 and downplayed the World Health Organisation's recommended safety measures, such as the wearing of face masks. Meanwhile, the coronavirus was spreading and causing mass hospitalisation and deaths. According to one Tanzanian doctor:

> We have elderly patients coming in, showing every symptom that we've seen around the world, but we cannot test… we are not allowed to mention even COVID-19. We have to call it pneumonia.

While President John Magufuli continued to downplay the seriousness of the pandemic, his sudden absence from public life was noticed. Word spread that he had caught the virus and was seriously ill. His death was announced after two weeks of his absence, whereas rumours that he succumbed to COVID-19 were given resonance by Tanzania's main opposition leader, Tundu Lissu.

In Israel, however, Prime Minister Benjamin Netanyahu tasked the Israeli Institute for Biological Research with developing a vaccine. By December 2021, the Israeli Institute for Biological Research had successfully developed the BriLife vaccine. Apparently, the scientific method, not Nyame Bɛyɛ, proved effective once again.

At the European Union Parliament on December 14, 2021, President Akuffo-Addo said:

> I am a firm believer in the statement that 'no one is safe until everyone is safe.' Let us help make vaccines available to all parts of the world, encourage our citizens to take the jab, and we will win the fight against COVID faster and together.

The speech above marked President Akufo-Addo's shift from superstition to a scientific standpoint. Some weeks later, in a sod-cutting ceremony for the construction of Accra STEM Academy, President Akufo Addo, in his speech, hit the nail on the head:

> Indeed, our world is essentially driven by technology. Energy, industry, agriculture, medicine and health, clean air and water, transportation, sanitation, the use, management and conservation of natural resources - the successful exploitation of all these sectors depend, ultimately, on the application of science and technology. So it is obvious that, to be part of this modern world, science and technology must be present at every stage of the development process.

Note that Israel isn't the most scientifically advanced country in the world, nor is it the country with the best education system. But they took a scientific approach in the face of a pandemic, took the initiative to develop a vaccine, and succeeded at it.

Take a cue from this: none of the 'religious economies' that exercised spiritual exertions in an attempt to curb the coronavirus was able to produce a vaccine or provide any antidotes. In the end, they took the vaccines that were produced by the 'scientific economies.'

The Danger of Dogma

Some years ago, I was with my daughter and her playmates when a lady and a gentleman came in to share their religious teachings with them. My wife welcomed them, and the children gathered to hear them. I was ready to go to work at the time, but I decided to sit with them to hear every word the visitors spoke to the children until they left.

I wasn't worried they would hurt the kids, but having grown up in a religious family, I know that the essence of accepting a belief system is to believe and obey without questioning or doubting. I've seen how this orientation can cause a child to become gullible and vulnerable to manipulation and exploitation by some clergymen and women. This is so common in a religious demographic.

I've seen how dangerous it can be when dogma sinks into a child's brain and influences their worldview. I've seen the same effect on many adults, including relatives and friends. These relatives and friends tend to believe everything their 'clerics' tell them in God's name and would do anything they told them, no matter how absurd. I've also noticed how a lot of children are being covertly brainwashed at many places of worship in order to be controlled and exploited when they become adults, at which point they'll choose to die for their brainwashers.

Furthermore, brainwashed religious adherents dwell in their own fantasies and act sanctimoniously towards open-minded people. Sometimes, they even think the latter are foolish for not thinking like them. This renders it nearly impossible to convert brainwashed fellows en masse to realism without risking being perceived as Satan or an enemy.

Due to this experience, I was determined to train my daughter to be logical enough to notice brainwashers and misleading religious teachings so common in my demographic. This was in order to prevent anyone from inculcating any dogma in her. I also wanted to train her to question any concept, teaching, or idea that doesn't add up, including her own beliefs and worldview, and never to allow herself to be influenced by superstition or be afraid to ditch any belief she will later find to be absurd and harmful to herself or that can incite her to hate or hurt someone. Simply put, I wanted her to grow up to be a critical thinker, a go-getter, and an open-minded woman.

Fortunately, there are still some religious entities that are proper, and I have no doubt that some clerics are noble. Personally, I have a heartfelt admiration for the Chief Imam of Ghana, Sheik Osman Nuhu Sharubutu, for his piety and commitment to oneness among Ghanaian Christians and Muslims.

However, due to the prevalence of unbridled chicanery and charlatanism in many religious establishments, you must tread cautiously in matters of faith, lest you be brainwashed and fall for the antics of the many charlatans who spread ignorance and misrepresent the Creator.

In January 2014, a South African pastor called Rev. Lesego Daniel of Rabboni Centre Ministries in Garankuwa, North Pretoria, told his congregants to dash to the lawn at the church premises and chew the grass, assuring them the act would bring them closer to God.

When he said this, dozens of his congregants, including a 21-year-old law student, threw themselves to the ground and voraciously munched the grass as though they were possessed. Following the grass-munching hysteria, photos on the internet showed women congregants clutching their stomachs in the restroom while men vomited into sinks.

Again, in September of the same year, Rev. Lesego Daniel made his congregants drink petrol, telling them the petrol would miraculously turn into pineapple juice. 'Do you believe in the Father [God]? Can you imagine not being able to have a baby, and you come here, drink petrol, and tomorrow, the doctor says, 'No more barrenness, you are pregnant because you drank petrol?'

In July 2015, another South African pastor called Penuel Mnguni of End Times Disciples Ministries in Soshanguve, North Pretoria, asked his congregation to eat live snakes, assuring them that the snakes would turn into chocolate in their mouths. His congregants did as they were told.

Penuel Mnguni, in the past, had made his followers eat human hair and rags, claiming God has the power to make a person eat anything and that his teachings were based on scripture.

These absurdities are prevalent in a religious demographic. However, the antics of Lesego and Penuel are only infinitesimal, considering the totality of the various acts of mass stupidity that people have been made to do in the name of religion.

Prophet Rufus Phala, the general overseer of the AK Spiritual Christian Church in Makgodu, Limpopo, South Africa, made his members drink disinfectant during a Sunday church service, claiming that God had instructed him to do so. Prophet Theo Bongani Maseko of the Breath of Christ Ministries, South Africa, also asked his congregants to drink engine oil, which they did.

In 2021, Prophet Kevin O. Smith, the Head Preacher of St. James Pathway International Kingdom Restoration Ministries, and his aides allegedly slit the throats of an unidentified man and a 39-year-old woman named Tanecka Gardner at church in Jamaica—in what was suspected to be a human sacrifice ritual.

Some weeks before the blood-letting ceremony, Smith told his congregants that there would be a flood. And on the day of the sacrifice, he posted on his timeline, 'The Ark is loading now! Leave immediately dressed in white…It is a Roman Catholic sacrifice—it will have no survivors.'

Had it not been for the timely intervention of the police, it was reported that some naked men had lined up, each ready to take his turn to be slaughtered.

Magdalena Solis: The High Priestess of Blood

In the early part of 1963 in Mexico, the Hernández brothers, Santos and Cayetano, both scammers, devised a ruse to make quick money. So they targeted Yerba Buena, an impoverished community with mostly illiterate inhabitants.

When the two arrived in the isolated community, they announced themselves as a prophet and priest of the Inca gods and told the villagers that if they accepted to worship and pay tribute to the Inca gods, the all-powerful gods would provide them with treasures in the mountain caves surrounding their village. They also told the villagers that their old kingdom would be rebuilt and that they would be given power to rule, while those who didn't believe would be punished.

The rhetoric sank in and won over the already superstitious villagers. Santos and Cayetano then established a cult fellowship with them.

In one of the mountain caves, which became their place of worship, Santos and Cayetano demanded money and sexual tributes from their adult members (both men and women) and indulged in drug-fuelled orgies with them.

These activities continued until the members were disillusioned: the promise of the treasure and the restoration of their ancient kingdom were not happening. Scepticism set in, and they began questioning their prophet and priest. Without any plausible explanation for them, the Hernández brothers devised another plan. They travelled to Monterrey in search of a prostitute to join their cause, and ran into Magdalena Solís and her pimp brother, Eleazar Solís, there.

Santos and Cayetano came back with her, presented her to the devotees through a flashy smokescreen trick, and introduced her to them as a reincarnation of the goddess Cōātlīcue. The ignorant devotees fell for the trick and didn't doubt Magdalena Solís' 'authenticity'. But suddenly, and usually under these circumstances, Magdalene Solís came to fancy herself as a true incarnate of the goddess Cōātlīcue and arrogated to herself total control over the cult.

Two members had become fed up with the recurring sexual exploitation and told the rest they wanted to leave the group. Word spread and reached Solís and the Hernández brothers; Solís ordered their deaths, and the two were lynched by the other members.

After the first murder of the two, Solís—who had become bored with the orgies—became bloodthirsty, devised a blood ritual, and began making demands for human sacrifices.

Her victims were the dissidents within the group, who were either lynched, burnt, or mutilated by the group members and left to bleed to death. She collected her victims' blood in a chalice, mixed it with chicken blood, weed, or peyote, and drank the blood mixture before passing it to the Hernández brothers, then to their devotees.

The devotees believed that drinking the blood-mix gave them supernatural powers, and so the blood ritual went on for six weeks, during which four people were sacrificed and had their hearts ripped out.

One night in May 1963, a 14-year-old boy called Sebastián Guerrero was wandering about the mountains when he noticed a light and noise coming from the caves. He prowled nearer and saw the cult members in the process of slaughtering another victim for sacrifice.

Horrified by what he saw, Guerrero ran for more than 25 kilometres to Villa Gran, the town where the nearest police station was, and reported what he had seen. The police, after listening to Guerrero's narrative, dismissed it as the delusion of a drugged boy. The next day, one of the investigators, Luis Martinez, offered to escort Guerrero home and check where he claimed he had seen those 'vampires.' But neither Guerrero nor Martinez returned.

Alarmed by Guerrero and their colleague's disappearance, the police took the narrative seriously and called in the army's assistance for a raid at Yerba Buena. Magdalena Solís and her brother, Eleazar, were found high on a farm, smoking weed, and were arrested. Santos was shot while resisting arrest; a dozen other cult members were also shot.

As for Santos' brother, Cayetano Hernández, he had already been murdered by a psychotic member of the group called Jesús Rubio. Jesús Rubio, knowing Cayetano Hernández as a priest, killed him, believing that keeping part of Cayetano's body would give him divine protection. Subsequent interrogation led to where the dismembered corpses of Sebastián Guerrero and Luis Martinez were buried, and it was near the farm where Magdalena and her brother Eleazar were living.

The two were handed a 50-year jail term each, whereas the rest of the members, considering their illiteracy and delusion, were given a 30-year prison sentence each.

How did these things begin, and how did they get there? If any man or woman succeeds in making you believe that they have divine powers, they can manipulate you. Even for any conventional religious organisation, if they succeed in brainwashing you in God's name or the name of any deity you revere, they can make you do anything!

Expunge Superstition and Embrace Rationality at All Times

To expunge superstition and embrace rationality doesn't mean you're rejecting God—as people who want to keep you ignorant would attempt to make you believe. Embracing rationality means turning to your God-given brain to solve problems.

This is what has brought progress to the human race. Besides, after centuries of experimenting with the God-will-do concept in Africa, it turns out that rationality and science rather orient us to God's nature and our primordial life purpose, which is for us to be fruitful, multiply, fill the earth, and subdue it.

This primordial life purpose has been realised and continues to be advanced by the pursuit of knowledge and scientific endeavours, which are substrata of rationality.

Unfortunately, superstition and excessive spirituality haven't conjured a toothpick (at least, not one that has been proven) or churned out a more straightforward explanation for why water wets glass. Yet, it distracts millions of religious adherents from endeavour, ingenuity, and common sense.

Key Takeaway: It is important to have a realistic worldview and to approach beliefs and practices with a critical and rational mindset. This can help protect against manipulation and exploitation, as well as support personal growth and progress. It is also important to be aware of the potential negative effects of superstition and to recognise that scientific knowledge and technology plays a significant role in human advancement.

Be that as it may, have science and rationality answered all questions or solved every problem?

Unravelling the dancing plague: a tale of superstition and science

In the summer of 1518, in the French city of Strasbourg, something very strange happened. It was called the **dancing plague**. It all began when a woman called Frau Troffea stepped out of her house and started dancing, even though there was no music. She danced throughout the day, puzzling her neighbours and onlookers. Exhausted, she took an overnight break, but when she woke up, she continued dancing despite her bruised and bloody feet.

Word spread, and a crowd began to gather to watch Frau Troffea's peculiar dance. They wondered if she had gone mad and feared that she might dance until her death. Surprisingly, more people joined her, and soon around 30 individuals were dancing with her, all without music. The crowd grew larger, with as many as 400 people joining the spontaneous dance.

The situation became a crisis, bewildering the city council. Every day, a group of men and women would wake up and uncontrollably dance, pushing themselves to exhaustion. The dancers were clearly in pain and begged for relief from whatever was afflicting them. Unfortunately, they couldn't stop dancing, and no one knew how to help them. As the summer persisted and the temperature rose, the situation worsened.

Concerned by the unusual situation, the city council sought help from the local physicians to diagnose and treat the dancers. After dismissing superstitious explanations, the doctors arrived at a diagnosis: the dancers' condition was likely caused by hot blood. Since it was summertime, the physicians theorised that the dancers' overheated brains had driven them to madness. They proposed bloodletting as a potential treatment, but this proved impractical as the dancers were constantly moving.

Feeling uncertain about their next course of action, the city council devised a plan to involve musicians, hoping that the dancers would exhaust themselves more quickly and stop dancing as the musicians played music alongside them. The musicians, however, played at a high tempo, making the dancing even more frenzied and attracting more people to join the afflicted group.

Realising that their efforts had inadvertently worsened the situation and feeling at a loss for what to do, the city council turned to superstition. They suggested that the dancing mania was a curse caused by the people's sins and a sign that they should repent. Fuelled by this belief, the city council ordered the police to crack down on gamblers and prostitutes.

This led to the shutting down of gambling houses and brothels, resulting in the expulsion of many individuals from Strasbourg. The city council believed that by ridding the city of these 'sinners,' they would appease their patron saints. Also, in an attempt to seek divine favour, they donated a large candle weighing 100 pounds to the cathedral. However, their efforts proved futile as the dancing mania persisted and people allegedly danced to their deaths each day.

After discovering that superstition wasn't the solution to the dancing mania, the city council used reason and decided to ban drumming and dancing. Anyone caught swaying their hips to any rhythm would be fined 30 shillings. String music, however, was allowed at weddings. Even with these measures, the dancing mania persisted, causing frustration for the city council and leaving the dancers trapped in the agony of their relentless movements with no control over their actions.

Interestingly, the 1518 dancing plague was not an isolated incident. In 1374, a similar dancing epidemic swept through the city of Aachen, quickly spreading across the Rhine Valley. Those afflicted held hands in a circle and danced endlessly as if they were under the influence of a powerful hallucinogen. Confused about this strange dancing, officials in Aachen attributed the phenomenon to demonic possession, disagreeing with any other explanation.

As a result, exorcists were summoned to intervene. They sprinkled holy water on the dancers while they were still engaged in their circular dance. They also chanted incantations over the dancers. However, these efforts proved ineffective, leaving Aachen in a state of helplessness, much like the situation faced in Strasbourg during the Holy Roman Empire in 1518.

During those times, the veneration of saints held great importance in Catholic religious practices, and people sought solace and protection through their devotion to saints in both public and private worship. Saint Vitus was one of these revered saints, often depicted as a young boy holding a palm branch in one hand and a rooster in the other, symbolising martyrdom and purity.

Vitus was martyred as a child in the 4th century on the orders of Emperors Diocletian and Maximilian. According to legend, despite being thrown into a cauldron of boiling lead and tar, and exposed to a lion, Vitus emerged unscathed from these ordeals, becoming a friend to the lion.

Over the centuries, Saint Vitus gained a reputation as a healer and protector against various ailments, particularly those associated with seizures and nervous disorders. Subsequently, he became widely venerated as the patron saint of those suffering from epilepsy.

As Strasbourg continued to grapple with the mysterious dancing epidemic, with dancers flinging their arms in the air, the people turned to Saint Vitus, praying for his intervention and healing. However, despite this, the dancing continued, and the reported number of deaths continued to rise.

In their search for a solution, the Strasbourg city council came up with another superstitious plan. They gathered the dancers and led them to a shrine devoted to Saint Vitus, situated on a mountain. At the shrine, the priest made the dancers wear red shoes that were anointed at the tops and soles and sprinkled with holy water. They were also made to hold small crosses, while incense and Latin incantations were included in the ritual. Surprisingly, the ritual worked, and the dancing stopped.

The dancing plague lasted for two months and became known as the Vitus Dance, either because Saint Vitus was believed to have caused it or because he miraculously cured it.

Explication

The dancing plague that swept through Strasbourg gave rise to various theories among medical experts, each trying to explain its peculiar cause. One renowned physician of the time was Paracelsus; he visited Strasbourg in 1526, eight years after the dancing plague, to conduct a post-mortem examination and offer a diagnosis.

According to Paracelsus, spontaneous dancing was an involuntary physical response, similar to a reflex, triggered by stimulation of certain parts of the body. Perhaps not convinced by his own diagnosis, Paracelsus revisited the origin of the dancing mania, focussing on Frau Troffea. He concluded that Frau Troffea was a rebellious wife who resorted to dancing in order to avoid fulfilling a household chore requested by her husband.

Modern experts, on the other hand, still hold conflicting views on the cause of the dancing plague. Some have suggested a possible connection to grain poisoning, believed to cause convulsions. However, this theory falls short, as the movements of the dancers were inconsistent with the convulsive reactions typically associated with grain poisoning. Another hypothesis suggests a group case of epilepsy, but this seems unlikely considering the contagious nature of the dancing mania, while epilepsy is not contagious.

There was even a conspiracy theory suggesting that the dancers were part of a secretive heretical cult that surfaced every decade to disrupt society. However, this theory doesn't seem credible since intentionally dancing to the point of death, as alleged, while enduring the pain of bleeding and injured feet, seems implausible. Furthermore, at that time, Europe was highly vigilant and hostile towards heretics, making it unlikely for the dancers to have belonged to such a cult without being discovered and suppressed.

Amid the confusion of competing theories, a more rational theory for the dancing plague emerged. Strasbourg had experienced difficult times with severe economic hardships: the city had endured not just one, two, or three famines but four devastating ones between 1492 and 1511. A fifth famine occurred in 1517, resulting in a significant loss of life. Leprosy and smallpox outbreaks followed in 1518, further contributing to the death toll. The city's orphanage became overwhelmed, accommodating at least 300 additional orphans.

This bleak socioeconomic situation had a negative impact on people's mental health, leading to some individuals displaying unusual behaviours. This, in turn, fuelled fears of demonic possession. In such situations, mass hysteria was highly likely, and with a population deeply steeped in superstition, many believed the dancers were under the control of supernatural forces.

Throughout the course of the dancing plague, there was indeed a contest between science on one side and superstition on the other. Both sides attempted to explain the bizarre phenomenon and find a cure, but they were mired in confusion.

The Renaissance physician Paracelsus, who was expected to provide a scientific and rational perspective, only added to the confusion with his questionable diagnosis. In contrast, considering the dancing plague as a result of stress induced by the gloomy socioeconomic situations in Strasbourg seems reasonable. But this explanation lacks consistency and concrete evidence, making it difficult to uphold in scientific terms.

In the end, the prevailing belief that attributed the affliction to an unseen supernatural power gained traction, despite the lack of concrete evidence, which is typical in matters of superstition and the supernatural. Incidentally, the belief in an unseen force causing affliction, along with the subsequent cure involving a visit to the shrine of Saint Vitus and the wearing of red shoes anointed with holy oil, left little room for further debate. As a result, superstition seemed to have triumphed over scientific reasoning.

In any case, it is important to note that this historical narrative, while highlighting the success of superstition, does not endorse superstition as a problem-solving approach. It remains crucial to advocate for an evidence-based approach to problem-solving. However, despite the failure of both science and superstition to fully diagnose the dancing plague, neither side offered a substantial explanation as a probable cause.

Indeed, while the attribution of such phenomena to an unseen supernatural force has been common throughout history, it cannot be considered a valid or substantiated explanation. It is important to recognise that the ability to solve a problem does not always validate the underlying belief or explanation used to do so.

Hence, before being swayed away from science, it is crucial to exercise caution and critical thinking. Beware of those who advocate for divine healing while secretly relying on medical professionals and treatments when they or their loved ones are ill. It is important to consider the inconsistencies and contradictions in their approach.

Furthermore, it is worth reflecting on the actions of people who are dismissive toward science yet heavily rely on scientific advancements in their everyday lives. They drive cars, use phones, televisions, and various other technological innovations that are products of scientific progress. They also read and write with reading glasses and pens, all made possible by science. Even the clothes they wear are products of scientific advancements rather than superstition.

In conclusion, it is important to maintain a scientific or rational perspective and not dismiss the worth of science based on a single historical event or the success of superstition in a specific context. History has shown that many phenomena initially attributed to the supernatural and superstition have eventually been explained by scientific inquiry. Case in point: the *Angel's Glow* took 139 years to unravel. Finally, it is reasonable to believe that, through diligent scientific investigation, the mystery of the dancing plague and the 'Jumping Frenchmen of Maine' will be unravelled.

CHAPTER NINE

Be Virtuous

Politeness and civility are the best capital ever invested in business.
– P. T Barnum.

Be Honourable

The habit of cheating people out of their share, withholding commissions from those deserving, and neglecting your part of the bargain stems from greed and ingratitude, and has jarred people's careers, brands, and businesses. Because cheated men are vindictive; as Tacitus put it: 'Men are more willing to repay an injury than a benefit because gratitude is a burden and revenge, a pleasure.'

In March 2021, news emerged that a scammer called Jacob had reported his accomplice named Awuni, who was domiciled in the US, to the FBI. According to the report, Awuni stole the personal details of US citizens and sent them to Jacob to file for unemployment benefits. The scam paid the accomplices almost $10 million, which Awuni got in the US. However, he was too greedy and didn't share the money with Jacob like they had agreed to.

Jacob was vexed with Awuni for double-crossing him, and he reported him to the FBI, who arrested Awuni promptly. Jacob was fully aware of the possibility that the FBI would come after him too, but he didn't care as long as he saw Awuni punished and suffering.

This is how vengeful a cheated man can be. A memory of being used and fooled cuts them to the bone, and they can spend the rest of their lives seeking revenge.

In a corruption-laden social milieu, however, generosity won't necessarily prevent people's dishonest tendencies, and you better look out for strangers, relatives, and friends alike. But being stingy when there's abundance and neglecting the hands that contributed to your gains is a mistake—as those same hands may collude to undermine your gains. In most cases, they do, and they can be so covert that you would hardly know who the culprit is.

In business, ill-treated employees and associates will find ways to treat themselves better at your expense than it would've cost you to treat them well.

To avert these happenings, keep a watchful eye on your enterprise, but never neglect to institute a reward system for your deserving team members. When you demonstrate that you have their best interests at heart, they will prioritise your needs as well.

Know when to surprise people with rewards. Sometimes, surprises are more valued, but don't be in a hurry to make promises; if you do, keep them.

Even in the throes of inadequacy, manage to pay for your needs and expenses. 'What has worth is worth paying for,' author Robert Greene says. 'By paying your own way, you stay clear of gratitude, guilt, and deceit. It is often wise to pay the full price—there is no cutting corners with excellence.'

Make a Difference in the Community

When you become successful, you will be influential, and your name and personality will carry weight, sometimes morphing you into a high-net-worth brand. To achieve this status implies that you've garnered a fan base that will listen to you.

One of the things you can do with this privilege is make a social impact. For instance, if there's endemic drug abuse among the youth, use your influence to help them overcome it. If there's prevailing laziness among them, inspire them to be hardworking, and they'll listen to you.

Family poverty reduces a child's ability to receive a high-quality education, which concerned the legendary LeBron James. In 2011, the NBA icon was researching the high school dropout rate of his hometown, Akron, Ohio, and upon his findings, he decided to found the I PROMISE Program to assist the disadvantaged children in his childhood community. In November 2017, he asked the Akron School Board for permission to open a public school to help kids from poor families do better in school.

The plan was approved that month, and in 2018, the I Promise School was opened, beginning with 240 third- and fourth-grade pupils, with the intention to include first-through eighth-grade pupils by 2022. Within the first year of opening, the school saw a 90% growth in its inaugural class and met or exceeded the growth goals in reading and mathematics. The pupils were also doing better than their peers in the other public schools in Akron.

And that was LeBron James' vision for the I Promise initiative: the I Promise School focuses on the city's most at-risk children to ensure that they succeed in the classroom, at home, and in the community. In April 2020, James said in an interview with *The People*:

> At the I Promise School, our goal is to let every single kid know they are special. That they can be whatever they want to be. And that starts with addressing everything they're going through before they even step foot in a classroom.

As a child in Akron, he relocated with his mother from time to time because she didn't have a permanent job and had to move to find work. Due to this frequent relocation, LeBron James was absent for 83 days in fourth grade, resulting in a significant shortfall in his education. This unfortunate experience motivated the now NBA star to champion the I Promise School initiative in order to provide special care and support for young children.

In a video on Twitter, LeBron James said, 'I know these kids basically more than they know themselves. I've walked the same streets, I've rode the same bikes on the streets they ride on, I went through the same emotions, the good, the bad, the adversity… Everything they're going through as kids, I know and for me to be in a position where I have the resources, the finances, the people, the structure, and the city around me, why not?'

In addition to founding the I Promise School, LeBron James, through the LeBron James Family Foundation, funds additional services for the children attending the IPS. These include uniforms, food for families, career placement services, bikes and helmets for each student, transportation, et cetera.

The distinctive part of LeBron James' I Promise School initiative is that the school belongs to the Akron City School District, not an NGO school owned by him.

In any case, he's committed to funding the school in partnership with the Akron School Board, having already committed an estimated $2 million in start-up costs and other supplemental support as of August 2018. And after all his successes, LeBron James regards founding the I Promise School as his most significant accomplishment. What will you do for your community when you also become successful?

Be Charitable

The US leads the world in philanthropy. But the philanthropists aren't necessarily giving their money to the poor. According to statistics, barely a fifth of the most affluent philanthropists' donations go to the needy; half go to education and healthcare, and the rest go to the arts, sports teams, and other cultural pursuits.

In the UK, from 2007 to 2017, two-thirds of all millionaire donations, which amounted to £4.79 billion, went to higher education; half of this amount went to just two universities: Oxford and Cambridge. And particularly for educational philanthropy, the wealthy elites donate to their children's schools or their own alma maters, which are already thriving.

All signs indicate that the wealthier a donor is, the less likely it is that their money will be directed towards helping the poor. Furthermore, in contrast to conventional expectations of philanthropy, the wealthiest philanthropists prioritise their personal interests over assisting those in need.

For instance, Ken Griffin, the billionaire hedge fund manager, gave $150 million to create scholarships in his name at Harvard University; Sandy Weill, the former chief executive of Citi, donated $250 million to Cornell University for a medical school to be established in his name; the list goes on and on. Apparently, addressing poverty isn't much of the elites' priority.

In Ghana, the social problems in the rural areas are pronounced and prevalent. They include the absence of hospitals in several communities, pupils having to commute long distances to school by foot, cross a stream at some point, attend schools without furniture to sit on, study without textbooks, and learn computing without a computer.

It would be self-aggrandising to overlook these dire social needs and pour your fortune into an already thriving elite cause in the name of charity. For this reason, the establishment of non-profit trusts and NGOs has snowballed over the years, either purposefully or ostensibly, to tackle deprivation.

These organisations thrive on donations; many have been of immense help and have earned a good reputation. But be mindful that some others are fraudulent, albeit legally registered and prominent. The latter capitalise on dire social problems to defraud unsuspecting victims.

In January 2021, when schools had resumed after a year of closure due to COVID-19, a young man I had met in 2020 on marketing errands visited me. He lamented how deprived the village public schools were and implored me to donate 100 copies of my Integrated Science textbooks to his NGO. He said he had already identified two public schools in the village and would visit them in two days to re-donate the books.

Being aware of the situation he had described and knowing pupils in rural public schools couldn't afford textbooks, I agreed to his solicitation. And he was all smiles until I told him I needed the names of the schools he'll be sending the books to as well as donation receipts from the headmasters. I was emphatic that I would follow up to confirm.

Ideally, this shouldn't be an issue; however, his smile disappeared, and he suggested that he usually took pictures of the distribution and sent them to his sponsors. I insisted we go by my terms, but the manner in which he responded made it obvious that he didn't want to be transparent and accountable. This made me doubt his integrity, and I ended the meeting without giving him the books.

Within the charity sector, there are also some racketeers whose modus operandi is to project an existing or non-existent social problem and pretend to be solving it in order to bamboozle donors.

An orphanage keeper pitched the idea of building a school for the less privileged in his community, and after a concerted effort, his donors secured for him a parcel of land and funded the school building project.

But when the school building project was completed, he closed the orphanage and returned the supposed orphans to where he had brought them from. He then converted the school to a fee-paying private school, in which he enrolled privileged pupils while keeping the school's status as an NGO to evade tax and fool new donors.

Apparently, the whole idea of starting the orphanage was a gambit to get donor funding for his personal gain. It was later revealed that the orphans he had been keeping and presenting to his donors were not orphans; he had brought them from their parents in the village, ostensibly to educate them in the city.

The credulous donors, who later regretted donating to the orphanage keeper, didn't consider that building a school for the less privileged wasn't a need for a community that already had enough non-fee-paying public schools with excellent enrolment and facilitated by qualified teachers.

In any case, from the donors who sank their monies into the orphanage and the school building project, corporations that brought them gifts from time to time, service providers that gave them generous discounts, and family and friends who supported in one way or another, the devious orphanage keeper fooled them all.

Understand: When you become successful, you'll be a target of solicitations for funding. However, for any charity project you want to consider, you must first ascertain its need. And if you're convinced, ask the solicitors to tell you exactly how the donation they're requesting from you will solve the problem they have presented. This stipulation can also be an opportunity for you to contribute your ideas to the cause or a way to be sure the fundraisers will put your donation to judicious use.

In an interview with CNN on October 26, 2021, the Director of United Nations World Food Programme, David Beasley, urged the super-wealthy billionaires, including Elon Musk, to donate $6 billion of their fortune to help solve world hunger.

Elon Musk noticed David Beasley's appeal and tweeted:

> If WFP can describe on this Twitter thread exactly how $6 B will solve world hunger, I will sell Tesla stock right now and do it.

Elon Musk followed up with, 'But it must be open-source accounting, so the public can see exactly how the money is spent.'

By principle, this stipulation wouldn't be an issue if the solicitation was real. And after giving a donation, be sure to verify that it was expended accordingly. After all, it's your money.

This modus, however, may not be very necessary for every philanthropic donation, and I don't think Elon Musk used it for every charity donation he made. But if internalised, it'll guide you to support only genuine causes, proper NGOs, and practical interventions.

Be cautious in this matter, as if your donation is used improperly, you won't be aiding anyone; instead, you'll fall victim to a scam, and it will be necessary to reclaim your donation.

In October 2019, two US-based donor charities petitioned the Commercial Division of the Ugandan High Court, praying the court to order a local NGO to account for the funds they donated to combat human trafficking and help the needy.

The Executive Director of the local NGO was to expend the funds and render an account after that, but though he spent the funds, he failed to be accountable, thereby necessitating the court suit. The court documents read:

> On November 19, 2016, the defendants (NGO and Ssewakiryanga) jointly by false pretences of following up on counselling for Uganda young women rescued from Saudi Arabia, with the intention to defraud, requested and received from donors $9,965, which work was never done.

In any event, giving to charity is always laudable and must be encouraged, though guided. Because it makes society a better place, and it's even more beneficial to the giver. As Robert Greene puts it: 'Be lavish with your money and keep it circulating, for generosity is a sign and magnet of power.'

> Of course, men should be charitable because it is a duty and a pleasure. But even, as a matter of policy, if you possess no higher incentive, you will find that the liberal man will command patronage while the sordid, uncharitable miser will be avoided. – P.T. Barnum.

But charity begins at home, so your family must be the first to benefit from your generosity.

After landing his first major role as an actor, Chris Pratt bought a house for his mother. He said, 'I bought my mum a house when I was 23 years old. I wasn't rich; I had just enough to buy the house. I was rich for a second, and then I was poor, but my mum had a house.' Dwayne Johnson surprised his mother with a new home in 2018 and did the same for his father in 2019. In January 2020, John Boyega surprised his parents with a new home in London. Cardi B bought a house for her mother in 2018, to name a few.

The second place to be most generous is your enterprise. One morning at Apple Inc., a secretary reported to work late, and Steve Jobs demanded an explanation. She responded, 'My car wouldn't start.' That afternoon, Steve Jobs walked into her office, threw a set of keys to a brand-new Jaguar at her and said, 'Here, don't be late anymore.'

Third, no matter how self-made your fortune is, other people likely contributed directly or indirectly to your success. From the friend whose advice led you to opportunities, your neighbour who gave you a generous discount, your teacher who inspired you for a higher purpose, and the stranger who helped pay your school fees, don't forget about them!

In 2013, George Clooney demonstrated a heartwarming act of gratitude towards 14 close friends who had been by his side for over 35 years, supporting him in various ways throughout his journey. As a token of appreciation, he generously gifted each of them $1 million. What made this gesture even more special was that Clooney took care of the taxes on these gifts, ensuring that each person received the full $1 million amount.

Upon presenting 14 suitcases brimming with dollar bills to his longtime buddies, Clooney expressed his deep appreciation, saying, 'Listen, I want you guys to know how much you've meant to me and continue to mean in my life. From the time I arrived in LA, sleeping on your couches, to where I am today, I owe it all to you.' He emphasised how fortunate he felt to have such amazing friends and acknowledged that his success wouldn't have been possible without their support.

For Clooney, giving back to his friends was a significant moment, and he wanted to cherish the time spent together. As they opened their suitcases, a meaningful chapter in their friendship was written, symbolising their lasting bond. Truly, this act of genuine appreciation by George Clooney left a profound mark on their history together.

In a similar act of appreciation, in 2016, shortly after Abraham Atta rose to stardom through his role in the film *Beast of No Nation*, he made a gracious visit to Hon. Kennedy Agyapong. The purpose of his visit was to express his heartfelt appreciation for the support he received from the member of parliament, which significantly contributed to his education. This genuine gesture of gratitude from the young actor touched the heart of the MP and served as a motivating example for other accomplished individuals to embrace acts of kindness and charity as well.

Without Personal Finance

While growing up as a boy, I observed that whether people earned a modest income or were gainfully employed, it took only those who had assimilated personal finance to be prudent with money. Because they had learned to budget and save, they avoided debt, invested their surplus, and created wealth earlier than their counterparts, who didn't give two hoots about personal finance.

In the book, *The Art of Seduction,* there's a narrative of an American soldier who seemed to have lived his career life without any inclination for personal finance:

> During World War I, a twenty-nine-year-old American soldier named Frederick, stationed in France, won $37,000 in a four-day crap game. On his next leave, he went to Nice and checked himself into the finest hotel. On his first night in the hotel restaurant, he recognised Otero sitting alone at a table. He had seen her perform in Paris ten years before, and had become obsessed with her. She was now close to fifty, but more alluring than ever. He greased some palms and was able to sit at her table. He could hardly talk: the way her eyes bored into him, a simple readjustment in her chair, her body brushing up against him as she got up, the way she managed to walk in front of him and display herself. Later, strolling along a boulevard, they passed a jewellery store. He went inside, and moments later found himself plopping down $31,000 for a diamond necklace. For three nights, La Belle Otero was his. Never in his life

> had he felt so masculine and impetus. Years later, he still believed it was well worth the price he had paid. (*The Art of Seduction*, page 396)

The excerpt above reverberated in my mind until it dawned on me that when people land fortunes they didn't earn, they're likely to assume a profligate lifestyle. Give them a little time, and they'll fritter all the fortune away. This is common with lottery winners.

In 2002, Michael Carroll won a fortune of £9.7 million with a £4 lottery ticket. Soon after becoming a millionaire, he splurged wildly on fast living and indulged with prostitutes and hangers-on, much to the disgust of his wife. She later left the marriage with a £1.4 million divorce settlement.

With enough money in his account, Michael converted his mansion into a venue for house parties and orgies in which nude girls served cocaine on silver plates. In these orgies, he slept with up to eight damsels per night and later boasted about bedding an estimated 4000 of them. He, therefore, earned the moniker 'Master Micky' and reportedly spent up to the tune of £90,000 on bail bonds for his druggy pals.

Michael also became a nuisance in his neighbourhood; he raced with his friends in old bangers and dirt bikes and hosted demolition debris, in which they smashed up cars for fun. On some occasions, he drove around the countryside in plush cars and hurled Big Macs and nuggets at pedestrians. This led him to make more than 30 court appearances.

In 2005, he was given an anti-social behaviour order for driving through town in his Mercedes van, shooting steel balls from a catapult, and smashing the windows of 32 shops and a car, thereby causing damage worth thousands of pounds. That year, his accountant wrote to inform him that he was down to the last million pounds sterling.

Meanwhile, he wasn't paying his bills, and his five-bedroom mansion was also dilapidated. With fences smashed, windows shattered, and debris in the garden, the self-acclaimed King of Chavs had to accept just £142,000 for the sale of his mansion.

His estranged wife was entitled to 50% of the sale's cash, and after deducting estate agent and legal fees, Michael was left with only £63,000.00 and had to return to his old job as a binman. He would've squandered his entire lottery win to the last penny if he hadn't doled out a million pounds sterling each to his mother, sister, and aunt in his hay day.

Nevertheless, the absurdity of Frederick's romance with La Belle Otero and the profligate lifestyle Michael assumed should give you an idea of how crucial personal finance is and why it shouldn't be ignored.

This is why I instruct my clients in personal finance. Personal finance is simple: first, create a budget based on your income, save before spending, and invest your surplus. It requires discipline and commitment, and if you adhere to it, it'll be your foundation for wealth creation.

Sense of Purpose is not Sense of Mischief

Having a sense of purpose means pursuing knowledge and skills that solve problems, committing to goals that create wealth, and creating opportunities that make life better for other people.

However, an endeavour devoid of integrity cannot be said to be driven by a sense of purpose but by a sense of mischief intended to make ill-gotten gains. Sense of mischief encompasses dishonesty and illegalities that undermine morality and the economy.

On the flip side, many people have been caught and locked up for fraud and theft; be mindful that the prisons are full of people who took that path. And even in instances where certain people, such as politicians and public figures, are let off the hook or handed less stringent penalties for impropriety, they never get away from the accompanying disgrace.

Disgrace can be suicidal. According to some studies, disgraced women are more prone to low self-esteem and depression than men, whereas disgraced men have reported losing their erections at least during the midst of their scandals.

Furthermore, in the pursuit of mischief, people have entangled themselves in criminal syndicates and fraternities. The consequence is eventual but dire and not worth the initial pleasures it brings.

Hence, for whatever success is worth, prioritise your peace of mind above anything else, even if it means that you'll linger in your struggles a bit longer. In the end, as Sigmund Freud said: 'One day, in retrospect, the years of your struggle will strike you as the most beautiful.'

A Catholic Priest Falls in Love and Quits the Church

Every individual, irrespective of their identity, experiences the desire to establish emotional closeness with another person and often finds themselves enticed by romantic fantasies, particularly when these feelings are intense. This reality extends even to individuals such as Catholic priests, who are expected to uphold celibacy.

Be that as it may, over the course of the Catholic priesthood's history, there have been stories and tales that have come up from time to time about priests making passes on nuns or being secretly involved in romantic relationships. One such tale I've reimagined unfolds as follows:

> A priest offered a ride to a young nun with preternatural beauty. As she settled and closed the door, she adjusted herself, revealing her thigh. The priest caught a fleeting glimpse of the nun's thigh, causing a start that momentarily led him to lose control of the car and narrowly avoid an accident. He managed to regain control of the car, but his thoughts remained fixated on the nun's thigh. He couldn't resist sneaking glances as he drove on and eventually let his hand move to caress. The nun took a deep breath and closed her eyes, uttering, 'Father, recall Psalm 129.' The priest swiftly withdrew his hand, his fingers unsure of where to settle, and he apologised for his inappropriate behaviour. He then shifted gears, but soon found his hand back on the nun's thigh. Feeling his touch, a shiver ran down her spine, and she repeated her plea, looking the other way, 'Father, recall Psalm 129.' Once again, the priest removed his hand and offered another apology, murmuring, 'Forgive me, Sister, but the flesh is weak.' Upon arriving at the convent, Sister remained seated in absolute silence, while Father looked forward in silence as though he were cooling off. Without hearing anymore words or feeling another touch, Sister let out a sigh, opened the door, and departed abruptly. Father shifted gears, and sped off to the chapel. When he reached his office, he promptly looked up Psalm 129, finding the words, 'Go forth and seek further up, you will find glory.'

While the tale above features a fictitious bible verse, the notion of a priest falling in love and embarking on a romantic relationship is undeniably intriguing. In the case of Father Xavier Novell, his feelings for Silvia Caballol surpassed mere admiration, and his profound desire for her led him to resign from the Catholic Church. Apparently, his decision to resign was driven by his yearning to be with Silvia Caballol openly, free from the weight of shame and guilt and the burden of keeping their relationship concealed.

But Father Xavier Novell's resignation surprised many people because he seemed really connected to his spiritual side. In 2010, at the age of 41, he achieved a notable milestone by becoming the youngest bishop in Spain, assuming his role in Solsona within the northeastern region of Catalonia. Regarded as a rising figure within the Spanish Catholic Church, he garnered attention for endorsing a contentious conversion therapy aimed at gay individuals.

Additionally, he actively conducted exorcisms—an ancient practice focused on expelling perceived malevolent spiritual entities, such as demons, from individuals. Yet his spiritual compass encompassed more than just these practices. For instance, he held conservative stances, notably expressing his views on abortion and maintaining strong opinions on homosexuality. It's interesting to note, however, that the public fascination and humorous commentary surrounding his resignation centred on the woman with whom he had fallen in love: Silvia Caballol. She is an erotic novelist specialising in satanic-themed erotic fiction.

Satanic erotic fiction is a literary subgenre that melds explicit sexual content, known as erotica, with themes centred around satanism or the occult. In this genre, stories often explore forbidden and shadowy subjects, intertwining ritualistic practices, unearthly desires, and elements of the supernatural and demonic. The term Satanic erotic fiction indicates a concentration of eroticism set against the backdrop of satanic elements.

Among Silvia Caballol's literary works is a book titled, *The Hell of Gabriel's Lust*. Also, in the description of one of her books, the blurb suggests that she offers readers an immersive experience delving into sadism, madness, and lust. The narrative unfolds as a conflict between opposing forces—good and evil, God and Satan—with a plot that challenges the reader's values and religious convictions, poised to unsettle the very foundations of their beliefs.

Imagine, if you will, what could have transpired if a devout Catholic exorcist and a writer of erotic fiction with a touch of satanic themes had developed a romantic relationship, and the exorcist had quit the church as a result during the era of medieval European witch-hunts. Contemplating this scenario helps to grasp the profound astonishment that people experienced upon learning about the romantic involvement of Father Xavier Novell and Silvia Caballol. Thankfully, the world has moved beyond the irrational hysteria of witch-hunts and the unjust persecution of women, leaving such uncivilised and ignorant practices in the past.

But come to think of it, could there be more to why Father Xavier Novell resigned other than falling in love with Silvia Caballol? Could it be that he was becoming ill and dying due to celibacy? Consider the case of Mihailo Tolotos, an Orthodox Greek monk who lived his entire life without ever seeing a woman and yet lived to be 82. His passing wasn't attributed to celibacy; thus, though staying celibate is difficult, it's unlikely that Father Xavier Novell's decision was driven by a life-threatening consequence of celibacy.

Again, could Father Xavier Novell's decision to quit his job as a priest be entirely due to the power of love? Many people claim that the strength of a woman holds great sway. Yet, beyond the chatter and playful comments about his resignation and romantic entanglement, drawing from my experience as a certified career coach who has worked with a wide range of individuals, I discern a deeper reason behind his resignation: a sense of disconnection from his priestly career. I see that his connection with Silvia Caballol acted as a catalyst, prompting him to consider a career change.

On the flip side, I'm confident that Father Xavier Novell would have changed careers regardless of falling in love with a satanic-tinged erotica novelist, a nun, or no one. Therefore, I wasn't taken aback when news surfaced that shortly after leaving the Catholic Church, the former bishop actively searched for a job as an agronomist in the Barcelona region, opting against pursuing a pastoral role within a denomination that doesn't require celibacy. This change in career direction reinforces my conviction that his resignation is predominantly linked to a sense of professional disconnection, rather than other factors, and evokes the concept of job or career alienation.

Study and Career Alienation

It is a common phenomenon for individuals to experience shifts in their interests and career aspirations over time. But the key is to pay attention to one's inner voice and pursue endeavours that truly excite and motivate them. My name is Francis Ansah. I am a communication consultant and a life and career coach with a Career Development Associate Certified Experts Career Coach (ACECC) designation.

Before enrolling in university, I was deeply passionate about pursuing a career in chemistry. This desire was largely influenced by my fascination with the book *Makers of Civilisation* and other literary works that featured prominent chemists such as Michael Faraday, Alfred Nobel, and Marie

Curie. In addition, the animated character *Dexter* from the popular Cartoon Network show *Dexter's Laboratory* also played a role in fuelling my interest in chemistry. Therefore, I was overjoyed when I received admission into University for Development Studies to study BSc. Applied Chemistry.

During my first and second years, I performed exceptionally well academically, earning a good number of A's and feeling optimistic that I was on track to achieving a first-class degree. However, during my third year, I noticed a decline in my academic performance, which was a departure from my previous successes. How did it happen?

In the second semester of my second year, I wrote an article expressing my discontent with the Student Representative Council and posted it on the campus notice boards. To my astonishment, the next day, my article gained a lot of attention, and students were discussing it everywhere on campus.

My coursemates were particularly impressed with my writing skills and commended me for my work. That moment marked the beginning of a newfound interest in creative writing that I had never experienced before, and my passion for chemistry began to diminish.

By the middle of my third year, I had redirected my career aspirations towards becoming an author, communication consultant, and career coach. Hence, I began self-studying by reading books on writing to improve my writing skills. At that time, my interest in chemistry had faded, and despite it no longer aligned with my career goals, I had to continue studying it to obtain my degree. It was a challenging balancing act as I struggled to maintain my academic performance in a field that no longer resonated with my career aspirations.

While pursuing my self-study endeavour, I stumbled upon a book that left a lasting impression on me – Professor Aron Mike Oquaye's *Politics in Ghana*. This voluminous historical account provided profound insight with impeccable expression, which I absorbed over the course of one semester.

As I read, I assimilated the professor's writing style, which greatly contributed to my development as a writer. Furthermore, I realised that to excel in authorship, communication, and career development, I needed to cultivate a deep and resourceful mindset. This led me to delve into extensive reading, particularly in areas of critical thinking and problem-solving – essential skills for success in management and leadership.

My preference for self-study stems from the fact that it allows me to focus solely on a particular subject without the added burden of taking **extraneous courses**, which is often required in a traditional college major. Of course, I understand that not everyone may share this view, but please note that by 'extraneous courses,' I mean extraneous courses, not supplementary courses.

Meanwhile, I continued writing articles and started a nonfiction book project. The articles were more for the moment, whereas the 200-page nonfiction manuscript I wrote, which remains unpublished, was intended for deliberate practice. Throughout this process, I developed a keen eye for improving the written word and began practising as an editor. However, as I became more invested in my self-driven pursuits, I felt increasingly like I was wasting time studying a major I had no desire to pursue professionally. I also found myself increasingly bored during chemistry lessons and began skipping classes altogether. As a result, my grades suffered, and I considered dropping out.

Ten years after UDS, I took some time to reflect on what led me to lose interest in chemistry and become drawn to authorship, communication, and career development. Through this reflection, I came to realise that what I had experienced was a phenomenon called **Study Alienation**. This is a feeling of detachment from one's studies that arises from a deep attachment to one's natural inclinations and interests. Also, even if a student's studies align with their natural inclinations and passions, they can still feel disconnected if there's a discrepancy between the teaching methodology and the practical aspects of their studies. This too can result in study alienation.

Some years ago, I knew a talented young man named Henry who showed exceptional promise in computing. He was encouraged to enrol in a computing school to obtain a certificate and pursue his passion further. However, after six months of attending the school, it appeared that all he had accomplished was diligently taking notes during lectures, studying those notes, and completing assignments and quizzes on paper.

While there were practical lessons offered, they were infrequent, simplistic, and only skimmed the surface of what Henry was capable of. Moreover, even the most basic practical session that should be done in minutes could be dragged on for days, which only added to Henry's frustration. As a result, he became disinterested in the course and began skipping classes, scoring low marks or neglecting quizzes, and failing to complete his assignments. Eventually, Henry made the difficult decision to withdraw from the course, foregoing any possibility of obtaining a certificate.

Fortunately, Henry's passion for computing remained strong, and he was determined to learn the skills he desired. He found a mentor who was willing to teach him in a more practical and hands-on manner. Daily lessons were held in the mentor's home, and within just three months, Henry had developed a comprehensive understanding of computing. His newfound skills were so impressive that his mentor hired him to work alongside him, proving that Henry's potential had been overlooked by the school he previously attended.

Indeed, study alienation is a common phenomenon experienced by many students. As a result, some students may struggle to find motivation or enjoyment in their studies, leading to poor academic performance or dropping out. It is important to recognise that the resulting non-performance due to study alienation is not a reflection of a student's intelligence or ability but rather a mismatch between their academic pursuits and their natural inclinations or passions.

This is why you might have encountered people who are undeniably intelligent, exceptionally skilled in their profession, and consistently produce high-quality work, but who either did not complete their degrees or finished them with average grades.

The esteemed Professor Christos Charilaos Papadimitriou once shared an anecdote from his time as an assistant professor at Harvard. According to him, during that period, Bill Gates was a junior undergraduate student, and he (Papadimitriou) was so impressed with Gates' intelligence. In fact, he went on to tell his girlfriend at that time that 'There's this undergrad at school who is the smartest person I've ever met.' Bill Gates is frequently cited as a prime example of a success story, where a college dropout went on to achieve incredible accomplishments.

Steve Jobs dropped out after one semester at Reed College in 1972 and went on to explore a career path that aligned with his natural inclinations. He later explained that he dropped out because he didn't see the value in spending his parents' savings on college when he didn't know what he wanted to do with his life. After co-founding Apple and launching the iPhone, he became acclaimed as 'father of the digital revolution.'

When Albert Einstein was ten years old, he was admitted to the Luitpold Gymnasium, a prestigious school in Munich. However, the school placed more emphasis on Latin and Greek than on mathematics and science, which resulted in a feeling of alienation towards his studies. As a result, Einstein turned to self-directed studies and eventually left the school. Also, though he completed Zurich Polytechnic with ordinary grades, Einstein's scientific contributions in later years earned him the Nobel Prize. Subsequently, he became an internationally acclaimed scientist whose name became a byword for *genius*.

Study alienation can be passive or active. For instance, a student may feel detached from their studies and yearn to pursue a different programme, but they manage to control this feeling without it affecting their academic performance. This type of study alienation is passive. Conversely, with active study alienation, the feeling of detachment is so intense that it affects a student's grades or even leads to dropping out.

Regardless of its type, no student intentionally seeks study alienation; it occurs spontaneously and affects each person differently. Nevertheless, students whose academic interests align with their natural inclinations tend to have a strong sense of motivation and are unlikely to experience study alienation.

Now, as professionals, we are not immune to the experience of study alienation, because it manifests itself in a new form known as **career alienation**. After ten or fifteen years in a profession, some people begin to feel a sense of boredom and disinterest, which leads to a feeling of detachment from their work and a desire to switch jobs or change careers in an attempt to find fulfilment. However, they often fail to recognise this feeling of detachment as career alienation and instead attribute it to factors such as a lack of motivation, a toxic workplace, a difficult boss, or a lack of challenge in their job. While these factors may play a role, it is more likely that the underlying cause of their boredom and disinterest is career alienation, and this is what brings about it:

Someone may have chosen a career path based on external factors like family expectations, societal pressure, financial security, or limited job opportunities rather than their true passions and interests. As time goes by, the lack of fulfilment in their job takes a toll on their emotional and mental well-being, leading to a feeling of detachment from their jobs.

After a 25-year career, Mr. Shaw became bored and disinterested in his job. In a dramatic and extreme act, he disrupted a board meeting by storming in uninvited and throwing live cockroaches onto the table from a jam jar he had brought with him. The board members reacted with terror and confusion, as they scrambled to escape the insects. Mr. Shaw then moved back to the entrance, where he continued to laugh and pull faces as he observed the chaos.

When the cockroaches were released, Mr. Anderson, the bully boss of Mr. Shaw, was the first person to flee through the backdoor exit, convinced that Mr. Shaw had gone mad and was after him. The chairperson, who was known as the 'Iron Lady' for her formidable personality, was so frightened that she fainted. Two other women and a man fled to the washroom and locked themselves inside, while the rest followed Mr. Anderson, leaving the Iron Lady helplessly unconscious. However, after she regained consciousness, she demanded the immediate dismissal of both Mr. Shaw and Mr. Anderson from the company. This was precisely what Mr. Shaw had wanted all along. He wasn't trying to harm his boss; he simply wanted to create chaos and get himself fired.

One month after the boardroom drama, Mr. Shaw began working as a female body massage therapist. It was a profession that paid him less than his previous job as operations manager. However, he found his new job exhilarating and fulfilling, as it aligned with his lifelong passion. Mr. Shaw later confessed that he had always been interested in female body massage therapy, and nothing else had ever motivated him as much.

In Wa, a trainee nurse appeared in a viral video threatening to harm any patient that would be put under her care. She stated in *Waali,* 'Okay, I never had the passion to be a nurse, but my relatives forced me. Fine, once you see me around your health facility, begin to run with your bag for your life, or else I will kill you.'

Upon further reflection, I realised that what caused my detachment from chemistry was the fact that my decision to pursue it was primarily based on external factors. In contrast, if I had pursued a degree in creative writing, communication, or career development, I am confident that I wouldn't have experienced this sense of disconnection.

As a certified career coach, I've come to understand that people are more likely to thrive in fields that align with their interests and values, and that when people pursue careers or academic paths solely based on external factors, they are less likely to feel motivated and fulfilled.

Furthermore, the feeling of being stuck in a job that is not aligned with one's natural inclinations can have a significant effect on job satisfaction and overall career success. Therefore, it is essential to recognise the signs of study or career alienation (boredom and disinterest) and take the necessary steps to address them. Here are some suggestions:

1. First, educating yourself about study alienation and its potential consequences can help you manage it on your own and reduce its impact on your academic performance. Fortunately, reading this piece to the end will educate you enough.
2. Second, consider consulting with a career coach when you begin to feel bored and disinterested in your studies. A career coach can assist you in finding a balance between your academic requirements and personal passions. This could prevent your grades from slipping.
3. Third, think about speaking with a career coach to assist you in choosing a college major. If I had had the opportunity to do so, I would have chosen creative writing, communication, or career development as a major and kept chemistry as a side interest.

4. Fourth, consider consulting with a career coach when you begin to feel boredom and disinterest in your work. It may be time to switch jobs or change career.
5. Fifth, consulting with a career coach can also help with your career decision-making. They can provide you with guidance and support in determining the best path forward.

Just like study alienation, career alienation can be either passive or active, though not every professional will experience it, even if their field of work doesn't align with their natural inclinations. This can be due to a high salary, satisfactory conditions of service, or job flexibility. In any event, when we experience career alienation long enough, we may become desperate to escape it, which can lead to mindless measures, as seen in the cases of Mr. Shaw and the trainee nurse. As such, the above-listed countermeasures shouldn't be overlooked.

During my time at UDS, when I was experiencing doubts about my chemistry major, I sought advice from my department head, who also happened to be my lecturer. However, his response proved to be unhelpful. And after learning about other successful individuals who had faced scepticism and discouragement from their lecturers regarding their career aspirations, I came to the realisation that I had sought career advice from the wrong professional.

For example, in 1874, Max Planck's university professor told him that there was no point in pursuing physics because 'almost everything has already been discovered, and all that remains is to fill small holes.' However, Planck's fascination with physics and his desire to learn the fundamentals were not deterred by his professor's discouraging words. He went on to launch quantum theory and win the Nobel Prize. Unlike Planck, another student might have taken the professor's advice to heart and missed out on becoming an extraordinary achiever.

Similar to Max Planck's experience, Bill Gates faced scepticism from his professor when he dropped out of Harvard to pursue a career in the tech industry. Professor Papadimitriou, with whom Gates had worked on a mathematical project, believed Gates was wasting his potential by running a small company in Albuquerque that wrote code for microprocessors. In his own words, Papadimitriou said, 'He had moved to Albuquerque, New Mexico, to run a small company writing code for microprocessors, of all things. I remember thinking, 'Such a brilliant kid, what a waste.'''

Nevertheless, Gates went on to co-found Microsoft and become one of the most successful tech entrepreneurs in history. In hindsight, Professor Christos Charilaos Papadimitriou's misgivings about Bill Gates's decision turned out to be incorrect, despite him being regarded as one of the smartest people in the world.

The point is that relying solely on our lecturers and teachers for career advice has its limitations. Firstly, career development is a specialised field, and while lecturers and teachers can offer valuable guidance on academic matters, they may not have the expertise to provide comprehensive guidance on career choices. In other words, teachers or lecturers may not be the best source of advice to turn to for career guidance.

Thankfully, I was able to navigate the challenges of study alienation successfully, earn my degree, and establish myself as a career coach, author, and communication consultant. Sadly, not everyone I knew who experienced study alienation was able to navigate it successfully.

Frank, one of my university friends, started off with a strong GPA, but he encountered a setback and ended up not graduating because he refused to retake a course he did not pass. Despite the fact that he was smart, he lacked specialised skills and knowledge and didn't have the motivation to start his own business. A decade later, he was still struggling to find work and barely making ends meet.

This is a stark example of how failing to address study alienation can have long-lasting consequences, particularly in a job market with limited opportunities.

So, after several career coaching sessions with Frank, held over my mobile site at **wa.link/mycareercoach**, I determined that he was a good fit for digital marketing. I recommended an online course, which he completed and then spent a year doing **deliberate practice** before landing a role as a member of a YouTuber's crew. As of the time of writing this piece, he works with three different YouTubers simultaneously and earns several thousand dollars per month in Ghana.

When I was a level 100 student, John was in level 300 and doing well academically. However, he suddenly decided to drop out without warning. Despite efforts by his lecturers to convince him to stay, he handed in a one-sentence deferral letter and disappeared from campus. His departure took everyone by surprise.

Thirteen years later, I ran into John again, and he didn't appear to be pursuing anything particularly meaningful. He mentioned that he didn't regret dropping out since he didn't feel any attachment to his studies, but he did express some regret over the limited job opportunities available to him in Ghana as a non-degree holder, as they were not the kind of jobs he liked. Suddenly, he hailed a taxi and jumped in before I could continue our conversation or exchange contact information. Despite my efforts to locate him on social media, I haven't been able to find him since.

Princess had previously been enrolled at a public university but was withdrawn due to non-performance. She then began her studies anew at another public university but faced similar challenges in her first semester, as evidenced by her poor exam result. A mutual friend introduced her to me, and we had a career coaching session through **wa.link/mycareercoach**.

During our session, Princess revealed that she had a true passion for cooking and wished to train as a caterer at a vocational school. However, her father, who struggled financially to pay for her education, had high expectations for her to become the first graduate in the family, and Princess felt the weight of that pressure. She told me that while her friends thought that she was studious because of how she frequented the university's library, on most days, she spent all of her study hours reading cookbooks, the same as she did at her previous university. I suspected that her lack of engagement with her studies was due to a deep-seated feeling of study alienation.

In just one hour of career coaching, I was able to help Princess shift her mindset and confront the realities of her situation. We discussed her true interests and aspirations, and I provided her with a clearer understanding of the different career paths she could take to achieve her goals. (I'm not permitted to disclose the details.)

With a newfound sense of purpose, Princess was able to make more informed decisions about her academic and career pursuits. After our coaching session, she was able to refocus and improve her academic performance, leading to her graduation with a degree in actuarial science. Her dedication and hard work continued to pay off, as she pursued a master's degree and is now thriving as a corporate executive.

Despite her success in a multinational company, Princess' passion for cooking never diminished. As of the time I was writing this piece, she was actively pursuing her dream of launching a restaurant and catering service, using her culinary skills and creativity to bring her vision to life. Princess's story serves as a testament to the power of refocusing and following one's passions, and I'm proud to have played a part in her career journey.

It is important to note that my decision to transition to career coaching, authorship, and communication was not influenced by any negative feelings towards chemistry. Instead, it was simply a matter of following my natural inclinations and pursuing a path that aligned with my aptitudes and passions.

That being said, I have great respect for the field of chemistry and the valuable skills it has taught me, particularly, the scientific method.

Thank you for taking the time to read my book. Whether you're a student seeking professional advice, a graduate looking for a job, or someone seeking a trustworthy professional to discuss a career decision or workplace challenge with, I invite you to visit **wa.link/mycareercoach** to book a session. My goal is to help you achieve your professional goals, and I am excited about the opportunity to collaborate with you.

Acknowledgement

I am deeply thankful to Doris Ampofo for being the driving force and inspiration behind my writing. Without her, this book would never have come to fruition. I also extend my heartfelt gratitude to my wife, Ruth; my children, Awurabena and Nana Yaw; and my sister, Sheila, for their steadfast support throughout the entire writing process.

Works Cited

Al Jazeera. "Coronavirus: What Is Madagascar's 'herbal Remedy' Covid-Organics?" *News | Al Jazeera*. Al Jazeera, 05 May 2020. Web. 03 Aug. 2020.

"Albert Einstein Looks for a Job." *The Scientist Magazine®*. Web.

"Almanac." *Wikipedia*. Wikimedia Foundation, 24 Feb. 2022. Web. 24 Apr. 2022.

"Annie Oakley." *Wikipedia*, 31 May 2023.

Anonymous. "What Was Elon Musk's GPA at UPenn? - Quora." *Quora*. Quora. Web. 4 Nov. 2021.

Anya. "Chocolate Helped a Old Man to Still 28 Million from a Bank Vauilt." *Alearned*. 21 Aug. 2013. Web. 05 Aug. 2020.

April 7, 2016 | Published By Parfit. "Remember When LL Cool J Jacked a Commercial and Made It "for Us by Us on the Low?" (video)." *Ambrosia For Heads*. 07 Apr. 2016. Web. 15 Jan. 2022.

"Arthur Eddington, the Man Who Invented Einstein." *OpenMind*. 29 May 2019. Web.

"Ashland University MFA Graduate Sets Record with 12th Graduate Degree." *Ashland University MFA Graduate Sets Record with 12th*

Graduate Degree | Ashland University News Center. 28 July 2020. Web. 23 Aug. 2020.

Asubonteng, Benard. ""Over-spiritualization" Is Making Many Ghanaians Non-critical Thinkers." *GhanaWeb*. GhanaWeb, 27 July 2016. Web. 14 Nov. 2020.

"Attack on Pearl Harbor." *Wikipedia*. Wikimedia Foundation, 26 Mar. 2020. Web. 08 Apr. 2020.

"Attention-deficit/hyperactivity Disorder (ADHD) in Children." *Mayo Clinic*. Mayo Foundation for Medical Education and Research, 25 June 2019. Web.

Bailey, Regina. "The Cerebral Cortex Is a Fascinating Part of the Brain's Anatomy." *ThoughtCo*. ThoughtCo, 04 Dec. 2019. Web.

Barca, Jerry. "Stunning Criticism of LeBron James and The Funding For The I Promise School." *Forbes*. Forbes Magazine, 12 Aug. 2018. Web. 12 Nov. 2020.

Bediako, Mark. "Common Causes of Building Collapse in Ghana." *Graphic Online*. 3 Aug. 2015. Web. 23 Nov. 2021.

"Benjamin Bolger - Biography." *Benjamin Bolger - Biography | Technology Trends*. Web. 23 Aug. 2020.

"Benjamin Bolger." *Wikipedia*. Wikimedia Foundation, 05 Dec. 2019. Web. 23 Aug. 2020.

"Benjamin Franklin." *Wikipedia.* Wikimedia Foundation, 28 Aug. 2020. Web. 01 Sept. 2020.

Berger, Sarah. "Notorious South African Preacher Arrested After Feeding Congregation Snakes." *International Business Times*. 19 July 2015. Web. 02 May 2020.

"Bernard Boursicot." *Wikipedia.* Wikimedia Foundation, 15 Feb. 2020. Web.

Biography.com Editors. "Winston Churchill." *Biography.com.* A&E Networks Television, 28 Aug. 2019. Web.

Brown University. "Study Describes Brain Changes During Learning." *ScienceDaily*. ScienceDaily, 20 Oct. 2000. Web.

Brown, Lee. "Virginia Pastor Who Defiantly Held Church Service Dies of Coronavirus." *New York Post*. New York Post, 13 Apr. 2020. Web. 03 May 2020.

"Brownsville Affair." *Wikipedia.* Wikimedia Foundation, 21 Dec. 2019. Web.

Buehler, Antonio. "Elon Musk Does Not Care Whether You Have a College Degree. Why Should You?" *Medium*. Medium, 05 June 2017. Web. 20 Apr. 2020.

Burdett, Carolyn. "Darwin and the Theory of Evolution." *The British Library*. The British Library, 06 Mar. 2014. Web.

Burke, Jason. "Tanzania Leader Says Prayer Will Cure Covid, as Hospitals Overflow." *Tanzania Leader Says Prayer Will Cure Covid, as Hospitals Overflow*. The Guardian, 28 Feb. 2021. Web. 10 Apr. 2021.

Burke, Jason. "Tanzania's Covid-denying President, John Magufuli, Dies Aged 61." *The Guardian*. Guardian News and Media, 18 Mar. 2021. Web. 4 May 2022.

Burke, Minyvonne. "Kim Kardashian's Bodyguard Sued for $6 Million for Not Protecting Her during 2016 Paris Robbery." *Daily Mail Online*. Associated Newspapers, 04 Oct. 2018. Web. 22 May 2020.

Busari, Stephanie, and Nimi Princewill. "Did Tanzania's Covid-denying Leader Die of the Coronavirus? It's One of Many Questions He Leaves behind." *CNN*. Cable News Network, 20 Mar. 2021. Web. 22 Apr. 2021.

"Cameroon: Obituary - Franklin Ndifor Passes On." *AllAfrica.com*. 19 May 2020. Web. 21 May 2020.

Carlton, Genevieve. "How Humanity's Response to Epidemic Disease Has Stayed the Same throughout History." *Ranker*. 12 Mar. 2020. Web. 10 Dec. 2021.

Carnegie, Dale. "Chapter Five." *How to Win Friends and Influence People*. United Kingdom: Vermilion, 2006. 228-29. Print.

Chingono, Nyasha. "'I Haven't Been Paid a Cent': Jerusalema Singer's CLAIM Stirs Row in South Africa." *The Guardian*. Guardian News and Media, 13 July 2021. Web. 21 Aug. 2021.

"Christopher Columbus Reaches the New World." *History.com*. A&E Television Networks, 24 Nov. 2009. Web. 09 Apr. 2020.

"Christopher Columbus." *Wikipedia*. Wikimedia Foundation, 05 May 2020. Web. 14 May 2020.

"Churchill: A Study in Oratory." *The International Churchill Society*. 27 Nov. 2019. Web.

Clear, James. "Absolute Success Is Luck. Relative Success Is Hard Work." *James Clear*. 21 Sept. 2018. Web. 16 May 2020.

Cohn, Scott. "Gold 101: Digging for Opportunity? Here's What to Know." *CNBC*. CNBC, 03 Jan. 2020. Web.

Coleman, Oli. "Floyd Mayweather Will Wish You a Happy Birthday for $999." *Page Six*. Page Six, 08 July 2020. Web. 22 Sept. 2020.

"Columbus and the Night of the Bloody Moon." *The Guardian*. Guardian News and Media, 15 July 1999. Web. 24 Apr. 2022.

"Columbus Sets Sail." *History.com*. A&E Television Networks, 09 Feb. 2010. Web. 09 Apr. 2020.

Corbet, Sylvie. "France: Macron Rewards Migrant Hero Who Saved Dangling Child." *AP NEWS*. Associated Press, 29 May 2018. Web. 14 May 2020.

Cork, Jen. "Jesse Martin OAM." *The Australian Museum*. Web.

"Coronavirus: 'Heal Our Land'– Akufo-Addo, Clergy Pray for Ghana." *Ghanaweb.com*. GhanaWeb, 19 Mar. 2020. Web. 03 May 2020.

"Craig Harrison (sniper)." *Wikipedia*. Wikimedia Foundation, 06 Nov. 2019. Web.

Curry, Colleen. "Psychic Who Said Amanda Berry Was Dead Silent After Berry Is Found." *ABC News*. ABC News Network, 7 May 2013. Web. 03 Nov. 2020.

"Dancing Plague of 1518." *Wikipedia*, 25 June 2023.

"Darwin's Voyages." *National Geographic*. 26 Mar. 2011. Web.

David, Topper, and E. Vincent Dwight. "Albert Einstein and the High School Geometry Problem." *Physics Today*. American Institute of Physics, 19 Dec. 2017. Web.

Dodd, Vikram. "A Party, Prayers, Then Mass Suicide." *The Guardian*. Guardian News and Media, 20 Mar. 2000. Web. 05 Apr. 2021.

Doherty, Ben, and Kate Lyons. "Australian and British Bloggers Arrested in Iran Named as Jolie King and Mark Firkin." *The Guardian*. Guardian News and Media, 12 Sept. 2019. Web. 06 Apr. 2020.

The Editors of Encyclopaedia Britannica. "Bologna." *Encyclopædia Britannica*. Encyclopædia Britannica, Inc., 14 Apr. 2016. Web.

The Editors of Encyclopaedia Britannica. "Brownsville Affair." *Encyclopædia Britannica*. Encyclopædia Britannica, Inc., 08 May 2015. Web.

"Education of Winston Churchill." *National Churchill Museum | Education of Winston Churchill, Winston Churchill in School*. Web.

Elkin, Mike. "The Veleia Affair." *The Veleia Affair - Archaeology Magazine Archive*. The Archeological Institute of America, Sept.-Oct. 2009. Web. 06 July 2020.

"Elon Musk." *Wikipedia*. Wikimedia Foundation, 17 Apr. 2020. Web. 19 Apr. 2020.

England, Lucy. "The Artist Who Painted Facebook's 1st Office Took Stock Instead of Cash - and Now He Is worth $200 Million." *Business Insider*. Business Insider, 09 June 2015. Web. 22 Sept. 2020.

Erlandsson, Ake. "Alfred Nobel and His Interest in Literature." *NobelPrize.org*. Web.

Feloni, Richard. "Former SpaceX Exec Explains How Elon Musk Taught Himself Rocket Science." *Business Insider*. Business Insider, 23 Oct. 2014. Web. 19 Apr. 2020.

"Ferdinand Waldo Demara - The Greatest Imposter among Us." *Things I Learned Last Night*, 2 Nov. 2021.

"Ferdinand Waldo Demara." *Wikipedia*, Wikimedia Foundation, 15 Nov. 2022.

"Fetish Priests Killed Ex-Soldier." *DailyGuide Network*. 04 May 2020. Web. 18 May 2020.

Field, Shivaune. "Hedy Lamarr: The Incredible Mind Behind Secure WiFi, GPS And Bluetooth." *Forbes*. Forbes Magazine, 08 Mar. 2018. Web. 23 Aug. 2020.

Fitzgerald, Edward W. "CHURCHILLIANA - TOY TROOPERS - SMALL STATESMEN." *The International Churchill Society*. 01 June 2015. Web.

Fowler, Julian. "Ancient Fermanagh Cure Gets Modern Makeover." *BBC News*. BBC, 29 Dec. 2018. Web. 26 Apr. 2022.

"Frank Abagnale." *Wikipedia*, Wikimedia Foundation, 21 Dec. 2022.

Froelich, Paula. "Jamaican Preacher Kevin O. Smith, Parishioners Arrested for Alleged Human Sacrifices." *New York Post*. New York Post, 23 Oct. 2021. Web. 23 Dec. 2021.

"Ghanaian ISIS Recruit Killed." *Ghanaweb.com*. GhanaWeb, 21 Mar. 2016. Web. 03 May 2020.

GhanaWeb. "Jammeh Ordered Us to Kill 44 Ghanaians – Gambian Soldiers Confess." *Ghanaweb.com*. GhanaWeb, 24 July 2019. Web. 06 Apr. 2020.

GhanaWeb. "Was Naming MTN SMP a Blackmail? – Part 1." *Ghana* GhanaWeb, 19 June 2020. Web. 03 Aug. 2020.

Gillett, Rachel. "An inside Look at How J.K. Rowling, One of the Most Influential People Alive, Turned Rejection into Unprecedented Success." *Business Insider*. Business Insider, 02 Apr. 2016. Web. 29 Apr. 2020.

Godfrey, Alex. "Jean-Claude Van Damme: 'I Tried to Play the System; I Was Blacklisted'." *The Guardian*. Guardian News and Media, 10 Aug. 2012. Web. 08 Dec. 2020.

Gonzalez, Nora. "The Bizarre Posthumous Journey of Einstein's Brain." *Encyclopædia Britannica*. Encyclopædia Britannica, Inc. Web.

Green, Erica L. "LeBron James Opened a School That Was Considered an Experiment. It's Showing Promise." *The New York Times*. The New York Times, 12 Apr. 2019. Web. 07 May 2020.

Green, Joseph. "Mihailo Tolotos: The Man Who Never Saw a Woman." *Historic Mysteries,* 3 Mar. 2023.

Greene, Robert. *Mastery*. Penguin Group, 2012. 52-53. Print.

Gunn, Angus M., Robert W. Richburg, and Rita Smilkstein. *Igniting Student Potential: Teaching with the Brain's Natural Learning Process*. Corwin, 2007. Print.

Gyamfi, Ameyaw Adu. "Christianity Is One Major Cause Of Suicide In Ghana - Psychologist Reveals." *Peacefmonline.com - Ghana News*. 10 Sept. 2020. Web. 22 Oct. 2020.

"Happy Land Fire." *Wikipedia*. Wikimedia Foundation, 17 Apr. 2020. Web. 24 Apr. 2020.

"Hedy Lamaar." *Hedy Lamarr*. Web. 23 Aug. 2020.

"Hedy Lamarr." *Wikipedia*. Wikimedia Foundation, 13 Aug. 2020. Web. 23 Aug. 2020.

Heydenreich, Ludwig Heinrich. "Leonardo Da Vinci." *Encyclopædia Britannica*. Encyclopædia Britannica, Inc., 22 Aug. 2019. Web.

Hill, Catey. "You Don't Need a 4-year College Degree for These High-paying Jobs at Google, Apple, Netflix." *MarketWatch*. MarketWatch, 17 Apr. 2019. Web. 01 Sept. 2020.

History.com Editors. "Alexander Graham Bell." *History.com*. A&E Television Networks, 09 Nov. 2009. Web. 29 Nov. 2021.

Hockaday, James. "New Zealand Declared Coronavirus-free and Removes All Restrictions." *Metro*. Metro.co.uk, 08 June 2020. Web. 20 Oct. 2020.

Holt, LIoyd. "Archimedes." *Archimedes*. Wichita State University. Web.

"Home." *About FedEx*. Web.

Horgan, John. "Why There Will Never Be Another Einstein." *Scientific American Blog Network*. Scientific American, 23 Aug. 2015. Web.

"How Churchill Prepared for His Speeches." *The International Churchill Society*. 24 Mar. 2017. Web. 15 Apr. 2020.

"How Two Fetish Priests Murdered and Buried a Biochemist, Others at Their Shrine." *MyJoyOnline.com*. 05 May 2020. Web. 18 May 2020.

"Human." *Wikipedia*. Wikimedia Foundation, 31 Dec. 2019. Web.

"Humphry Davy." *Wikipedia*. Wikimedia Foundation, 14 Mar. 2022. Web. 30 Mar. 2022.

"I Promise School." *Wikipedia*. Wikimedia Foundation, 10 Apr. 2020. Web. 07 May 2020.

Ibeh, Nnenna. "STRANGE TIMES: Pastor Gives Church Member Dettol to Drink." *Legit.ng - Nigeria News*. 09 Dec. 2016. Web. 23 Oct. 2020.

Isaac, Susan. ""Phossy Jaw" and the Matchgirls: A Nineteenth-century Industrial Disease." *Royal College of Surgeons*. Royal College of Surgeons, 13 May 2019. Web. 24 Apr. 2020.

"J. K. Rowling." *Wikipedia*. Wikimedia Foundation, 24 Apr. 2020. Web. 29 Apr. 2020.

"Jack Coe." *Wikipedia*. Wikimedia Foundation, 07 Sept. 2019. Web. 19 May 2020.

"Japanese Americans: The War at Home." *Scholastic.com*. Web. 08 Apr. 2020.

"Jesse Martin." *Business Blueprint*. 29 June 2015. Web.

"John D. Rockefeller." *Wikipedia*. Wikimedia Foundation, 13 June 2022. Web. 15 June 2022.

"John Gurdon." *Wikipedia*. Wikimedia Foundation, 22 Nov. 2019. Web.

"John Magufuli." *Wikipedia*. Wikimedia Foundation, 27 Apr. 2022. Web. 4 May 2022.

"Joseph Priestley." *Wikipedia*. Wikimedia Foundation, 17 Aug. 2020. Web. 01 Sept. 2020.

Kaku, Michio. "Nazi Backlash and Coming to America." *Encyclopædia Britannica*. Encyclopædia Britannica, Inc., 14 Jan. 2020. Web.

Kamasah, Andreas. "Take a Cup of Hot Water and 2 Lemons - T.B Joshua Advises as Covid-19 Failed to Vanish." *Pulse.ng*. 31 Mar. 2020. Web. 22 Oct. 2020. <https://www.pulse.ng/news/metro/take-a-cup-of-hot-water-and-2-lemons-tb-joshua-advises-as-covid-19-failed-to-vanish/tf6sp61>.

Kamasah, Andreas. "This Month 27th, Covid-19 Will Be Over Whether We Like It or Not - T.B Joshua Declares." *Pulse.com.gh*. 16 Mar. 2020.

Web. 22 Oct. 2020. <https://www.pulse.com.gh/filla/this-month-27th-covid-19-will-be-over-whether-we-like-it-or-not-tb-joshua-declares/xyhww80>.

Karuga, James. "Did You Know Albert Einstein Was Offered The Israeli Presidency?" *WorldAtlas*. WorldAtlas, 18 May 2017. Web.

Kaufman, Scott Barry. "What Is Talent – and Can Science Spot What We Will Be Best At?" *The Guardian*. Guardian News and Media, 06 July 2013. Web.

Kids Discover. "Angel's Glow: The Bacterium That Saved Civil War Soldiers." *Kids Discover*. 08 Aug. 2016. Web. 05 Apr. 2021.

Kieffer, Sara. "How the Brain Works: Johns Hopkins Comprehensive Brain Tumor Center." *How the Brain Works | Johns Hopkins Comprehensive*. 03 Dec. 2018. Web.

Kiger, Patrick J. "Benjamin Franklin Established the Post Office to Connect and Unite the Colonies." *History.com*. A&E Television Networks, 10 Aug. 2020. Web. 01 Sept. 2020.

"Kim Kardashian Bodyguard Sued for $6.1m over Paris Robbery." *BBC News*. BBC, 04 Oct. 2018. Web. 22 May 2020.

"Kim Peek." *Wikipedia*. Wikimedia Foundation, 26 Apr. 2022. Web. 10 May 2022.

King, Gilbert. "The Rise and Fall of Nikola Tesla and His Tower." *Smithsonian.com*. Smithsonian Institution, 04 Feb. 2013. Web. 21 Aug. 2021.

Klos, Naomi Yavneh, and Stanley Yavneh Klos. "Alexander Graham Bell." *Alexander Graham Bell*. Historic.us, 01 Jan. 1970. Web. 29 Nov. 2021.

"KNUST Graduate Joins ISIS." *Ghanaweb.com*. GhanaWeb, 25 Aug. 2015. Web. 03 May 2020.

Kouimtsidis, Dimitris. "Spanish Archaeologist Sentenced to More than Two Years in Prison for Faking Finds That Would 'rewrite History'." *Olive Press News Spain*. 19 June 2020. Web. 06 July 2020.

Kremer, William. "The Strange Afterlife of Einstein's Brain." *BBC News*. BBC, 18 Apr. 2015. Web.

"Kylie Moore-Gilbert, Jailed Academic, 'rejected Iran's Offer to Become Spy'." *BBC News*. BBC, 21 Jan. 2020. Web. 06 Apr. 2020.

Kämmerer, Annette. "The Scientific Underpinnings and Impacts of Shame." *Scientific American*. Scientific American, 09 Aug. 2019. Web. 23 Apr. 2022.

Landsverk, Gabby. "Face Shields Did Not Protect People from the Coronavirus in an Outbreak in Switzerland, but Masks Did, Health Officials Say." *Insider*. Insider, 21 July 2020. Web. 10 Aug. 2020.

Learning, Lumen. "Introduction to Psychology." *Lumen*. Web.

Lebowitz, Shana. "Professor Who Knew Bill Gates as a Student at Harvard: He Was the Smartest Person I've Ever Met." *Business Insider*, Business Insider.

Ledbetter, Carly. "George Clooney Explains Why He Gave 14 Close Friends $1 Million Each." *HuffPost*, 16 Dec. 2020.

Lee, Dave. "Nokia: The Rise and Fall of a Mobile Giant." *BBC News*. BBC, 03 Sept. 2013. Web. 16 Apr. 2020.

"Leonardo Da Vinci." *Wikipedia*. Wikimedia Foundation, 26 Jan. 2020. Web.

Lewis, Hilary. "Donald Trump Defends Not Accepting Melania Speechwriter's Resignation." *The Hollywood Reporter*. 21 July 2016. Web. 07 Sept. 2020.

"List of Child Prodigies." *Psychology Wiki*. Web.

Live Science Staff. "Top 10 REASONS Alexander the GREAT Was, Well ... GREAT!" *LiveScience*. Purch, 10 Dec. 2004. Web. 07 Sept. 2021.

Luce, Edward. "Is Wealthy Philanthropy Doing More Harm than Good?" *Financial Times*. 21 Dec. 2018. Web. 07 Nov. 2020.

"Magdalena Solís." *Wikipedia*. Wikimedia Foundation, 12 June 2022. Web. 26 June 2022

Malado, Jardine. "South African Pastor Makes Congregants Drink Engine Oil for Healing." *Christian News on Christian Times*. Christian Times, 19 Jan. 2017. Web. 23 Oct. 2020.

"Mamoudou Gassama: Mali 'Spiderman' Becomes French Citizen." *BBC News*. BBC, 13 Sept. 2018. Web. 14 May 2020.

Manga, Dhiren. "US Indian Man Hires Woman to Slap Him If He Visited Facebook." *DESIblitz*. 12 Nov. 2021. Web. 25 Nov. 2021.

"March 1504 Lunar Eclipse." *Wikipedia*. Wikimedia Foundation, 09 Apr. 2022. Web. 24 Apr. 2022.

Mark, Joshua J. "Aristotle." *World History Encyclopedia*. World History Encyclopedia, 05 Sept. 2021. Web. 07 Sept. 2021.

Mark, Joshua J. "The Battle of Pelusium: A Victory Decided by Cats." *Ancient History Encyclopedia*. Ancient History Encyclopedia, 01 Apr. 2021. Web. 02 Apr. 2021.

Mark, Joshua J. "The Seven Wonders." *Ancient History Encyclopedia*. Ancient History Encyclopedia, 16 Jan. 2020. Web.

Martinez, Jessica. "After South African Pastor Makes Church Members Eat Grass, He Now Forces Them to Drink Petrol." *The Christian Post*. Web. 02 May 2020.

"Marvin Pipkin." *Wikipedia*. Wikimedia Foundation, 14 Sept. 2021. Web. 30 Mar. 2022.

Matousek, Mark. "Elon Musk Says You Still Don't Need a College Degree to Work at Tesla. Here's What He Looks for in Job Applicants Instead. (TSLA)." *Ghana News, Business, Sports & Entertainment*. 24 Dec. 2019. Web. 19 Apr. 2020.

McCoy, Alli N, and Siang Yong Tan. "Otto Loewi (1873-1961): Dreamer and Nobel Laureate." *Singapore Medical Journal*. Singapore Medical Association, Jan. 2014. Web.

Mead, Wendy. "Alexander Graham Bell: 5 Facts on the Father of the Telephone." *Biography.com*. A&E Networks Television, 28 Sept. 2021. Web. 29 Nov. 2021.

Mensah, Jeffrey. "Sarkodie GHC1000; D-Black Paid GHC5000 for Fake UN Awards - Shatta Wale Claims." *Yen.com.gh - Ghana News*. 07 Sept. 2020. Web. 08 Sept. 2020.

Mensah, Mary. "Murdered Pensioner Was Biochemist - CID." *Graphic Online*. Web. 18 May 2020.

"Michael Kearney." *Wikipedia*. Wikimedia Foundation, 14 Dec. 2019. Web.

"Michelangelo Style and Technique." *Artble*. 19 July 2017. Web. 24 July 2020.

"Mileva Marić." *Wikipedia*. Wikimedia Foundation, 19 Jan. 2020. Web.

Money, Smart. "10 Things Your Lawyer Won't Tell You." *Fox News*. FOX News Network, 25 Mar. 2015. Web. 16 July 2020.

Montag, Ali. "Billionaire Alibaba Founder Jack Ma Was Rejected from Every Job He Applied to after College, Even KFC." *CNBC*. CNBC, 10 Sept. 2019. Web. 29 Apr. 2020.

Morgan @jnoahmorgan, Jessica. "Lavinia Woodward Stabbed Her Boyfriend and Didn't Go to Prison Because She Was 'too Clever' – Does That Count as Justice?" *The Independent*. Independent Digital News and Media, 29 Dec. 2018. Web. 09 Aug. 2020.

Munishi, Deogratias. "President Magufuli, We Need Leadership, Not Prayers." *African Arguments*. 27 Apr. 2020. Web. 4 May 2022.

Nathan, Alec. "LeBron James' I Promise School to Cost District Taxpayers Around $8M Per Year." *Bleacher Report*. Bleacher Report, 06 Aug. 2018. Web. 12 Nov. 2020.

Ndagire, Betty. "US Donors Sue NGO over Misuse of Needy Funds." *Daily Monitor*. Daily Monitor, 24 Oct. 2019. Web. 16 May 2020.

Nicholas, Herbert G. "Winston Churchill." *Encyclopædia Britannica*. Encyclopædia Britannica, Inc., 21 Jan. 2020. Web.

Nigeria, Biesloaded. "Coronavirus: Ogboni Cult Head Releases Statement, Offers to Perform Rituals to Cleanse Nigeria." *Biesloaded NG*. Blogger, 21 Mar. 2020. Web. 20 Oct. 2020.

"Nigerian Singer Sentenced to Death for Blasphemy in Kano State." *BBC News*. BBC, 10 Aug. 2020. Web. 20 Oct. 2020.

"Nobel Prize: Scientist Sir John Gurdon Had Disastrous School Report." *Daily Mail Online*. Associated Newspapers, 09 Oct. 2012. Web.

"Occipital Brain Lobe: Function, Anatomy, Position, and Structure." *The Human Memory*. 31 Oct. 2019. Web.

O'Kane, Caitlin. ""Resident Evil" Stuntwoman Sues Producers after Losing Her Arm, Says They "abandoned" Her." *CBS News*. CBS Interactive, 16 Sept. 2019. Web.

Oluwole, Victor. "Nigeria, South Africa, Kenya among Top 5 African Countries with the Most Developed Startup Ecosystems – Report." *Business Insider*. Business Insider. Web. 15 Sept. 2022.

"On the Trail of Albert Einstein." *Le Bon Travel & Culture*. Web.

Oppenheim @mayaoppenheim, Maya. "Anti-LGBT Politician Resigns after He's 'caught Having Sex with a Man in His Office'." *The Independent*. Independent Digital News and Media, 23 Apr. 2019. Web. 15 May 2020.

Ortega, Ralph R. "Egypt Invites Elon Musk to See Great Pyramids after He Tweeted They Were 'built by Aliens Obviously'." *Daily Mail Online*. Associated Newspapers, 02 Aug. 2020. Web. 03 Aug. 2020.

Ott, Tim. "Isaac Newton Changed the World While in Quarantine From the Plague." *Biography.com*. A&E Networks Television, 25 Mar. 2020. Web. 30 June 2020.

"Paulo Coelho." *Biography.com.* A&E Networks Television, 06 Nov. 2019. Web. 26 Apr. 2020.

"Paulo Coelho." *Wikipedia.* Wikimedia Foundation, 17 Apr. 2020. Web. 26 Apr. 2020.

Payton, Bre. "Why Sparta Collapsed After Defeating Athens And Building An Empire." *The Federalist.* 25 July 2018. Web. 16 Apr. 2020.

Pester, Patrick. "What Did the Ancient Egyptian Pyramids Look like When They Were Built?" *LiveScience*, Purch, 5 Feb. 2023.

Petkar, Sofia, Holly Christodoulou, and Emma Lake. "Who Is Lavinia Woodward? Oxford Uni Student Who Stabbed Cambridge Boyfriend at Christ Church College." *The Sun.* The Sun, 27 June 2018. Web. 09 Aug. 2020.

"Philosophiæ Naturalis Principia Mathematica." *Wikipedia.* Wikimedia Foundation, 25 June 2020. Web. 30 June 2020.

"Phossy Jaw." *Wikipedia.* Wikimedia Foundation, 25 Mar. 2020. Web. 24 Apr. 2020.

"Political Connection Not Needed for Business Success in Ghana – McDan." *MyJoyOnline.com.* 06 July 2020. Web. 01 Sept. 2020.

Preston, Allan. "'ancient Cure' in Fermanagh Soil May Lead to Antibiotic Breakthrough." *Belfasttelegraph.* BelfastTelegraph.co.uk, 06 Nov. 2018. Web. 26 Apr. 2022.

"Project 523." *Wikipedia.* Wikimedia Foundation, 12 Apr. 2020. Web. 27 Apr. 2020.

Pruitt, Sarah. "8 Inventions We Owe to the Ancients." *History.com*, A&E Television Networks, 19 Nov. 2015,

Quartey, Daniel. "Mike Tyson Names Floyd Mayweather as the Greatest Boxer in the past 100 Years." *Yen.com.gh - Ghana News.* 18 May 2020. Web. 22 Sept. 2020.

Reilly, Jill. "South African Preacher Makes Congregation Eat GRASS to Be Closer to God." *Daily Mail Online.* Associated Newspapers, 10 Jan. 2014. Web. 02 May 2020.

Reuters. "Indian Doctors Warn Against Cow Dung AS Covid Cure." *@businessline.* The Hindu BusinessLine, 02 July 2021. Web. 07 Sept. 2021.

"Richard Montañez Speaking Engagements, Schedule, & Fee: WSB." *Wsb.* Washington Speakers Bureau. Web.

"Robert Kearns." *Wikipedia.* Wikimedia Foundation, 26 Mar. 2020. Web. 08 May 2020.

Roberts, Sam. "Julio Gonzalez, Arsonist Who Killed 87 at New York Club in '90, Dies at 61." *The New York Times.* The New York Times, 15 Sept. 2016. Web. 24 Apr. 2020.

Robertson, Colin. "How Kobe Bryant Willed Himself to Greatness." *Willpowered.* Willpowered, 04 Oct. 2015. Web.

Robinson, Brandon. "LL Cool J Rapped This in a Gap Commercial to Help Another Clothing Company." *Heavy.com.* Heavy, 25 Apr. 2019. Web. 15 Jan. 2022.

Rogers, Kara. "Sir John Bertrand Gurdon." *Encyclopædia Britannica.* Encyclopædia Britannica, Inc., 28 Sept. 2019. Web.

Roget, Stephan. "The Still-Unexplained Phenomenon Of The Jumping Frenchmen Of Maine Disorder." *Ranker.* Ranker. Web.

Roget, Stephan. "This Unknown Hero Saved A US President's Life And Was Rewarded By Having His Life Publicly Destroyed." *Ranker.* Web. 15 May 2020.

"Russian Gallery Security Guard Accused of Drawing Eyes on Painting." *BBC News*. BBC, 10 Feb. 2022. Web. 15 Sept. 2022.

Sample, Ian. "UK Mathematician Wins Richest Prize in Academia." *The Guardian.* Guardian News and Media, 10 Sept. 2020. Web. 10 May 2022.

Sarpong, Akwasi. "Melcom Shop Collapse in Ghana: Negligence Blamed." *BBC News*. BBC, 08 Nov. 2012. Web. 24 Apr. 2020.

"Saul Kripke." *Saul Kripke.* Jewish Virtual Library. Web.

Schecter, Anna, Kathryn Nathanson, and Tracy Connor. "Farid Fata, Doctor Who Gave Chemo to Healthy Patients, Faces Sentencing." *NBCNews.com*. NBCUniversal News Group, 17 Aug. 2015. Web. 05 Apr. 2021.

Scully, Emer. "Cameroon Pastor Who 'healed Coronavirus Sufferers by Laying His Hands on Them' Dies from Covid-19." *Daily Mail Online*. Associated Newspapers, 19 May 2020. Web. 21 May 2020.

Seanm. "The Wright Brothers: Pioneers in Aviation." *Smithsonian Institution Archives*. 14 Sept. 2012. Web.

Sedlak-Hevener, Amanda. "11 Common Household Products From Victorian England That Could Kill You." *Ranker*. Ranker. Web.

Selby @JennSelby, Jenn. "Paul Walker's Gift: Actor Secretly Bought Iraq War Veteran Engagement." *The Independent*. Independent Digital News and Media, 06 Dec. 2013. Web. 07 May 2020.

Shanklin, Emily. "Elon Musk." *SpaceX*. SpaceX, 27 Mar. 2017. Web.

Shen, Lucinda. "Here's How Much Nobel Prize Winners Get." *Fortune*. Fortune, 03 May 2018. Web.

"Shi Pei Pu." *Wikipedia*. Wikimedia Foundation, 24 Feb. 2020. Web.

Sigman, Suzanne. "Discovering Winston Churchill: Teaching Ideas and Resources." *Scholastic*. Web.

Singh, Olivia. "13 Celebrities Who Bought Homes for Their Parents after Making It Big in Hollywood." *Insider*. Insider, 02 July 2020. Web. 30 Dec. 2021.

Sky News. "Judge Criticised after Taking 'exceptional' Course for Oxford Student Who Stabbed Boyfriend." *Sky News*. Sky News, 17 May 2017. Web. 09 Aug. 2020.

Smith, John. "English Factory Laborers Were Forced to Work with Toxic Chemicals until Their Faces Became Deformed." *HT*. 05 Aug. 2019. Web. 23 Nov. 2021.

"SpaceX." *Wikipedia*. Wikimedia Foundation, 16 Apr. 2020. Web. 19 Apr. 2020.

"Spanish Bishop Quit for Love for Erotic Writer." *BBC News*, BBC, 8 Sept. 2021.

"Spartan Army." *Wikipedia*. Wikimedia Foundation, 07 Apr. 2020. Web. 16 Apr. 2020.

Srinivas, Sydney. "Hunt for a Job." *Albert Einstein*. Prism Pvt., 2014. Print.

"Steve Jobs Bought This for a Secretary to Ensure She Was Always on Time and 32 More Interesting Facts." *TechEBlog*. 22 Jan. 2015. Web. 07 May 2020.

Surowiecki, James. "Where Nokia Went Wrong." *The New Yorker*. The New Yorker, 03 Dec. 2017. Web. 16 Apr. 2020.

Taylor, Mildred Europa. "Daniel Abodunrin, the Nigerian Prophet Who Was Eaten by Lions While 'replicating' a Bible Story in 1991." *Face2Face Africa*. 05 Aug. 2018. Web.

"Terence Tao." *Wikipedia*. Wikimedia Foundation, 13 Feb. 2020. Web.

"The Plague That Made People Dance Themselves to Death." *YouTube*, 11 Sept. 2019.

"Titanic (1997 Film)." *Wikipedia*. Wikimedia Foundation, 09 Mar. 2020. Web.

Web. 28 Aug. 2020.

"Two American Entrepreneurs: Madam C.J. Walker and J.C. Penney--Reading 1." *National Parks Service*. U.S. Department of the Interior. Web.

"University of Bologna." *Wikipedia*. Wikimedia Foundation, 02 Jan. 2020. Web.

Utkarsh. "How Did Elon Musk Learn Enough about Rockets to Run Spacex?" *Inc42 Media*. Inc42, 28 June 2016. Web. 04 Nov. 2021.

Valentine, Matt. "The Most Overrated College Degree, According to Mark Cuban." *Goalcast*. 13 Sept. 2019. Web. 01 Sept. 2020.

Vallely, Paul. "How Philanthropy Benefits the Super-rich." *How Philanthropy Benefits the Super-rich*. Guardian News and Media, 08 Sept. 2020. Web. 07 Nov. 2020. Web.

Vardhan, Harsh. “Elon Musk Gets Reply from WFP on How $6 Billion from His Fortune Can Solve World Hunger.” *Republic World*, Republic World, 16 Nov. 2021. Web.

"Victims in NYC Dance-club Arson That Killed 87 to Be Commemorated." *New York Post*. New York Post, 25 Mar. 2015. Web. 24 Apr. 2020. Web.

Warah, Rasna. "Tanzania: The Curious Case of John Pombe Magufuli." *The Elephant*. 26 Mar. 2021. Web. 24 Apr. 2021.

Wendorf, Marcia. "How Robert Kearns Took on Ford and Chrysler and Won." *Interesting Engineering*. Interesting Engineering, 10 Sept. 2019. Web. 08 May 2020.

West, Thomas. “13 Fascinating Facts We Just Unraveled about Egyptian Pyramids.” *Ranker*, Ranker, 27 Mar. 2023.

White, Abbey. "The Real Reason LeBron James Opened the I Promise School." *Looper.com*. Looper, 06 July 2020. Web. 12 Nov. 2020.

Williams, L. Pearce. "Michael Faraday." *Encyclopædia Britannica*. Encyclopædia Britannica, Inc. Web. 30 Mar. 2022.

Wilson, Xerxes. "Kim Kardashian West Claims Bodyguard’s Negligence Led to Robbery of Millions in Jewels." *USA Today*. Gannett Satellite Information Network, 05 Oct. 2018. Web. 22 May 2020.

Wintour, Patrick. "Britain-Iran Relationship Caught up in Mutual Blame Game." *The Guardian.* Guardian News and Media, 11 Sept. 2019. Web. 11 Aug. 2020.

Wires, News. "'Hero' Malian Migrant Saves Child from Paris Balcony." *France 24.* France 24, 28 May 2018. Web. 14 May 2020.

Wolfson, Alisa. "'Less Education Can Be Worth More.' While College Grads Have a Net Worth about 5x Higher than High School Grads, Here's What Can Matter Even More than That College Diploma." *MarketWatch*, MarketWatch, 22 Dec. 2022.

Wollaston, Sam. "The Rise and Fall of Nokia Review – Fascinating Insight into the Finnish, and Now Finished, Tech Firm." *The Guardian.* Guardian News and Media, 10 July 2018. Web. 12 Aug. 2020.

Wood, Gordon S., and Theodore Hornberger. "Achievement of Security and Fame (1726–53)." *Encyclopædia Britannica.* Encyclopædia Britannica, Inc., 13 Apr. 2020. Web. 01 Sept. 2020.

"Wright Brothers." *Wikipedia.* Wikimedia Foundation, 02 Feb. 2020. Web.

Yeboah, Isaac. "#Coronavirus: Ghana to Observe National Day of Fasting and Prayer." *Graphic Online.* 22 Mar. 2020. Web. 20 Oct. 2020.

Yeboah, Thomas Freeman. "Man of the Match in Kotoko-hearts Game Receives Malaria Mixture as Reward." *Pulse Nigeria.* 28 Aug. 2018. Web. 10 June 2022. Web.

Zitelmann, Rainer. "The Jack Ma Story: Why Thinking Big Is More Important Than Technical Knowledge." *Forbes*. Forbes Magazine, 04 Nov. 2019. Web. 29 Apr. 2020.

Index

Made in the USA
Las Vegas, NV
27 January 2024

84653504R00184